Beyond the Plan

About the Book and Author

The aims of postwar Eastern Europe governments included, first and foremost, the restructuring and controlling of economic and social domains. Since 1945, planning in rural Hungary has been focused on the collectivization of agriculture. However, activities at the village level not only deflected the intended outcomes of government policies, but also generated new, innovative results. Families managed to redirect their efforts into a variety of job sectors and to forge essential ties with the industrial, non-agricultural job sectors. Labor withheld from the collectives was invested in plot farming, a development that proved of paramount importance to both the national and household economies. Today, most rural families continue to participate in more than one sector of production, making it difficult for the central government to design selective policies aimed at the "peasant."

The broadening of Hungary's interpretation and application of socialist principles was largely a result of the ways in which government plans were reinterpreted and reapplied at the local level. By examining agricultural changes in one Hungarian village, Dr. Vasary explores some of the possibilities and limitations inherent in collectivization.

Ildiko Vasary is a research Fellow at the University College of London.

Beyond the Plan

Social Change
in a Hungarian Village

Ildiko Vasary

Westview Press / Boulder and London

Westview Special Studies on the Soviet Union and Eastern Europe

----
This Westview softcover edition is printed on acid-free paper and bound in
softcovers that carry the highest rating of the National Association of
State Textbook Administrators, in consultation with the Association of
American Publishers and the Book Manufacturers' Institute.

Copyright © 1987 by Westview Press, Inc.

Published in 1987 in the United States of America by Westview Press, Inc.;
Frederick A. Praeger, Publisher; 5500 Central Avenue, Boulder, Colorado
80301

Library of Congress Catalog Card Number: 87-8219
ISBN: 0-8133-7412-X

Composition for this book was provided by the author.
This book was produced without formal editing by the publisher.

Printed and bound in the United States of America

The paper used in this publication meets the requirements
of the American National Standard for Permanence of Paper
for Printed Library Materials Z39.48-1984.

6   5   4   3   2   1

For Tamas

Contents

PART 1
ANTECEDENTS

PART 2
AGRICULTURAL COLLECTIVIZATION

Tables, Maps, and Figures

xiv

Preface

Research in Hungary attracted me because of my intriguing relationship to that country. I am both an insider and an alien. I was not born there, nor had I lived in Hungary before the fieldwork visits, but by parentage, language and culture I belong there.

I chose the village of Pécsely for fieldwork for several reasons. Transdanubia has received somewhat less attention than more ethnographically colourful or remote regions of Hungary, so a study of contemporary life in one of its rural communities promised to be rewarding. I sought a village in which the major social categories typical of pre-war Hungary were represented and on this count Pécsely was admirably suited. More than a passing glance is needed to assess a village's character in Hungary today. Resettlement programmes, massive depopulation or other demographic movements have broken the continuity of development in many and they no longer appear as they did, say, forty years ago. Although not looking for a 'typical' village, I wanted to find a settlement in which the transition from traditional peasant existence to a socialist society and collectivized agriculture could be traced. Pécsely had the continuity I was looking for.

Although I expected to meet the traditional hospitality of Hungarian rural communities, long drawn out fieldwork needs more than a casual welcome. Distant kinship ties with some families in Pécsely helped to justify my presence there in the villagers' eyes and to allay initial suspicions. My interest in piecing together the history of the village legitimized my inquiries and ensured the friendly cooperation of both ordinary villagers and local officials. I eventually completed thirteen months of fieldwork in Pécsely in three-month long stays between April 1978 and October 1981, followed by shorter visits.

Pécsely has about 600 inhabitants, and I was able to get personally acquainted with most and develop close friendships with many. My research was based on participant observation, informal interviews and gathering information on many facets of everyday life in the village. Census data collection, index card making for each family, etc. served to organize more casual observations and experiences. Fieldwork was complemented by research into the written sources found in the village such as an unusually complete set of church registers, records of the local council and the collective of production. Documentary research was also carried out in the Zala County Archives and Land Registry of Füred. More general statistical information was collected from the Statistical Office's Library in Budapest.

The nature of the material presented made it unnecessary to conceal identities, but, to avoid identification through quotations or references of a more personal nature, subjects are marked by initials or first names alone. Proper names have been written in the English manner, with Christian name first.

It was not possible to use a uniform measure of land throughout this work. Earlier sources give measurements in cadastral holds, and statistical categorizations are based on this. Since 1945, hectares have been more commonly used. Rather than tamper with the tables, I have given them as found with keys for conversion where appropriate.

Ildiko Vasary

Acknowledgments

I am indebted first and foremost to Rosemary Harris and
László Péter for their guidance, advice and support through
the fieldwork period and subsequent organization of the material that forms the basis of this book. I owe thanks to the
Hungarian Ethnographic Institute and in particular to Tibor
Bodrogi for providing all the assistance I needed, both
practical and academic. I am grateful to Caroline Humphrey
for reading and commenting on portions of this work.

I am grateful to Józsa Tivadar, medical doctor in
Pécsely and dedicated observer of the life and history of
the community, for sharing with me his insights generously.
I also thank István Kocsis, pastor, and Gyula Henn, council
president, for their friendly cooperation and assistance.

During the fieldwork period I was generously supported
by a grant from the Social Science Research Council.

I also wish to thank the villagers of Pécsely for their
trust, patience and friendly support.

Finally, I thank my husband, Tamas, who made it all
possible.

I.V.

Introduction

Over the past four decades Hungary has been transformed, through fundamental political and social changes, into a socialist state committed to industrialization. Until 1945 the Hungarian economy was mainly agricultural and its society was riddled with material and social inequalities. The impact of post-war changes was perhaps experienced more than anywhere else in the rural communities.

Collectivization of agriculture has effectively brought an end to the peasantry as a social class.[1] Through collectivization, traditional farms previously controlled and worked by individual families are brought together into larger units, to be worked and managed by members who share profits in proportion to their contributions in labour and land. Since 1960, the number of individual peasant farms in Hungary has dwindled into insignificance, concluding a ten-year campaign of collectivization.

In socialist Eastern Europe governments have attempted to restructure and control far larger social and economic domains than has happened in Western Europe, where political programmes for agriculture, for example, have been less ambitious and piecemeal (Franklin, 1969). In Eastern European countries, particularly those introducing collectivization, governments have planned, guided and, many would argue, imposed change. This process raises urgent questions about the effects of political and economic programmes on the communities at which they are aimed. The economic and social functions of peasant families have changed radically as a result of collectivization. The analysis of these changes, far from being finished, has gathered momentum in Hungary only since the 1970s. The social variables which influence the outcome of specific political and economic programmes

deserve special attention. Even in countries like Yugoslavia where collectivization has been only partial it has
been found that the social context may significantly
restrict the outcome of economic and social programmes (cf.
Barić, 1978). The question is of equal relevance to Hungary.

In contemporary complex societies, formal regulation
through various forms of rule-making implies confidence in
the predictability of results. Considerable trust is placed
in the effectiveness of legislation and its derivative forms
of regulation and nowhere has that trust been so consistent
as in Eastern Europe in recent decades.

After a radical political change, parts of the previous
ideology and social organization are often cast aside and
replaced both by a new ideological charter and new regulations (Moore, 1983:12). This has certainly been the case in
Hungary since 1945. New laws and regulations, however,
often fail fully to achieve their aims and have unforeseen
side effects. Social forces appear to have areas of relative autonomy and self-regulation which have their own momentum and can undermine effects of government planning. I am
thinking here not only of traditional attitudes to labour,
ownership and patterns of interaction but also of new strategies adopted by families and village communities.

How non-regulated social processes can significantly
remake or unmake regulations of social domains by the state
has been shown by S.F. Moore (1983). The analytical model
she proposes is based upon the definition of areas of 'in-
determinacy' alongside those amenable to formal regulation.
Social change is approached through the interplay between
regulated and non-regulated domains. This model, a development of F. Barth's (1966) model of form and process, avoids
a too rigid dichotomy of structure and change, instead
strengthening the link between them. Moore's case studies
illustrate two types of social domains which exert a formative and distorting influence on formal regulation: the
interest networks generated by group and individual self-
interest in the US rag-trade (1983:59-64), and the resilient
traditional kinship networks operating beneath the surface
of the reformed formal regulations of the African Chagga
(1983:65-77). There are few analyses of this type and the
potential effects of 'wild growths' of non-regulated interest networks upon highly regulated and rationally ordered
social systems need to be examined in more detail.

Anthropological and ethnographic literature about Hungary in English has been scarce, with the notable exception
of E. Fél and T. Hofer's (1969) account of traditional peas-

ant life before World War II. C. Hann's (1980) perceptive study of specialist cooperatives in Tázlár is a welcome recent addition. However, the cooperatives that Hann describes are rather atypical and regionally specific, allowing the author little scope for examining aspects related to the agricultural collectives, currently dominant throughout the country.

Anthropological literature related to the present is also scarce in Hungarian. This is partly due to the dominant interest in Hungarian ethnography and folklore, and partly to political reticence about field-work based research and analysis of present-day social conditions. There has, however, been a significant change in recent years, and a number of rural sociological surveys have been published; Varsány (T. Bodrogi, ed. 1978) is one example. There are also publications by demographers, economists and political writers; many can be drawn upon with profit, particularly those analysing collectivization, economic reforms, the system of household plots and the 'second economy.'

In Hungary the Soviet model of collectivization was followed - or rather the collective agriculture system of the Soviet Union as it was in the 1950s. However, Hungary allowed significant variations from the stricter Soviet model. For example, simpler and more varied types of collectives were tolerated for longer periods than was the case in Russia (Erdei, 1979:250).

Collectives[2] in Hungary were envisaged initially as organizations thoroughly integrated into the village in which they were based. Official terminology reflected this aim; in the 1950s 'collective community' (termelőszövetkezeti község) was the standard appropriate term (Erdei, 1952; Márkus, 1969). Identification of the collective with the village followed from the assumed relationship between the peasant family and the collective. Socialist policy makers reckoned that whole peasant families rather than individual members would make up the constituent units of collective membership. Members were expected to dedicate their full labour capacity and undivided interest to the joint enterprise (Márkus, 1968; Orbán, 1972). As a consequence a 'homogeneous class of collective-member peasants' was expected to arise (Erdei, 1969:77). Connection between village and collective through peasant families did not develop as expected, however, and government agricultural programmes had to be revised repeatedly, a process by no means finished in Hungary, even today.

Erdei's hope of a unified, homogeneous peasant class emerging within the collective system has been only partially achieved: since 1960, the year when collectivization was completed, the peasantry has no longer been stratified by land ownership. However, nor is there much justification for speaking of a 'peasant class' any longer. The agricultural and rural population in general has undergone new forms of differentiation, in ways that were neither intended nor foreseen by policymakers.

As shown by C. Humphrey (1983) in relation to the Soviet Union, in the socialist system, there is a model of the economy which is lacking in non-socialist countries. In Humphrey's words this consists of '... not only the statutes and instructions of what people ought to do, but also the explanations of them in the countless publications of the Ministry of Agriculture; these, in effect are what people ought to think' (1983:74). This model referred to by Humphrey exists in Hungary too, alongside much of the ideological package imported from the Soviet Union since 1945. If this aspect of the ideology appears a lot less relevant in Hungary today than it is in the Soviet Union, this is because of socio-political changes over the past two decades in Hungary, with the emergence of a more pragmatic approach to economy and society, exemplified by the chain of reforms carried through since 1967. Despite the reforms, it has never been easy to reconcile ideological prescriptions and socio-economic reality in Hungary and understanding their interrelation remains a challenge.

In collectivized agriculture the problem deserving attention is the extent to which policies of collectivization have been realized or adapted throughout their implementation. In the early stages of collectivization in the 1950s, gaps between expectations and results were already acknowledged. These were attributed to the peasants' inadequate understanding of the advantages of collectivization, lack of resources (such as capital and machinery) and the demoralizing intrigues of rich peasants (Erdei, 1952:3-32). During the 1960s, the more crude simplifications and assumptions of 'sabotage' of collectives by rich peasants gave way to more conciliatory views. The problem of relations between membership and collective was assessed less dogmatically and in more subtle terms. Leading authors (Erdei, 1969: Markus, 1968) distinguish two types of collective members. One type concentrates on plot farming, remains uncommitted to the collective, and preserves traditional values and a 'peasant existence.' The other relates to the collective as to any contractual employment and is nearer to the worker than peasant in outlook. Neither type conformed to the expected commitment to the collective of families as units. Rural families continued to maintain strong, family-based interests, values and even productive activities independently from the collective.

The government had to decide whether the integration of the family within the collective should be pursued in the face of the members' apparent resistance and to the detriment of economic growth, or whether to abandon this course in favour of more flexible policies. In the late 1960s Party politics had become less ideologically dogmatic, and the latter course was chosen. Act III of 1967, which made individual members rather than families entitled to the standard plot allotment from the collective, is one example of policy change (see page 141).

The duality, which the original conception of the collectivization sought to avoid, was henceforth officially acknowledged. On the one hand, the collective stands as an industrial-type enterprise with specific interests and development, and on the other hand, members' families preserve their independent interests which may be unconnected with, or even contrary to, those of the collective. For some Hungarian analysts the implication was that the village has remained a strong vital community at the expense of the collective: '... the collective commands but the village binds ...,' was one conclusion (Márkus, 1968).

Hungarian sociography has devoted relatively little attention to several central aspects of collectivization, such as the ways in which elements of the traditional peasant system helped or hindered collectivization, or the extent to which the villagers influenced political and economic directives imposed on them by 'reinterpreting' directives in ways other than those intended by the policy makers.

In this work the aim is to define domains of social life which, no matter how tight social planning is, remain open; that is, in Moore's terminology, 'normatively indeterminate' (1983:50), and which may have far reaching effects on formalized domains. It is argued that the family is one major entity which has the ability to interfere with social planning. L. Barić (1978) has already shown how, in socialist systems, resilient elements of the traditional family structure may act as a deadening influence on economic planning and block investment and innovation. Carrying this proposition further, the Hungarian example suggests that the responses of the family unit may not only deform or deflect the intentions of socio-economic planning but may also generate new and creative outcomes. In other words, intentional rational planning may be enriched by new elements which, given even a small measure of structural flexibility in the

state apparatus and political receptiveness to movements upwards, can force their way into what E.R. Wolf (1968) has
called 'the formal table of organization.' Clearly much
depends on the scale on which such processes take place and
on the pressure exerted on economically sensitive areas.
Socialist administrations are not credited with an easy flow
upwards of grass-roots response to central policy making
(Hann, 1980), yet relatively simple but wide ranging self-
regulation at a core point of the social aggregate, such as
the family, may be more able to exert a formative influence
than is generally expected.

In post-war Hungary, fundamental agricultural reforms
set on a comprehensively pre-defined course - that of collectivization - left few options open for the peasantry.
Options were open, however, as regards the engagement of
family labour in different sectors, either agricultural or
non-agricultural. The form this engagement takes had, and
continues to have, wide ranging consequences for the development of the different sectors themselves. Development may
diverge from or coincide with the aims of central economic
planning at various points. For example, since the 1960s
manpower has flowed from agriculture into industry, enabling
growth plans to be met. The emergence of a new and resilient sector of private production alongside collectivized
agriculture, however, was unforeseen and unsought.

Employment trends helped to polarize the two domains
within the national economy: a 'first economy' comprising
the state-controlled large scale enterprises and collectives, and what is known as a 'second economy' (see pp. 135-
136) which includes all private undertakings such as plot
farming. As will be shown later the first and second
economies differ fundamentally: in the way they operate,
their amenability to state regulation, the constitution of
their units of operation and, finally, in the attitudes to
labour and profits which they foster - in spite of the fact
that the same people are employed often in both domains. At
a technical level, the socialized and private sectors are
complementary (Tepicht, 1975): they depend on each other
for their operation, with the private sector taking on production and services in areas that the socialized sector
cannot assume. Nevertheless, their relationship is one of
conflict (Gábor, 1985); the existence of one sets limits to
the other and their fundamentally different ways of operating prevent them from growing into each other, merging their
interests.

In the second economy, the single most significant
development factor has been the growth of plot farming.

Originally intended as merely a relic of traditional farming, temporarily tolerated in order to ease collectivization, plot farming went from strength to strength, becoming an essential part of the national economy. The nature of the small plots left in individual cultivation deserves emphasis. In both form and function these plots are new and unplanned, yet they combine elements of both tradition and contemporary socialist practice. What distinguishes their development is the way in which the members of each family have allocated their working hours, first dispersing into various sectors during formal working time, and then coming together again to work on the plots after formal working hours. This manner of labour allocation determines many of the secondary features of plot farming, such as what it produces, labour division within the family, and how the household budget is allocated. Locally, plot farming draws the villagers into relationship with one another to a greater extent than the collective and it allows the family to remain an important unit of production and common interest. At the same time, rural families have sought and forged new ties with the non-agricultural labour market to an extent that has only recently been recognized (Donáth, 1980; Kulcsár, 1982). This makes redundant the distinction between 'peasant' and 'worker,' current in the formulation of state policies until the mid-1970s.

Overall plot farming neither fits into the formal socio-economic socialist plan, nor can it be easily dismissed as a mere survival of traditional form, since it differs from traditional farming in both form and function.

Questions relating to the collectivization of agriculture are relevant not only to Hungary but to all countries where socialist changes of a similar nature are taking place or have taken place already. Within Hungary, the Transdanubian village of Pécsely, chosen to exemplify the problems raised in this book, is atypical inasmuch as its ecological features are regionally specific - but that would be true of any village one might choose. However, Pécsely is particularly suited on several counts; its natural resources are neither exceptionally good nor very poor and its categories of peasants are typical of Hungary as a whole: rich, middle and small peasants, self-sufficient on their farms, and the landless employed by either individual landowning peasants or the manorial estate.

Pécsely is set in a valley surrounded by hills. There are records of three separate hamlets in the valley from the thirteenth century onwards. In Hungarian there are distinct terms for 'community': the first, 'kőzség,' denotes a local administrative unit and the second 'kőzősség,' a group or collectivity in the social sense, a distinction of meaning similar to the German Gemeinde/Gemeinschaft. Before 1940, there were two kőzségs proper in the valley, that is, two administratively autonomous villages and one semi-autonomous manorial estate. They were merged officially in 1940, forming the village of Pécsely.

It is more difficult to define the three localities in the second sense of the word 'community.' The two villages of the valley, Nemespécsely and Nagypécsely, had fairly comprehensive interrelated institutions covering most aspects of social life: familial, political, religious and economic, with associated values and beliefs. The manorial estate, Kispécsely, though in many ways self-contained, was incomplete in the sense that it did not have separate political and religious institutions. Agriculture was the main occupation until 1945 and the localities may be defined 'occupational communities' with a common occupational culture, close-knit cliques of friends, neighbours and kinsmen and a sense of group identity marking them off from surrounding localities (cf. Newby, 1977:327; 1980:156-164). More importantly there were rigid hierarchical divisions of landholding, religion and local residence which changed gradually between 1848 and 1945.

Nemespécsely ('Noble-pécsely') the largest of the trio, was a 'curialis' village;[3] that is, it was inhabited by the special brand of petty nobles i.e. 'nemes' of Hungary, independent of any landlord. Its twin, Nagypécsely ('Great-pécsely'), was inhabited by serfs under the authority of several landlords. Kispécsely ('Small-pécsely') was a manorial estate where landless serfs of the estate resided. These differences reach back to the 1848 period of serfdom. Merged in 1940 to form the present village of Pécsely, the three communities of the valley did not immediately lose their separate identities; therefore when certain aspects are discussed, such as the formation of collectives after 1949, it is useful to refer to the officially redundant but de facto still relevant tripartite division.

Until 1945, social divisions in the valley were based on land ownership, religion and locality of origin. It was primarily by these criteria that residents were classified and classified themselves. Relations between people and groups were ordered and ranked hierarchically. Broadly, landholding categories ranged from wealthy and middle peasants to small peasants and the landless. Religious denomination divided Catholics and Protestants. Religious divisions in the valley coincided with different landholding patterns: it was mainly Protestants and not Catholics who owned self-sufficient farms. Local identity of the residents of Nemes, Nagy and Kis went beyond simple geographical divisions because different landholding strata predominated in each (see Chapter 1).

These divisions did not prevent social and economic relations between the different groups and localities; rather, they determined their nature. Relations between the groups and localities as well as the significance of the groups they represented altered significantly during the nineteenth and early twentieth century. For example, the division of Protestants and Catholics lost much of its edge through secularization and the integration of many Catholics in the villages.

In Chapter 1, the socio-economic structure of the pre-war village is introduced, elements of which went into the building of the system that we find today. It is intended to be somewhat more than a requisite historical introduction. What are described here are events in the past to which the villagers refer to this day and which had relevance in the shaping of the post-war socialist system. The formation of the first collectives, the resistance to relinquishing control over the peasant farms and the development of plot farming are just some examples. Although traditional peasant committees are relatively homogeneous, the status and interest groups in rural communities turn out to be highly differentiated when seen from close range. After 1945, when the old order gave way to government-controlled change, the reactions, resistance and support of the various groups within the village cannot be understood without reference to their historical origins.

In socialist countries the concept of social change is given greater emphasis than in non-socialist countries and the implications are different. Progress away from the old order, towards a frankly idealized future, is central to the socialist ideological self-representation, with intermediate steps charted out dogmatically along the way. Socialist sociological analyses tend, therefore, to assess social processes as 'forwards' or 'backwards' in relation to a goal of near-mythical proportions. Much of contemporary Hungarian sociological literature polarizes and places in opposition the traditional elements and new planned course of socialist change. This approach is problematic on several counts. First, it tends to place undue emphasis on the social problems of pre-war peasant existence, although admittedly these were many and should not be ignored. Second, it leads to a preference for 'before' and 'after' static pictures, with only the most cursory glance at the processes that lead from one period to the next; for example, the period between 1948 and 1960 is often given much less attention than it deserves (cf. Sárkany, 1978; Simó, 1983), although the need to reassess this period more precisely is becoming recognized by some authors (cf. Donáth, 1980; Kulcsár, 1982). The greatest disadvantage of a narrowly static approach is the lack of an assessment of how elements of the traditional peasant culture and way of life have been absorbed into the present social structure.

Chapters 2 and 3 introduce the post-war years preceding the more active campaigns of collectivization. The land reform of 1945 initiated transformation of the traditional peasant community and this was closely followed by the comprehensive agrarian programme starting in 1948 to 1949 which aimed at wide ranging control over production, marketing and ownership of land. These two chapters are the background against which subsequent developments are assessed throughout this book.

In post-war Hungary the collectivization of agriculture was pivotal in the planned recasting of the economy and society along socialist lines. Collectivization implies fundamental change from the peasant system; it involves tens of thousands of individual units of production which require the full cooperation of the peasantry in order to remain operational. Hence it was not possible to change the system - by making collectivization compulsory for example - without jeopardizing the production of essential food supplies. Collectivization, therefore, had to be approached gradually and with caution. In Part 2 the course of agricultural collectivization proper, leading up to its completion in 1959, is presented; subsequently the cycle of mergers and consequent changes in the structure of collectives are examined. Each phase of collectivization (Chapters 4-6) belongs to a defined period reflecting the country's political climate; different groups and categories of the peasantry were variously affected in the course of successive phases, and the functioning and organization of collectives was, it will be argued, strongly influenced by the members' attitudes and strategies (Chapters 7-11). The methods of collectivization had to be repeatedly revised and the worst anti-peasant measures abandoned before collectivization could be brought to completion. In particular, the continuance of some form of private farming had to be conceded.

In Part 3, economic and production activities of the villagers outside the collective and outside agriculture are examined. As will be shown, these sectors - plot farming and non-agricultural employment - have significantly affected the development of the collectives. The relationship between the collective and the plot farming sector is critical in rural Hungary today. Chapters 12 to 19 define the place of plot farming within the national and domestic economy, its official and popular status; they examine the form and function of plot farming, together with the division of labour within the family. It is a major aim of these chapters to assess to what extent the plot farming sector perpetuates features of traditional peasant farming or, on the contrary, introduces new patterns of production and lifestyle.

Hungarian agriculture today is credited with considerable achievements, but this success depends as much on the plot farming as it does on the collectives. The original aim of collectivization appears to have been fulfilled by not one but two different institutions: the collectives and the household plots, in an interdependence described by J. Tepicht's model of 'sectoral complementarity' (1973:14-45). Although the household plot and collective sector are - as will be seen from the example of Pécsely - technically interdependent and complementary, they remain, from the social point of view, sectors which are often contradictory and opposed to each other. This is shown, for example, in attitudes to labour: in the collective, withholding outputs is a strategy that pays, in the plots it does not. Doing as little work as possible in the collective saves energy for the after-hours work stint on the plots, since pushing oneself hard in the collective does not bring rewards in proportion to the effort (p. 82). In the plots, on the other hand, income rises in proportion to the energy expended. This example illustrates the differences between the sectors which, no matter how technically complementary, still represent different types of organization in the attitudes they encourage and social groups they involve.

In Chapter 21 we turn to non-agricultural employment outside the village, an activity of growing significance to the villagers and related to changing attitudes to consumption, labour, career aspirations and the agrarian programmes of collectivization. In present day Pécsely, most families have members in non-agricultural occupations. Families have high expectations for their children and aim above all for education leading to non-agricultural jobs. Such aspirations are not altogether unrealistic; in the last forty years social mobility in Hungary away from agriculture has been considerable (see Ferge, 1969) and higher education has enabled significant proportions of young people from a rural background to reach good positions in non-agricultural jobs.

The role of collectivization in pushing the peasantry into non-agricultural occupations should not be underestimated, for it has drawn the peasantry into a wider social environment. Tepicht (1975) has argued that the peasantry has been the main beneficiary of the social and economic policies in post-war Eastern Europe, because these policies have allowed them - or rather their children - to abandon the peasant mode of life. This assumes that the peasant does not want to be a peasant, because this class is socially the most disadvantaged and, intrinsically, wants to 'liquidate itself.' This has also been suggested in relation to the peasantries of Western Europe, where factors such as the aspirations of the peasants to educate their children, the high ratio of unmarried peasant men and the unwillingness of peasant daughters to marry peasants have been construed as indications of the peasants' desire to annihilate their class (Bourdieu and Boltansky, 1978:215-220). For the post-war peasantry of Hungary, however, the decisions regarding the future of the peasantry as a class were made elsewhere.

Until World War II, the valley represented the boundaries of the residents' social world. This is no longer so today, but the village is still a significant source of values and meanings. The community at present has more than one system of values upon which to draw: values surviving from the pre-war traditional peasant system, post-war introduction of the socialist values and - the latest to reach the village - urban attitudes and lifestyles. These reflect the different types of work in which families in the village engage: the plots, the collective and non-agricultural employment. In the social life of the village the different value systems do not yet seem fully integrated. They reflect the varying and often opposing nature of the various economic sectors. The community institutions, social stratification, family and systems of value are examined in the last four chapters of Part 4, these leading on to consideration of the outstanding feature of Hungarian rural society and economy today: the duality of the 'first' and 'second' economies.

NOTES

1. The difference between 'peasantry as a social category' and 'peasant economy' should be borne in mind. What I refer to here is that in Hungary there are no longer appreciable numbers of full time peasant family farming units. The existence of a 'peasant economy' is subject to debate. Tepicht (1973) argues convincingly that the peasant economy or peasant mode of production cannot be connected to only certain types of land ownership patterns or certain socio-economic formations (e.g. feudalism, capitalism or socialism). He argues that social and technical characteristics more aptly define the existence of peasant mode of production, and, as such, it may adapt to or persist over successive socio-economic formations: feudal, capitalist, socialist (1973:127). Tepicht argues that if collectivization precedes industrialization of agriculture, the result is no more than 'peasant economy multiplied' (1973:75). Tepicht took his point of departure from the observation that large collectives have taken over mainly grain production branches in agriculture, whereas stock breeding has remained largely in the hands of small farmers or plot farmers, re-enacting on a grand scale the organization of the peasant farm. Hungarian economy also involves the kind of 'sectoral complementarity' noted by Tepicht in Poland. In this sense it is valid to talk about elements of a peasant economy being preserved, but in Hungary, since collectivization has been brought to full term in 1960, it is no longer possible to talk of peasantry as a class.

2. Throughout this work 'agricultural collective of production' or 'collective' for short has been used for Mezőgazdasági Termelőszövetkezet in Hungarian. It is preferred to 'cooperative' to avoid confusion with the consumer, savings and other cooperatives and cooperative type associations and, the term also seems to be more expressive of the type of organization in question, which includes working collectively, for example.

3. Curia: free holding, noble estate (Szabad telek, nemes udvar). (K.B. Puky, Honni Törvény Szótár, Pest, 1930:54.) There were curialis serf villages too; these should be distinguished from the nemes curialis villages such as Nemespécsely. Curialis villages were settlements of defence, with a free population that could be called to arms (insurrectio). Nemespécsely is likely to have been a settlement of that origin.

PART 1

Antecedents

1

The Three Villages
in the Valley

Pécsely is in the Transdanubian part of Hungary, inland
from the shore of Lake Balaton (Maps 1.1 and 1.2). It
nestles in a small valley surrounded by gentle hills that
open towards the lake like an amphitheatre. The flatland
areas within the valley are adequately fertile for grain and
pasture, while the hillsides are eminently suitable for
vinegrowing. Several small streams criss-cross the valley,
some marked by ruined water mills. The enclosing hills form
a natural boundary separating the basin from the surrounding
villages and marking a natural limit to the határ, that is,
land belonging to the village.[1] The geographic unity of the
Pécsely valley (see Map 1.3) draws attention to the rigidity
of the socially created boundaries that kept apart three
tiny local communities in the basin until 1940.

Today, the village in the valley can only be pictured
as two villages with some difficulty. The stylish white-
washed Protestant Church stands in what appears to be the
exact centre of the present village. Closer inspection
shows that the church marks the precise pre-1940 boundary;
to the right lies Nemespécsely, to the left Nagypécsely. A
small stretch of land, no more than a couple of hundred
yards wide, now used for vegetable gardening, separated the
two sides. It is locally called a 'no man's land' (senki-
földje) and only recently have a few houses been built
there, materially expressing a slowly consolidating unity
between the two sides.

Kispécsely, the third local unit within the valley, was
not a village proper but a manorial estate (puszta) inhabited by a landlord and the labourers he employed. It is
about 1 km away from the two villages, towards the lake. At
present, the manorial house, outbuildings and labourers'

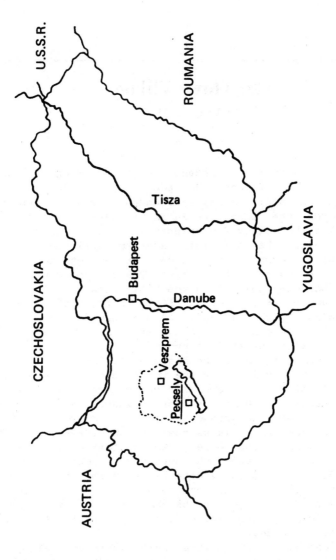

Map 1.1   Pécsely in Hungary

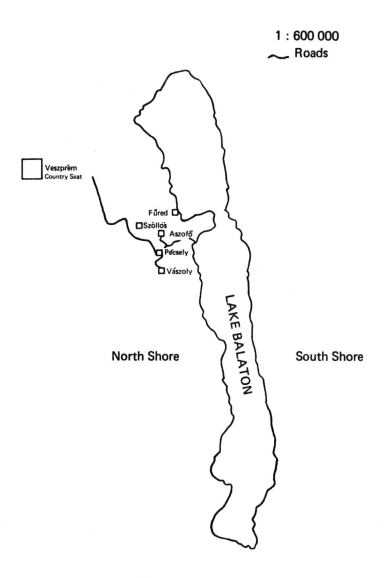

Map 1.2   The Balaton Region

20

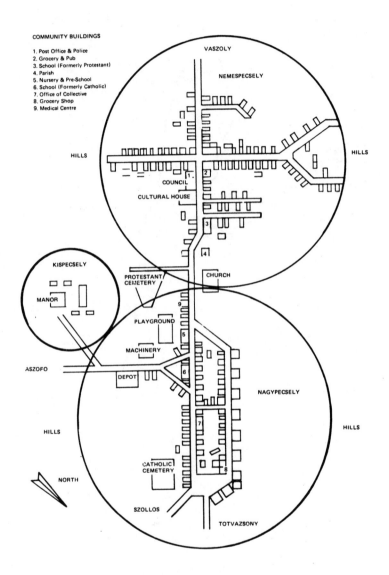

COMMUNITY BUILDINGS

1. Post Office & Police
2. Grocery & Pub
3. School (Formerly Protestant)
4. Parish
5. Nursery & Pre-School
6. School (Formerly Catholic)
7. Office of Collective
8. Grocery Shop
9. Medical Centre

VASZOLY

NEMESPECSELY

HILLS

HILLS

COUNCIL

CULTURAL HOUSE

KISPECSELY

MANOR

PROTESTANT CEMETERY

CHURCH

PLAYGROUND

MACHINERY

ASZOFO

DEPOT

NAGYPECSELY

HILLS

HILLS

CATHOLIC CEMETERY

NORTH

SZOLLOS

TOTVAZSONY

Map 1.3   Pécsely (schematic)

quarters are used as the animal farming centre of the agricultural collective (Map 1.3).

The side of the village that was formerly Nagypécsely
is made up of two parallel streets, lined with houses built
mainly in the traditional peasant style of the region, facing sideways. The houses are fairly evenly spaced and are
similar in style and size. There are also some recently
built villa-style houses, and a new street is taking shape
from the bare stretch of land which separates Nagy and
Nemes. Two large modern buildings draw attention: the new
administrative centre of the agricultural collective built
in 1969 and the new nursery and school building completed in
1975.

On the opposite side Nemespécsely is much less orderly
in its layout: its streets are tortuous, there are many
small alleyways and unlikely entrances to houses, which vary
in size, with the larger houses being interspersed with one
or two room pre-war labourer quarters. The larger houses
bear the 'NS' (noble insignia) with the name of the family
who built the house. The council building, post office and
Culture House are located in the centre of Nemes, as well as
the house of the Protestant clergyman.

The layout of the two villages clearly shows how dis-
similar they were: Nemes was a village of mainly noble,
landowners' families, whereas Nagy was a village of serfs
until 1848. Pécsely today ranks among the smaller villages
in Hungary, with about 600 inhabitants in 197 households.
It is characteristic of both the Nagy and Nemes side of the
village, that a large array of stables, granaries, sheds and
other agricultural outbuildings stands in ruins in the
courtyards, material remnants of a lifestyle of traditional
peasant cultivation that has nearly ceased to exist.

In the first month of fieldwork I was intrigued by the
frequency with which local informants referred to their own
and others' descent from serfs and nobles. Made redundant
as far back as 1848, these terms sounded anachronistic in a
socialist society. This is not to say that distinctions of
serf and noble have retained much significance - they are no
more than echoes from the past - but just as on the material
level the villages' layout preserves the historical heri-
tage, so these concepts reflect its vestiges in people's
minds (cf. K. Szentgyörgyi, 1983).

There are records of the villages of the Pécsely valley
dating back to the thirteenth century and it is likely that
three hamlets existed before that time. From the fourteenth
century they were the object of ownership disputes among
various contenders. Among others, the Bishop of Veszprém,

the Provost of Obuda, St Catherine's Monastery and the Abbey of Tihany claimed ownership of the serf holdings of the valley. By 1629 the Bishop of Vesprém and the Provost of Obuda had successfully recovered their feudal rights from the rival contenders. From this period onwards the inhabitants of Nagy and Kis Pécsely were reported to be the serfs of the Bishopric of Veszprém and the Provostship, while Nemespécsely was inhabited mainly by nobles and a small minority of serfs, that is, it was a 'curialis' village.

In Hungary before 1848 the terms 'serf' and 'peasant' cannot be seen to be opposed to the term noble (nemes). Not all serfs were peasants - there were, for example, artisans and craftsmen among them - while the great majority of nemes were small landowners with peasant culture, lifestyle and means of subsistence.

The social divisions between the nemes and serfs was not as clear cut as the legal definitions suggest; wealth and landownership frequently cut across these divisions. Within the nemesség (nobility) only a small minority enjoyed the 'noble mode of life' (nemesi életforma) and were 'bene possessionati' (well-to-do gentry), who formed the social elite of the counties, held offices and upheld nemes pride and consciousness. The nemes of the curialis villages rarely shared the privileges of this lifestyle; they were mostly poor, their lands fragmented through inheritance. The majority of the nemes worked their farms themselves and their lifestyles were similar to those of the serfs. They were confined to their villages and their farms, weighed down by the drudgery of physical labour with almost the same level of culture, housing and dress as the serfs. In other words, they belonged to the same class as the serfs. Yet there were consistent differences in outlook and attitudes and the nemes families of Nemespécsely live in relatively better economic conditions than the serfs of Nagypécsely. Although peasants in lifestyle, the nemes were proud of their de jure superiority over the serfs of Nagypécsely and Kispécsely and these attitudes persisted until well after the abolition of serfdom in 1848.

The twin villages of Nagy and Nemes and the manor of Kis had different landholding structures which rested on different principles of landownership and tenure. In 1842 the lands of the villages in the valley were constituted as shown in Table 1.1.

In Hungary the unit of serf holdings was the telek, the size of which was regulated countrywide.[2] The serfs of Nagy and Nemes held mainly quarter serf holdings, that is quarter teleks and only one household held a full serf holding.

Table 1.1
Constitution of land of the Pécsely valley in 1842 (in holds[a])

	All	Ploughing Fields	Vine-yards	Meadows	Woods	Other
Nagy	1,313	536	127	259	329	62
Nemes[b]	2,172	883	142	455	643	49

From: Community Records, Zala County Archives

[a]Hold: measure of land used in Hungary equal to 0.57 hectares or 1.42 English acres.
[b]Lands of the manor of Kis belonged for administrative purposes partly to Nemes and partly to Nagy.

Table 1.2
Distribution of land among serfs by size (in holds)

	20 & over		20-10		10-5		5-1		1-0		All	
	NGY	NS	NGY	NS	NGY	NS	NGY	NS	NGY	NS	NGY	NS
1779	1	1	3	1	30	2	22	8	19	31	75	43
1810	-	-	3	-	28	2	16	9	17	18	64	29
1842	-	1	3	3	27	3	21	-	16	36	67	43

From: Conscriptio Dicalis Possessionis Nagy et Nemes Pecsül pro Anno Militari 1779, 1810, 1842/3 ZML

In addition to the arable fields and meadows, most villagers had vineyards;[3] only one third of the serfs had none. These vineyards were an important source of cash for the villagers - very probably the only source for the majority - and they compensated somewhat for the small size of their farmland.

About half of the serfs of Nagypécsely had enough land, draught animals and vineyards to make them self-sufficient at a subsistence level without the need to contract for labour regularly. However, their self-sufficient status might be considerably modified by the quality of their farmland as well as by the ratio of workers to dependants in the household.

As the nemes residents of Nemespécsely were not taxable they were not listed in the records and information on their farmlands is lacking. In the 'Cadastre of Nobility of the Country of Zala' of 1790, however, the nemes of that village are listed. There were at that time 9 nemes families in Nemespécsely, comprising 29 households. They owned 1,213 holds of the local farming land, but there is no information about how it was distributed. If that land were equally distributed, each household would have had control of about 40 holds, that is 22.8 hectares, but in fact a much more unequal distribution is likely to have been the case. The land the nemes owned was about twice as large as the lands of the serf families, with correspondingly better economic conditions overall.

Neither the nemes nor the serfs had any chance of acquiring more land before 1848 because of the large allodial domain of the Catholic Church that took up part of the valley. All that could happen was redistribution of the land they held among their own numbers.

Although the declaration to emancipate the serfs in the spring of 1848 was the work of one day, the dismantling of the serf system went on for years, indeed almost three decades.[4] On balance, while serfs won emancipation and full ownership of the farms they worked, they also lost a great deal of land which had hitherto been in their control. In addition they had to raise considerable sums of money to redeem part of the lost land.[5] The new landowner peasants were, in fact, faced with many difficulties, for their farms had diminished and their debts increased. The new tax system[6] was heavier than previously and had to be met in cash. This led to the impoverishment and ruin of a large number of farms; between 1870 and 1910 about 100,000 small farms were ruined.

After 1848 peasant production for the market increased,

mainly because of the need to raise cash for taxes. Improvement of peasant production was facilitated by several innovations, such as the appearance of iron ploughs. Root crops and maize cultivation were more widely adopted by the late nineteenth century, resulting in better use of the soil. Improved strains of animals replaced the hardy, low milk and meat producing cattle and the good fat and meat producing mangalica pigs became common. Fodder crops, such as lucerne and sainfoin, were produced in greater volume so that the animals did not have to be pastured in the open all year round (Unger, 1973:224).

The dynamic growth of agriculture in the late nineteenth century was also associated with the development of capitalism and stimulated by the extensive market for Hungary's agricultural products within the Austro-Hungarian Empire. The newly built railway network, as well as improved river and road transport, allowed for a more efficient distribution throughout the country as well as aiding export, although they did little for villages far from the major regional centres. Developments favoured the larger agricultural production units and rich peasants rather than the smaller peasants, who, lacking the necessary capital, were less able to switch over to better techniques. Unable to compete, large numbers of this class were impoverished and swelled the ranks of the agrarian proletariat seeking subsistence as itinerant workers on the railway lines and embankment building (kubikos). Others joined industry as unskilled workers or emigrated overseas.

This process was less marked in the Balaton region for a variety of regionally specific reasons. There was less emigration; indeed, on the contrary, there was a vast influx of immigrants from other parts of the country. Between 1870 and 1952, for example, the population of the north shore increased from 26,830 to more than 50,000 (Orbán, 1953:43). There was no industry in the area to attract newcomers until the 1920s when factories were established in Füzfő and Vörösbereny. The significant factors for the region's development were, in fact, tourism and viticulture.

From the 1880s onwards the lake shores became popular holiday resorts for the gentry, and the region was developed to cater for this demand. A boat service was inaugurated by the turn of the century and the Fured-Tihany-Keszthely railway line was completed by 1907. Almádi, beyond Fured, was the first resort to develop in this way and a large number of villas were built all along the north shores, offering good labour opportunities for the rural landless both from the region itself and to newcomers.

Quality wines were grown extensively and in 1870 there were 7,655 holds (about 4,363 hectares) of vineyards on the north shore in the hands of 5,575 owners (a mean of 1.33 holds per owner). Vine growing was not suited primarily for large-scale cultivation on large estates and was mainly in the hands of individual smallholders. These comprised not only peasants but also tradesmen, non-agriculturalists and the intelligentsia that lived in the region (Orbán, 1958: 44). However, between 1878 and 1880 phylloxera spread unchecked over the entire region and destroyed the greater part of the vineyards. Their re-establishment, using grafts to wild, disease-resistant stock, was started immediately afterwards, providing labour for many people. However, the previous extent of vineyards was never reached again, although by 1935 there were 5,127 holds (about 2,922 hectares) which were of superior quality to the strains they had replaced.

Throughout the late nineteenth century there was a constant flow of newcomers to the region who formed the bulk of the landless stratum. During World War I, development of the region slowed somewhat but picked up again in the 1920s and continued steadily in spite of the general economic recession of the 1930s. Building proceeded at a great pace and by the 1930s about 1,000 villas, many of them occupied throughout the year, had been erected around the north shore of the lake.

In view of these regionally specific circumstances, distribution of land among the peasantry was less unequal than elsewhere in the country (Orbán, 1958:45). The small and middle peasants could find markets for their wines and other products in the region itself, and were able to hold their ground better. The landless had more labour opportunities (for example, in construction) than elsewhere and were less dependent on seasonal labour on large estates and on individual peasant holdings. Vineyards are very labour intensive, though mainly on a seasonal basis, and the re-establishment of vines in the area absorbed a great deal of labour.

The Pécsely valley is not located directly on the shores of Lake Balaton, but inland, in what may be described as the second ring of villages surrounding it. It is more isolated than the villages on the lake and no holiday villas were built in Pécsely in the 1930s. Generally, however, influences similar to those in the lakeside villages were at work.

In Pécsely the pattern of land distribution in particular and the lot of the villagers in general, were overwhelm-

ingly influenced by decisions regarding the local manorial
estates. In 1848, the Bishop of Veszprém and the Provost of
Óbuda granted tenure of their estates to two wealthy families, who remained in control of these lands and lived locally until 1912. When both tenants renounced their lease
and the owners decided to sell the estates, about 700 holds
(about 399 hectares) of land came up for sale in small lots.
This type of sale was uncommon: in Hungary such domains
usually changed hands undivided.

The land sale of 1912 provided a much needed opportunity for the villagers to improve their lot and increase
their holdings. Altogether, 63 local families bought land
in this deal, a third of all families. Twenty four were
from Nagy, thirty nine from Nemes and none from Kis.
Clearly, there was ample market for land locally, and the
villagers had the means to seize that opportunity. It is
also clear that the opportunity could best be seized by
those who had some land already and not the landless.

The main effect of this sale was to establish firmly a
base of middle and rich peasants as well as to broaden the
base of small farmers who after the sale became virtually
self-sufficient. The sale was indicative of the needs and
scarcities of the valley's farming land. Of those buyers
who had very little land, most are found to have owned 1-2
hold vineyards - which shows that in this area the possess-
ion of vineyards gave a man the best chance to acquire a
farm of viable size. Two thirds of the lands bought in 1912
were woods, which were always scarce in the valley and hence
at a premium. More importantly, they could be cleared to
make way for the establishment of vines; indeed, this is
what happened and several hillsides were deforested in the
1920s and planted with good quality vineyards. In most
cases the 1912 buyer was adding to his farm. He may have
had some arable land, but not enough; he therefore aimed to
add to it, and he may also have invested in some holds of
woods. As a result, the number of farms well endowed with
arable fields, meadows, woods and vineyards increased significantly. By 1930 the distribution of land in the valley
was as shown in Table 1.3.

The sale of the Bishopric's estate in the Pécsely valley represented a major change and break with the past. It
brought to an end the situation where the peasant farms were
in the stranglehold of one large, indivisible estate - a
situation which in most parts of Hungary did not come to an
end until 1945. Henceforth the owners of large farms in the
valley were people who lived locally, had extensive kinship
ties within the villages and were not as remote and alien as

Table 1.3
Land distribution in 1930 (in holds)

1930	100+	100-50	50-10	10-1	1-0	Sum
Nemes	1 1.5%	- -	24 27%	35 40%	23 26%	83
Nagy	1 1.5%	1 1.5%	17 24%	30 48%	13 20%	62

From: Magyar Királyi Statisztikai Kötetek 1930, vol 86, p. 34.

Table 1.4
The area of holdings by size category in Nemes, 1935

Farms under 1 hold	1-5	5-50	50-100	100-500	All
Total of holds and percentage of the villages' farmland					
44 1.9%	447 20%	1,164 53%	216 10%	292 13%	2,163

From: Magyarország Földbirtokviszonyai 1935 Statisztikai Kötetek, p. 118.

the landlords before 1912.

In the nineteenth century the stratification of Hungarian peasantry hardened into a rigidly hierarchical land-centred system. Scarcity of land and a growing rural population gave rise to a relentless drive for land acquisition and the landowning strata were set in an almost 'caste' like form. The three localities of the Pécsely valley well illustrate how landownership patterns shaped the social composition and character of rural communities.

After 1848, the categories of landed nemes, landed serf and landless serf (zsellér) were carried over and loosely applied to wealthy and middle peasants, small peasants and landless labourers. The local concentration of each category in Nemes, Nagy and Kis-pécsely respectively served to crystallize these divisions and emphasize their distinctness.

In the Pécsely area, landownership categories were compounded and reinforced by other divisions, more importantly the Protestant and Catholic division. The former corresponded to the landowners (either of serf or nemes descent) and the latter to the smaller landowners and the landless. The Catholics were mainly exogenous newcomers while the Protestants formed a core of torzsokos families, that is, those families that had been settled locally over several generations or even centuries. They can be considered the core of Pécsely's peasantry, whereas the Catholics formed the more mobile, transient, but ever-increasing part of the population.

The core of the village of Nemespécsely was composed of a group of larger Protestant landholding families of long-standing local residence, many of them nemes.

In the nineteenth century and up to 1945, members of the wealthy landowner stratum almost all belonged to the extensive Protestant families. Those owning more than 40 holds (about 23 hectares) generally assumed a directing role in the management of their farms but did little physical labour themselves. Among these richer peasants there were some who were interested in farming and technical innovations and were, for example, in a position to buy the first threshing machines. With more surplus to sell they were more involved in the market beyond the village than their poorer fellows. Their role in village affairs was significant in that they had an assured place in the body of village representatives as virilists (members of the highest tax paying group) and were in the best position to obtain offices such as that of mayor. In the Protestant church they were the leading contributors and filled prestigious positions in the Church Council. The leading landowners were more likely to have their children educated beyond the six elementary grades, even though most preferred their sons - or at least one son - to remain on the farm. Those few villagers who had higher schooling between 1850 and 1930 - two lawyers, two engineers and two notaries - were all from the wealthy peasant families.

The wealthier peasants had the means to increase their holdings but in Pécsely there is no evidence to suggest that they came to control ever greater shares of land at the expense of the small peasants. Of the wealthy peasants, some leaned towards gentry (úri) habits: gambling, carousing, hunting and leaving the farm to be worked by employees. Many dissipated much of their wealth in this way and earned themselves the reputation of kenyeretlen urak, 'breadless gentlemen,' and even though their wealth was dwindling fast they kept up their leisurely lifestyle.

The middle peasants were entirely different. Characteristically, they were set on the accumulation of assets, worked relentlessly, drove their families hard and adopted an austere lifestyle. In Nemes there were about 20 landowner families in this category in the 1930s, fully peasant in lifestyle, their lands large enough to allow self-sufficient, independent subsistence. As in other Hungarian villages, within the peasant household control over material resources and production was in the hands of the elder couple: gazda and gazdaasszony (Fél and Hofer, 1969). The gazda was the head of the household, usually the oldest married man and the owner of the farm. Gazda status refers not only to the position of authority within the family but also to the ownership of enough land to allow self sufficiency; it also refers to being a farmer by birth, upbringing and expertise. Financial independence and leadership in the organization of production on the family farm are also implied by the status of gazda. The term is equivalent to 'chef d'entreprise' as used by S.H. Franklin (1969). Gazdaasszony is wife of the gazda and his female counterpart in charge of the farm and household.

The economic and landownership structure in each local unit of the valley found its way into stereotypic definitions. The former nemes landowner families of Nemes had been established in their farms and within the community for centuries. They were self-sufficient, less in need of one another, and had therefore gained a reputation for haughty independence. They did not have active and lively informal organizations such as existed in their twin village of Nagy where there was a good Farmers' Circle and several informal

Table 1.5
The area of holdings by size category in Nagy, 1935

Farms under 1 hold	1-5	5-50	50-100	100-500	All
Total of cadastral holds and percentage of the határ					
52 4.3%	266 20%	307 23%	54 4%	624 47%	1,303

From: Magyarország Földbirtokviszonyai 1935 Statisztikai Kötetek, p. 118.

cooperative groups in the 1930s (see pp. 54-56). They did, however, have extensive individual ties of reciprocal help, which was an important factor governing the organization of village life in rural Hungary at all levels. Even after 1848, the nemes retained and displayed awareness of their ancestry and the curialis status of Nemes, even though it was no longer the source of any special privileges. In terms of address they distinguished themselves by insisting on titles of deference as 'honourable' (Tekintetes, Méltosagos), of which the Hungarian language has such a rich and subtle store. As the smallholders of Nagy remember: 'The nemes landowners of that village were a sort of caste,' referring to their proud bearing and preferential association with people of the same status which endured well into the twentieth century.

In Nagypécsley the core of residents was formed by small peasants, descendants of former serf families who had established themselves in independent, or nearly independent, smallholdings principally thanks to the land sale of 1912. Compared with Nemespécsely, a much smaller proportion of the határ - only about one quarter - constituted holdings from 5 to 50 holds.

The smallholders of Nagy who were already landholders needed merely to increase their holdings to ensure and consolidate their existence. They strove to achieve this by contracting for seasonal or daily labour, or devising other forms of income-raising activity such as, for example, horse dealing. The smallholders of Nagy were reputed to be hardworking and intent on raising themselves to independent middle peasant status; in this aim they were ready to cooperate with one another. Their Farmers' Circle and their informal cooperative groups (see p. 55) were known for their dynamism and efficiency. Their common aims and the similarity of their economic position welded them into a hard working, cooperative and upward-striving community.

The smaller the farm was, the less fully could the ideal of self-sufficient independence be achieved, and the role of the gazda was proportionately less complete in scope and authority. The smallholder with insufficient land for independence had to augment his income by contracting for labour on an occasional or seasonal basis and team owners - of whom there were 34 in 1941 - were in a better position to do this by, for example, engaging in sharecropping. This offered the best prospects for the accumulation of cash for the purchase of further parcels of land. Smallholders and owners of 'dwarf' holdings of Nagypécsely had many relationships with the middle and rich gazdas of Nemespécsely for day and seasonal labour. Until 1910 the landless and owners of dwarf holdings of Nagy congregated daily in front of the church, and the gazdas would come and engage daily labourers from among them as required. After 1910 these gatherings were discontinued and the gazdas in need of labourers had to solicit them in their homes. Thus the villages of Nagy and Nemes were in an employer-employee relationship, the employers always living in the latter village.

With a population of about 100, Kispécsely was not a village proper although it was mentioned separately in documents until the late eighteenth century; thereafter it became administratively part of Nemespécsely. Even for a manorial estate, that is puszta, it was very small by Hungarian standards. The size of its population varied and was at its greatest between 1860 and 1899. Thereafter the number of resident labourer families declined and, when most of it was sold in 1912, only 15 to 18 families continued to live there, employed by the new owner of a much reduced estate of about 300 holds (174 ha).

Few of the adult residents of Kis were born there as very little continuity of residence existed. Typically, labourers were employed for a few years and their children invariably moved away. Residents of the puszta were landless and were employed in different occupational branches of traditional agriculture, either as unspecialized labourers or as herdsmen, shepherds, teamsters or craftsmen.

For the steady flow of newcomers, the first choice of employment was to work on the puszta of Kis. From here some could eventually secure employment on the farm of one of the gazdas of Nagy or Nemes. By finding employment in the villages, newcomers stood a better chance of settling permanently and to being drawn into the network of community relationships. At present there are about 36 Catholic families in Pécsely who initially worked on the puszta and have succeeded in establishing themselves in the village.

The conditions of the landless labourers was by far the most insecure and unfavourable. They belonged to Hungary's agrarian proletariat, often described as the country's 'three million beggars' in the inter-war period. Their living quarters in either the manor or the individual farms, were dismal, with often several families to a room. Empty and ruined quarters such as these can be inspected even today. The landless labourers' food was poor and lacking in protein and their clothing was inadequate for the harsh Hungarian winter. Their health was poor and tuberculosis was endemic (Held, 1980:255-264). Their security of existence depended entirely on their employment, whether working for the estate or individual gazdas.

In the eyes of the landowner peasants in the villages, the landless labourers were lazy and unable to manage themselves independently, lacking in initiative and relentless dedication and expertise, with which the independent gazdas were credited. Such subjective definition disregarded the de facto difficulties of obtaining land and the socio-economic structure of the time. The landless themselves were, of course, aware of the objective limitations of their situation and felt unjustly penalized by such stereotypic generalizations. Differences such as these had the effect of putting distance between the landed peasant and the landless labourer, a fact that was to acquire great significance in the post-war years as we shall see in later chapters.

The component social groups found in the Pécsely valley were typical of Hungary in general: landowners and landless, Catholics and Protestants, descendants of serfs and nemes, were to be found in most villages throughout Hungary, in various proportions and strengths. In Pécsely the pattern of arrangement of these groups had its own locally specific features. First, the division between landless and landed coincided very neatly with the division along religious denominational boundaries. Second, the different landholding strata were clustered in different localities, which were fairly autonomous. Most Hungarian villages were divided into 'Upper' and 'Lower' ends, each with its predominant landowning stratum (cf. Fél and Hofer, 1969; Hann, 1980; Bodrogi, 1978), but in Pécsely this division was more than just different 'ends' of one administratively united community: Nemes and Nagy were totally autonomous until 1940.

Another feature of the specific conditions in Pécsely was that its landless did not have to go out in search of seasonal labour as was the case in most other villages. Indeed, Pécsely's landless stratum was constantly being replenished by newcomers attracted by the relative abundance of labour opportunities offered by extensive viticulture. Thus, the villagers' contact with the outside took place neither through seasonal employment in agriculture elsewhere nor through industry, but mainly through limited, though regular, contacts, for example through marketing their wines. In many villages in Hungary where the landless were numerous and unable to subsist on labour provided locally, a type developed which approached the 'worker' in mentality as compared to the traditional peasant (Jávor, 1978:296). In Pécsely no such type of individuals emerged; the conversion from traditional peasant to the new 'worker-peasant' was delayed until after 1945, in response to the situation that arose at that time (see pp. 195-196).

Several trends working in opposing directions may be identified among developments in the Pécsely valley in the first half of the twentieth century. First, the strengthening of the land-centred rigidly hierarchical 'land acquisition complex' took place; this has, with some justification, been elevated to almost mythical importance in Hungarian ethnographic literature. Second, the weakening of the hold of the local large estates took place: as has been shown, an important part of these was broken up in 1912 and fragmented into smaller farms of which the villagers themselves acquired a large share. In effect, the independent land-holding stratum was strengthened in the pre-World War II period, and the villagers of Pécsely were no longer in the stranglehold of large estates as was the case elsewhere in rural Hungary until 1945. However, the landless stratum was being continuously replenished by newcomers, and both land-hunger and the struggle for land remained pressing problems.

Landownership was the basis on which Pécsley's community rested. Until 1945 it was the main source for subsistence for the bulk of the population, 83% being employed in agriculture. A family's relationship to the land, or to those who owned it, largely determined its security of existence, as well as its social and economic status within the community. The central point of reference and social categorization was the 'middle peasant,' the ideal type of which is the independent, self-sufficient farming unit based on family alone (Chayanov, 1966; Franklin, 1969). In Hungary, however, although the middle peasant was pivotal within the peasantry mainly as a model, numerically the middle peasant was always a minority[7] - in contrast to Russia where, according to Chayanov, the middle peasant comprised a numerical majority in the early 1900s. In Hungary therefore the peasantry was not characterized by the constancy and numerical predominance of self-sufficient family farming units, but by the fluctuation of the strata just above and below that of the middle peasant. The strata merged at the immediate upper and lower levels, but grew further and further away from the peasant ideal at the extreme ends of the spectrum. That is, by merging into the landless proletariat at one end or growing into the lower strata of the rural gentry at the other. After World War II, however, the 'pull' of the middle peasant ideal was clearly revealed; the landless who came into land ownership through the Land Reform in 1945 saw in that reform their opportunity to approach that ideal at last - a barren hope as it will be shown (pp. 43-45). On

the other hand, the measures aimed at liquidating the rich
peasant stratum after the war achieved little more than to
bring that stratum down to the middle peasant level, to
which they clung with unforeseen tenacity. The result was
the strengthening of the hold of the middle peasant ideal,
which was to become the main point of resistance to collectivization. In fact, elements of the peasant 'family economy' (Chayanov, 1966) were built into the socialist economy
in a variety of ways. Even in the 1950s, when the greatest
pressure was exerted on the peasantry, in conditions which
would have eliminated other forms of economic enterprise,
the peasantry of Hungary showed remarkable ability to absorb
that pressure. They worked longer hours, sold at rock-
bottom prices, went without any surplus - and still kept up
farming. That process certainly confirms Chayanov's view of
the competitive edge and power of the peasant family economy
in the face of advances of large-scale farming, capitalist
and socialist alike.

Although the peasantry as such has become numerically
insignificant in Hungary since 1960, elements of the 'peasant economy' or the peasant mode of production' (Tepicht,
1973:50-68 and 75) have remained. As one example, one may
point to plot farming which utilizes family labour. Here,
no wages are involved and hence the exact cash value of
labour is not calculable; this leads to readiness to put up
with the drudgery of labour involved, a willingness which is
not in evidence in relation to wage labour. However, as
will be shown, in the 1980s in relation to the work on plots
there are already signs of moving away from the peasant's
vague sense of 'it is worth it' to exact calculations of
profit, and 'family needs' are no longer defined in terms of
pure subsistence, rather on urban models of consumption. In
other words, the peasant family economy currently serves
non-peasant, urban consumer aspirations in many instances.
So in the chapters that follow there will not only be a
discussion of the changes in the structure of land ownership
and the demise of the peasant family economy, but also of
the great flexibility with which elements of the traditional
peasant system adapted to fundamentally altered conditions,
whether economic, social or political.

NOTES

1. <u>Határ</u>: the precisely delimited tracts of land which
have been used and tilled by the people of one village for
centuries. Ditches mark the boundary line. Serfs were for-
bidden to move beyond it; they were bound to the <u>határ</u>.
(Szabó I, 1965:55)

2. <u>Telek</u>: serf-holdings of between 20 to 40 holds, of
which serfs could control half, a quarter or an eighth. It
usually also included a house, and serfs were bound to
supply corvée and tithes in proportion to the fraction of
<u>telek</u> they controlled.

3. Vineyards were not part of the serf <u>telek</u>, although
a ninth part was due to the landlord from the wine produced.
Usually landlords did not prevent their tenants extending
their vineyards. (Szabó I, 1965)

4. The laws of 1848 which abolished serfdom, left many
questions unsettled. The identification of lands which
counted as parts of a manorial tenement, compared with allodial lands of the landlord, was a major question. It was
found that serfs had been working lands which could not be
unambiguously classified as part of their <u>urbarial</u> holdings
- such as recent clearings, vineyards and the plot of the
<u>inquilini</u>. The <u>Urbarium</u> which recorded the lands worked by
the serfs, served as proof of the size of the serfs' holdings, but with the tacit approval of the landlord some portions of the lands de facto worked by serfs had not been
entered in the <u>Urbarium</u> to avoid taxes. These lands were
not covered by the 1848 laws and the serfs had to negotiate
with the landlord to redeem them for payment. Apart from
the loss of these lands themselves, the definition of the
size of the serf tenement mattered because in 1848 the meadows and pastures hitherto used in common with the landlord
were divided and each serf had a part in proportion to the
size of his tenement. Recent clearings, unrecorded in the
<u>Urbarium</u>, were, in the county of Zala to which Pécsely bel-
onged, almost as large as the tenement lands. Landlords did
not as a rule agree to the full redemption of such lands;
for example, the Bishop of Veszprém allowed only one third
of residual lands to be redeemed in the Füred-Pécsely area.
(Für, 1965:98)

5. The <u>inquilini</u> (serfs without <u>telek</u>) who owned a
house had right to only 500m^2 of internal fundus around the
house and could redeem, by private arrangement with the
landlord, the 1-2 holds of land they had been working
hitherto. Otherwise they were not covered by the 1848 laws

and were more disadvantaged than helped by the serf emancipation. Vineyards on the hillsides ('promontorium') had never been technically part of the serf tenement, unlike the few rows of vine a serf might have around his house. Hillside vines were assets established by the serfs at considerable cost and labour. The vineyards had not been covered by the 1848 laws, which led to widespread discontent, the majority refusing to deliver the ninth to the landlord. The question of vineyards took many years to settle and was concluded only in 1897 when a law was passed to allow them to be redeemed for an agreed sum. The economic importance of the vineyards was particularly great in the Balaton region as they were for many serfs the main source of livelihood, especially the inquilini, who had little or no other land.

6. After 1848 the most important tax was on land. For the assessment of this, countrywide, cadastral surveys were made in 1853, corrected in 1875, and finalized in 1883. Assessments were based on a complex system of grading land in seven quality categories. In addition, there were taxes on house and income which, although small, were hardest on the landless and poor. There were also supplementary taxes levied regularly after 1852 - road tax, supplementary county tax, and church tax - as well as other charges on pasturing, market places and death duties. Overall, taxes were of a regressive kind, so that smaller landowners paid up to three times the rate paid by wealthy peasants and 5-6 times per hold as the owners of thousands of holds. (Varga, 1965:292-295.)

7. The middle peasants were seen as the core and strength of Hungarian peasantry. In one sense this is misleading; in another quite correct. The middle peasants were by no means the most numerous - in 1935 those with between 5 and 25 holds comprised no more than one quarter of all landowners countrywide. On the other hand, the middle peasant was the ideal type aimed at by the less prosperous: '...numerically the "proper peasants" were in a minority but their way of life was the more or less generally accepted model for the village...' (Fél and Hofer, 1972:481)

2

The Land Reform of 1945

The land reform of 1945 was the first measure which struck at the basis of land ownership, significantly altering the economic structure of rural Hungary. After completion of the land reform, matters did not rest, for collectivization followed on its heels and, in many ways, the reform had opened the way towards it.[1] The land reform was indeed a significant antecedent to the establishment of a socialist sector of production.

With the end of World War II, the tasks of reconstruction facing the country were immense. A Provisional Government, set up in Debrecen in December 1944, began to attend to the most pressing needs. Among the political parties, the Communist Party in particular was quick to activate and organize its local cells countrywide and, supported by Soviet troops, to undertake urgent tasks such as clearing ruins and collecting provisions. It was essential that agricultural production be resumed fast and this provided the impetus to push through the bill of land reform with exceptional speed in the spring of 1945. The land reform, in turn, helped the Communist Party to activate cells in every village and establish a basis of popular support among the recipients of new land. In the event, support was not as strong as expected, as shown by the poor results achieved by the Communist Party in the elections of December 1945, which collected only 17% of the votes. Votes were cast overwhelmingly for the Smallholders Party (56%).[2] Yet, both nationally and locally this victory had little influence on the subsequent development of the political power structure. By 1948 the Communist Party had succeeded in discrediting or absorbing all the other parties, in a struggle which polarized into one with the Communist Party on one side and all other parties on the other. The merger of the Social Democrats with the Communist Party in March 1947, in fact marks the definitive disintegration of all other parties. The Hungarian Workers Party became the sole political power.

The land reform was long awaited by the landless agricultural population; its final terms were announced in March 1945 and, with exceptional speed, actual redistribution of land was under way by April. It involved 35% of Hungary's agricultural land: 5.6 million holds (1 hold = 0.57 ha = 1.42 acres), one third of which was redistributed among eligible claimants, the remainder being retained by the State for the establishment of State Farms, collectives and forestry. Estates above 200 holds were seized for distribution and the proportion of large estate owners fell from 7% to 2.8% after the reform. The number of smallholders of less than 1 hold was reduced from 45% to 17%, while the owners of between 1 and 25 holds rose from 47.2% to 80.2% (Berend, 1979:28).

The land reform was executed through locally elected land-claiming committees, the Községi Földigénylő Bizotság, or KFB for short. Members of the KFBs were chosen from among people who were themselves eligible claimants: that is, who were either landless labourers or who had holdings below 10 holds. The function of the KFBs was to decide who was entitled to land, but not to decide which lands would be distributed and in what way; in principle this was the function of the higher county land reform councils. In practice, all over the country the KFBs not only marked the lands for distribution, but, overstepping their original functions, also proceeded to distribute them.

This was condoned by the State authorities, for the emphasis was on speed not only for fear of political reaction against the reform but also to allow resumption of agricultural production as soon as possible (Donáth,1977:52).

The decentralized system of execution, through the local KFBs, allowed the reform to be completed within a very short time. Emphasis was on speedy execution, without allowing adminstrative minutiae and strict adherence to legal specifications to slow it down or stop it. The official stance was to disregard procedural irregularities as long as they remained 'within the spirit of the reform' (Béli, 1977:155).

Parts of estates of over 100 holds (57 hectares) were liable to be reclaimed, and estates over 1,000 holds (570 hectares) were reclaimed entirely. Estates of between 100 and 200 holds could be exempted from distribution if they could be proved to be farmed by their owners: that is, a distinction was made between peasant holdings and gentry estates (úri birtok). Vineyards and woods of over 10 holds (5.7 hectares) could also be distributed. The lands of war criminals, traitors, Nazi leaders and those 'guilty of crimes against the people' were confiscated, regardless of size.[3] Cash compensation was promised to the people whose lands had been reclaimed, but was never paid. Recipients had to redeem the land from the State, not from the previous owners, paying about one quarter of the land's market value over 10 to 20 years. The State did not press for instalments that were not paid regularly but, in the 1950s, pressure to recover these debts was started as a means of forcing new landowners into the collectives that were formed at that time (see p. 56).

The impact of the reform varied from village to village. Several chance factors determined the impact, most importantly, the size of the estates that could be claimed locally and the number of claimants in relation to the available land. Some villages were well-endowed, while in others there were hardly any estates that could be claimed. In a report on the reform in the county of Zala, to which Pécsely belonged until 1940, Z. Béli describes the wide spectrum of effects the reform could have in different villages (Béli, 1977).

In Pécsely itself the impact of the reform was limited. The only two estates that fell into a category liable for redistribution were the Merza and Marton estates. The Martons were a Jewish family killed in the war. Their estate, partly on the Nagypécsely side and partly in Kispécsely, comprised well over 200 holds and, because its owners were dead, could be claimed in its entirety. The Merza estate, comprising about 117 holds of land around Kispécsely, was smaller than the stipulated claimable size but counted as a 'gentry' holding because the Merzas were related to Count Zichy and did not farm it themselves. The other two holdings in Pécsely that were around 100 holds were not claimed, as their owners were themselves farmers.

The villagers heard rumours of the impending reform, but even when it was announced there was a great deal of uncertainty about its terms, as well as its finality. The reform was closely monitored by the local and regional Communist Party cells, who helped and advised the KFBs. A close correlation between party membership and advantage in the land allocation was rumoured to exist. In Pécsely, the local Party cell appears to have been formed directly in relation to the prospect of the land reform: it was founded on 20th April 1945 and the reform started on 25th April. Of the eight KFB members, six were members of the Communist Party. Many land recipients were Party members, but, in Pécsely, Party membership does not seem to have been an obvious source of favouritism in the redistribution.

The reform concerned and mobilized mainly the poorer strata and those few who feared their lands would be claimed. The majority of landowning villagers and community representatives remained aloof. In the pre-1945 period poorer villagers played a very limited role in community affairs, the land reform perhaps being the first occasion on which they came forward as a group and became active in an affair of community interest. But the land recipients from Nagy, Nemes and Kis-pécsely were mainly Catholic newcomers or labourers employed in the manor, who did not form a group with enduring common interest. When the reform was over, they dispersed and social life in the village went on as usual.

The KFB of Pécsely included members from the poorer strata of the village. The chairman was a smallholder from Nemes and the controller a shoemaker, a pre-war Communist of long standing. Two members were community shepherds, two were farmhands and there were also two smallholders.

The distribution was not contested by either the previous owners or the recipients. The outcome of the reform depended largely on the ability of the KFBs in charge: in some villages they were more militant on behalf of the landless, while in others they were more or less determined to secure the maximum amount of land for redistribution. The KFB of Pécsely was not militant and neither were the land recipients who acknowledged the share allotted to them and did not press for a new distribution or a new committee, as happened in many other villages (cf. Béli, 1977).

Of the seized estates about 89 holds were distributed to 54 claimants, and the remaining 300 holds of land were held back in reserve and eventually formed the basis for the first collective. It is not altogether clear why only one third of the available land was distributed, but it suggests that both country and district authorities exercised close control over the redistribution, for clearly the villagers' interest would be to distribute as much land as possible among individual claimants. The KFB of Pécsely did not appear to have stood up in favour of a larger scale redistribution.

The claimants mainly requested vineyards, which were four to five times more valuable than grain fields of equivalent size and could be worked without draught animals, few of which were available after the war. Large parts of the

Merza and Marton estates consisted of grazing land and as such they were not particularly coveted; that may have been one reason why nobody in Pécsely contested the redistribution. Some eligible poor families did not have a share either because they were too timid to come forward or were intimidated by the high-handed manners of some of the KFB members. But on the whole the KFB's decisions were accepted and the reform was carried out in a quiet, not to say insignificant, manner.

The KFB established the order of priorities among the claimants and decided, for example, whether a landless family with one child was in greater need than another with some land but many members. Other factors, such as the prospect of inheritance, ability to farm, and good character, also mattered. Such broad guidelines allowed individual cases to be discerningly considered, but they also opened the way towards nepotism. In Pécsely, where the distributed lands were of approximately similar size, competitition was in relation to quality rather than the size of land. Predictably, members of the KFB could never quite be absolved, according to the village opinion, from the charges of favouring themselves in the distribution by allocating themselves the best vineyards. To confirm these suspicions, it is notable that seven out of the eight KFB members subsequently succeeded in establishing themselves as individual farmers, increasing their lands, while the majority of the other land recipients gave up agriculture shortly afterwards or remained unprosperous. On the other hand it cannot be ignored that KFB members had been selected from the most resourceful, respected and industrious members of the poorer stratum, and their subsequent prosperity, therefore, cannot be entirely attributed to their advantageous position as committee members.

The pieces of distributed land were very small (Table 2.1), no more than mere plots which could not form the basis of self-sufficient farms. However, out of the 89 holds of land distributed, about 53 were vineyards, which represented greater value than grain fields.

The land reform created few viable, self-sufficient farms, and the new recipients faced immense difficulties: they had hardly any implements, tools, animals or fertilizers to enrich the soil impoverished after the war. The equipment of the manorial estates was mainly of an indivisible kind, and in the heat of the reform much of it was damaged. For example, a valuable threshing machine was taken apart and the pieces dispersed. War had depleted animal stocks and only three teams of horses remained on the Marton and Merza estates, which were retained by members of the

Table 2.1
Land distributed in the land reform of 1945 (in holds)

Size of land:	5 h & over	4	3	2	1 & less
No. of recipients:	3	4	3	4	28

Unaccounted for: 12 recipients

From: Gáldonyi, B., 1975:12

Table 2.2
Land distribution in Pécsely before and after the land reform (in holds)

Size of farms	0-1	1-5	5-10	10-20	20-50	50 & over	All
1941	15 13%	39 34%	29 25%	22 19%	6 5%	2 1%	113
1949	31 17%	71 39%	33 18%	22 12%	18 10%	3 1%	178

Részleges Mezőg. Eredmények, Történeti Statisztikai Kötetek 1941, vol. 1;
Népszámlálás 1949, vol. 3.

KFB. They were intended to be used by all new land recipients, but the tendency was for KFB members' kin and friends to be favoured while those unconnected had no access. In any event, three teams were not enough for all.

The land reform did not significantly alter the overall landholding structure in Pécsely (Table 2.2). Half the farming population were owners of between 1 and 50 holds before the reform; for them the reform made little difference. Approximately half of all families owned 1 hold of land or less and the fact that they were given a further 1 to 3 holds did not significantly alter their way of life, improve their lot or modify their place in relation to other groups in the village. They still remained the village poor.

Very few land recipients succeeded in establishing themselves as independent gazdas by adding to their farms through the purchase of further parcels. Most successful were some of the KFB members; the others appear to have led a very chequered existence, twelve joining the first collective formed in 1949, the others drifting into industry, or into other non-agricultural employment, or finding occasional labour with the local gazdas. All these alternatives were problematic. The collective was at this period very poor both in terms of organisation and productivity (Chapter 4) and members drifted in and out of it, unsettled. Some examples of relative success in individual farming can be found, but for the majority the land reforms brought little relief. Of the original land recipients, there are thirty-two still living in Pécsely today; the others have either moved away or have died. Of those remaining in Pécsely, twenty have retired from the collective, six are still working there and six are in non-agricultural employment, mainly in manual, unskilled labour.

In the early years after 1945 the difficulties encountered by the new land recipients were serious, and experience impressed upon them that they could not survive on their small farms alone. In 1949 they were therefore the most receptive to the idea of collectivization.

The land reform may be regarded as an important antecedent to collectivization in its results, if not in its aims; it eliminated the large estates countrywide, without, however, giving rise to a significant number of viable, self-sufficient small farms that could provide subsistence for the whole of the agricultural population. In Pécsely, as elsewhere in the country, the first collectives were formed on lands that had been objects of the land reform or on reserve lands that had been retained by the State and had attracted members who had been recipients of small parcels of land in 1945.

NOTES

1. Some consider the post-war land reforms in Eastern Europe to have been more ambiguous in aim, with some justification. In relation to Yugoslavia, for example, '... the real aim [of communists] was the implementation of collectivization rather than land reform' (Klein G. & Klein P. 'The Land Reform in Yugoslavia, in Völgyes, 1979, p. 39).

2. For a full account of politics in Hungary between 1945-1948 see I. Völgyes 'Politics in Hungary' 1979, and F. Donáth 'Reform and Revolution' 1980.

3. The reform guidelines were, of course, more complex than outlined here. See F. Donáth, 1977 and 1980; I. Berend, 1979.

PART 2

Agricultural Collectivization

3

Agrarian Policies
in the 1950s

The campaigns of collectivization started in 1948 took about a decade to be completed countrywide and another two decades for collectives to be irreversibly integrated into the country's economic and social system. It is beyond doubt that even this pace proved too fast and very difficult for the peasantry.

One of the crucial questions in the course of collectivization was how far the peasantry were prepared to cooperate. Despite the power the State could bring to bear upon them, the peasants could exert some indirect influence upon the course of agrarian programmes - for example by delaying and hampering collective production directing their labour into certain sectors and withholding from others. The initial collectivization drive in 1948 to 1953 undoubtedly employed coercive methods and did not significantly achieve the effect it was designed to produce: to convince the peasants of the superiority of collective production over individual peasant farming.

Collectivization began in Hungary in the very unfavourable period of political transition in the late 1940s and early 1950s.

The newly-nationalized heavy industry was set on a course of forced development, in line with socialist policy which required a strong industry and a broad worker stratum. Agriculture, based on traditional peasant farming, was still recovering from war damage when the burden of supporting this industrialization was laid on it.

Agriculture was subjected to State intervention and centralized control through three main means: control over production and marketing; liquidation of the wealthy peasant stratum; and collectivization. This three-pronged approach went a long way towards fundamentally changing the

relationship of the peasantry to the land and towards altering the rural socio-economic structure. However, during the
first ten years, which may be considered as a first phase,
the establishment of a socialist mode of production as the
dominant form was not entirely successful.

Close control over agricultural production and marketing was exerted through heavy taxation, a system of compulsory delivery quotas to the State at nominal prices,[1] and a
system of compulsory production of a specified range of products. The obligation for peasants to market their surplus
products, which had been introduced during the war, was developed into a complex system of compulsory quotas of production and deliveries which, by 1949, included all forms of
farm products: grains, fruit, meats, wine and fodder. Each
peasant had to contribute specified amounts of goods covering a large range of products, even if his farm was small
and better suited for a narrower range of specialized products. Many peasants teamed up together and exchanged goods
so that each could meet the full range of his quotas. The
quotas increased progressively in proportion to the size of
the farms and the wealthier peasant was faced with three to
four times larger quotas than, for example, the owner of
5 holds.

In a drive to eradicate 'exploitation' among the peasantry the so-called anti-kulák system was set up, on the
Soviet model. All peasants who owned 25 holds of land and
above were classed as wealthy, 'exploiter' peasant gazdas,
i.e. kuláks. Vineyards and other plots of intensive cultivation were rated at five times their acreage and regular
employment of farm-hands was considered a criterion of kulák
status in borderline cases. Secret lists of kuláks were
prepared by the council of each village and were regularly
revised, mainly in order to add further names, so that a
climate of uncertainty prevailed. The aim was, indeed, to
liquidate all those branded kuláks. Burdens were constantly
increased; in 1953 the taxes demanded from the kuláks were
168% higher than two years previously. Collections were
made locally and there were heavy penalties for non-
compliance or default, which produced a staggering number of
prosecutions: 400,000 peasants were interned, incarcerated
or fined between 1949 and 1953 (Donáth, 1977:149).

Who was and who was not included on the kulák list
depended, to some extent, on the goodwill of the local council and the Party; personal considerations were important
in borderline cases. Many middle peasants were included in
the lists. In Pécsely, twenty-five were listed as kuláks:
eight from Nagypécsely, the others from Nemespécsely. Of

these, fifteen owned less than 25 holds but had vineyards, which counted for five times their size. Only six could be classified as <u>nagygazda</u>, that is, as wealthy peasants in terms of the traditional local evaluation (owning about 35 holds and employing labourers on a permanent basis).

The <u>kulák</u> regulations, and the system of compulsory deliveries and requisitions, made a complex local system of control necessary, through which the village was linked to the district and county authorities. The main agency of control was the local council which had been reorganized along new lines in 1950 (Chapter 23). Its members were drawn entirely from the poorer landowners and landless, who could be trusted to be in political agreement with the socialist government. It was a large body of thirty-six members, none of whom had previously played any role in village administration.

The villagers were regularly summoned by the council or the district authorities to receive production directives, to account for their production, and so on. They were also regularly visited at home, both by fellow villagers acting as controllers and by individuals from outside the village. Through this new and complex system of control, the village was subject to an unprecedented level of outside interference.

It may, however, be pointed out here that at this time such new agencies of control and supervision were not limited to rural areas but were also active in non-rural areas to a greater or lesser degree. Undoubtedly the villagers were aware of the political and social problems elsewhere in the country and, even if they perceived their own difficulties as being of special immediacy, they knew that this was part of a greater, national process.

In 1952 there was a severe drought throughout the country and the enforced collection of grain left about 800,000 peasant families without enough wheat for the year (Berend, 1979:103). Thus it was not only the <u>kuláks</u> who were disadvantaged. The conditions of this period were very significant in transforming the relationship of the peasantry to the land. Land ceased to be a source of security and status and increasingly became a liability, while the peasants became vulnerable to a variety of extortions and harassment. The owner of land remained under an obligation to cultivate it; if he did not, he could be fined or imprisoned. Many attempted to relinquish their lands to the State in order to cast off the burdens attached to them, but when this movement reached unmanageable proportions, such offers were often rejected. It was safer for the peasant first to find himself employment in industry and then to offer his land to the State through his employers; in this case the offer had a better chance of being accepted. In other words, as a 'worker', he could be exempted from the obligation to farm the land he owned, while as a 'peasant' he remained under that obligation.

Concurrently, collectives were being formed, their formation being followed by land-consolidation. Land offered to individual peasants in exchange for stretches that lay in the path of continuous collective tracts was often of inferior quality and at the periphery of the village. About two-thirds of peasants who were displaced by consolidation did not farm the land offered in exchange, but left agriculture altogether and the collectives were swamped with lands which they had no means of cultivating. After 1948, no peasant farm could be larger than 40 holds, and all surplus parcels were confiscated by the State and attached to the collectives.

The relationship between individual cultivators and the first collectives was, in general, antagonistic, since the collectives were perceived as the root cause of many of the disadvantages afflicting individual peasants (see p. 247).

To sum up, in these years agricultural policies in Hungary amounted to the limitation as far as possible of the scope and attraction of individual peasant farming and pressure towards new forms of cultivation for which the peasants were neither ready nor willing. In the absence of previous experience, non-agricultural labour was considered a 'last resort,' not as a proper alternative (see p. 195). Collectivization was regarded as a threat rather than an alternative and at this time none of the advantages claimed for the system were apparent.

NOTES

1. Donáth quotes the following figures comparing delivery quota prices and contractual market prices in 1950 (1977:160):

		Compulsory quota prices	Contractual and free market prices
Autumn wheat	Ft/q	75,00	276,60
Wine	Ft/l	1,99	5,56
Pork	Ft/kg	5,40	19,60
Eggs	Ft/pc	0,38	1,11

4

The First Phase
of Collectivization

The approximate starting point of collectivization was the summer of 1948; its course was closely bound up with the economic and political circumstances outlined in Chapter 3.

Progress in the beginning was slow; by 1949, only 1,300 collectives had been formed. The rate of collectivization then accelerated, and by 1953 there were 5,224 collectives with an increase in membership from 36,400 in 1949 to 376,088, and an increase of collectivized holdings from 2.7% to 26% of the country's agricultural lands (Berend, 1979: 101).

Initially, different types of collectives were founded, regulated by Government guidelines in December 1948. Three types were officially set down, categorized by the proportion of production resources and labour required to be collectivized or left in individual control.

In collectives of the first type, group members agreed to a common yearly production programme and certain phases of production, such as ploughing and sowing, were undertaken collectively. Farming throughout the year and harvesting continued, however, to be done individually. Members contributed towards the expenses of the group in proportion to their participation in the production programme, but they did not pool and redistribute their profits.

In collectives of the second type, the production process throughout the year was similar to those of the first type. They differed in that at the end of the production cycle, produce was brought in collectively, pooled, and after deduction of the expenses of the group, the balance was redistributed among the members, in proportion to their inputs in land and labour.

The difference between the groups of the first and the second type was, briefly, that in the former the risks of

53

production were shouldered individually, while in the latter they were shared by the group as a whole (see Fazekas, 1976: 57-58). Both these types were elementary forms of collect-ivization: members were allowed to participate in the group's programme with only a portion of their land and assets and they were not bound to work collectively on a regular basis but went on farming individually. In fact, these groups represented only relatively minor departures from individual peasant farming.

Collectives of the third type, on the Soviet artyel model, were more comprehensive. Members agreed to contrib-ute all lands and animals they owned or controlled to the group they joined. Only a standard size household plot was allocated to each family for private cultivation. All phases of the production were agreed to collectively and were included in a programme of production. Members farmed collectively on a day-to-day basis and shared out the net revenues in proportion to their inputs of labour and land throughout the year.

The villagers in Pécsely - as elsewhere - had almost no experience of participating in or running cooperative vent-ures, although there had been various forms of cooperative associations in the pre-war period. The savings and loan cooperatives, formed throughout the country from around 1860 onwards, had been very rapidly centralized and removed from local control by the creation of the Országos Központi Hi-telszövetkezet (National Savings Association). A consumer cooperative had been formed in rural areas from 1898 onwards - the Hangya (Ant), which aimed to ensure distribution of essential goods in villages, at advantageous prices. The Hangya was a very successful organization and was soon to be found in the majority of villages. It soon developed an efficient centralized organization and at the village level mainly the middle and upper strata of the peasantry were involved in its management. Marketing cooperatives, mainly for milk, wine and grains, were sporadically formed but were mostly short-lived and made little impact on village popula-tions as a whole. None of these organizations appears to have provided any valuable experience towards the management and participation in the post-war production collectives.

In Pécsely, however, there had been forms of informal cooperative associations which, though different in many ways from the socialist collectives, could be seen as some sort of precedent. Significant differences do not allow direct parallels to be drawn between these and the post-1948 collectives, but it might be worth noting that they were formed in Nagypécsely, the locality that subsequently achieved the greatest economic success with socialist collectives.

Close reciprocal cooperation between both kinsmen and fellow villagers was traditionally an important organizing principle of village life and peasant production before the war. But, as informants remember, in the 1930s this traditional network of occasional reciprocal help was carried one step further by several groups of smallholders of Nagypécsely. Participants were holders of between 7 and 20 holds, who worked their lands together when it was practical to do so, purchased seeds, fertilizers and so forth jointly, and marketed their surplus products - principally wine - together. The gazdas in these associations came from the same stratum; that is, they had farms large enough for self-sufficient subsistence but not large enough to put them in the 'rich peasant' category. They had approximately similar status and background, in that they were of non-nemes descent, Protestant and residents in Nagypécsely, and were linked to one another by kinship or komaság (fictive kinship, godparenthood, friendship). Members were close neighbours on the Nagy side and their lands were adjacent. These informal associations were little more than an attempt to systematize the informal cooperation which took place among members along traditional lines of reciprocity. In Nagypécsely four such groups are remembered which were operational between 1930 and 1940, each including six to eight gazdas.

These associations did not imply a notion of 'collective ownership,' a concept central to socialist collectives. The emphasis was on joint action and labour in relation to privately owned farms. Informal, ad hoc meetings were held, to decide on the tasks to be carried out jointly, and there was no formal leadership or book-keeping.

This type of association could not be extended much beyond the given small size, nor could cooperation be increased much further, as the framework was loose and vulnerable and the associations' existence depended entirely on the continued goodwill and trust between the members. The objective was the strengthening of individual farms through the joint effort, not the strengthening of the associations themselves through the pooling of individual resources, as is the case in socialist collectives proper.

Despite these limitations, such pre-war associations bear witness to the enterprising spirit of the smallholders of Nagypécsely. Many of the gazdas involved in these associations were later to be prominent members, organizers, and chairmen of the socialist collectives to follow.

As a consequence of these home-grown cooperative associations the idea and principles of cooperative association
were that much more familiar when collectivization began –
not that this made the idea more attractive. In the formation of the first collective in Nagypécsely in 1951 one may
detect the intention of perpetuating the less radical features of these pre-war cooperative groups rather than adopt-
ing the more comprehensive collective form of organization,
such as collective labour on a daily basis, inclusion of
landless members and participation in the revenue in proportion to the work performed rather than land contributed. In
this effort to avoid full collectivization of resources and
labour the smallholders of Nagypécsely were only temporarily
successful (pp. 61-62).

The first socialist collective to be founded in Pécsely
was, in the summer of 1949, the Új Élet Termelőszövetkezet,
that is, New Life Collective of Agricultural Production. It
was a collective of the third, artyel type, centred on the
lands and manorial estate of Kispécsely.

Membership in the Új Élet was sought by the agrarian
proletariat and by those who had received some land in the
reform of 1945 but had not been able to subsist on such
small farms. It is not recalled that the Új Élet needed to
be forcibly imposed by external authorities. The prospect
of gaining control over the reserve land held by the State
was certainly a major incentive for its inception. This
land had been appropriated in the course of the land reform
in 1945 but had not been redistributed among the claimants
(see p. 42). Further parcels had been added to it in 1948
when the maximum land that could be owned privately was
reduced to 40 holds (22.8 hectares). Since the new landowners were faced with considerable difficulties in making a
living from their small farms in these years, and their
opportunities of finding occasional labour were very much
reduced, the collective offered good prospects for their
remaining in agriculture, through pooling the modest individual resources and taking advantage of the support provided
by the State in the form of extra land. Many land recipients were in such a poor situation that they could not even
pay the instalments due for the land they received in the
1945 land reform. The prospect of having to pay the arrears
was held up by the authorities in charge of collectivization
and that acted also as a powerful incentive.

The founder members of the Új Élet contributed in all
only 23 holds (13.1 hectares) of land, the remainder being
provided by the State. The collective's holdings were made
up of the types of land shown in Table 4.1.

Table 4.1
Holdings of the Új Élet Tsz in 1949

151 holds	ploughed fields
100 holds	woods
40 holds	pastures
35 holds	meadows
3 holds	vineyards

329 holds (187.5 ha) = 9.7% of the határ

From Gáldonyi, 1975:18.

The Új Élet collective preserved separation between the 'people of the puszta' and the villagers of Nagy and Nemes. The majority of members continued to live in - or moved into - the manorial buildings, which consisted of one imposing villa, separate labourers' quarters, and a set of barns, stables and similar structures. The manor was the centre of the collective. Members lived there, worked together, and spent most of their time in each other's company, which increased their separation from the two villages proper. There were altogether 23 families in the Új Élet, most of whom had previously been landless or new landowners, or former labourers in the Marton and Merza estates before 1945.

In this artyel type collective (see p. 54), members worked the lands together and shared in the revenue in proportion to the labour they put in during the year, which was calculated by means of a uniform measure of work units.[1] Different types of labour were each classified as worth a certain number of work units, but only at the end of the year, when the final reckoning was carried out, did it become apparent how much each work unit was worth in monetary terms. The value of each work unit, determined by the net profits of the collective, was therefore a sensitive index of the collective's economic strength. The State delivery quotas and taxes - which on agricultural products were very high - applied to the collectives as well and, in relation to the members' annual pay, the 'principle of surplus' (maradék elv) applied. This meant that the value of the work units was only calculated after all dues to the State had been met. As these obligations were high and varied from year to year, members did not have any basis on which they could forecast the value of their share out of the yearly net profit. Thus, if in one year a collective had a fairly

poor rate of production, the loss was borne not by the State
but, first, by the collective, which would not have had the
funds for essential investments and, second, by the individual members themselves, whose labour units would be worth
very little indeed.

The first collective in Pécsely was both economically
and organizationally weak. It had no machinery, very few
animals and no capital. Without the animals and equipment
which had been destroyed both during the war and the land
reform the manpower of the Új Élet proved inadequate for its
holdings, particularly because of the wide range of goods
needed to be produced to meet prescribed production and delivery quotas. In 1950, the Új Élet received from the district authorities eight horses, twenty-five head of cattle,
two hundred sheep and ten pigs, a meagre but essential contribution. Members were each entitled to a small household
plot of approximately 1 hold (0.57 ha) and they tended to
concentrate on the cultivation of this rather than work in
the collective brigades, in order to make ends meet.

Leadership was indecisive and inexperienced, on the one
hand weighed down by the task of managing such a radically
new type of farming enterprise, and on the other restricted
by the control of the council and district authorities, who
prescribed production plans, collected large shares of the
gross production and generally allowed a minimum of autonomy
to members and management. Machinery stations, which the
collective could make use of, were established on a regional
basis, but in effect these served also as a means of control
and interference in the affairs of the collectives (cf. Fazekas, 1976:63). In the Új Élet, for example, some of the
chairmen, who for political reasons fell into disfavour,
found it extremely difficult to acquire the machinery they
needed; this made the management task almost impossible,
according to local informants. In the six years of its
existence, the Új Élet had six successive chairmen, each
changeover being preceded by disputes and uncertainty.
Chairmen were selected from among the members, and had formerly been landless labourers, and they found it extremely
difficult to command the authority required to control the
body of members. And when the results were poor - for reasons not necessarily in their control - this also went against them. None of these problems were appreciated by the
membership at the time nor by the external authorities who
had a greater say in the choice of chairman than the members
themselves.

The villagers of Nemes and Nagypécsely viewed this
collective with little sympathy and blamed its lack of

success not on the objective difficulties but on its members' inefficiency, lack of discipline and lack of experience in independent farming. None of the members had been landowner _gazdas_ formerly, and many members were recent incomers to Pécsely who did not have the dense kinship network and friendship ties that more established residents commanded. They were to a large measure considered suspect outsiders, not credited with the dedication, thrift, expertise and hard work traditionally expected from a good local _gazda_. Anecdotes illustrating the carelessness and inefficiency of the members of the Új Élet are even today recounted with relish by older informants who were not themselves members.

The unfavourable image of this first collective rendered the entire collectivization campaign more difficult in Pécsely by confirming and increasing the peasants' suspicions and fears.

During this period most collectives formed in the country were similar to the Új Élet, with members recruited mainly from the landless proletariat (Erdei, 1972:199); they encountered similar organizational and economic difficulties (Berend, 1979:100).

The second collective of Pécsely emerged from a somewhat different configuration in 1951, at a time when collectivization was stepping up in Hungary.

In that year the Verseny Termelőszővetkezet - that is, the Competition Collective of Production - was founded in Nagypécsely. Among the founding members there were many smallholder _gazdas_ who had been members of the informal prewar cooperative associations referred to earlier (pp.54-55). The Verseny started off with twenty-eight members, all landowners with holdings approximately similar in size, linked by ties of kinship, friendship and neighbourhood. None were _kuláks_, or of _nemes_ descent, and all had some land. Thus in resources, landholding, background and status, the members of the Verseny were a very homogeneous group. The territory which formed the collective had all been contributed by members. The mean size of holdings contributed by each member was around 8 holds. Members also contributed in total eight horses, twenty-four heads of cattle and five pigs, but also retained an unknown number of animals, as well as their household plots, for individual use.

The Verseny did not have a separate centre like the Új Élet. The animals remained dispersed in different stables, and management was conducted from the house of the chairman. The holdings controlled by the collective were scattered, lying to the north and east of Nagypécsely, and were not

Table 4.2
Holdings of the Verseny Tsz in 1951

120 holds	ploughed fields
70 holds	woods
21 holds	pastures
15 holds	vineyards

226 holds (128.8 ha) = 17.2% of the határ

From Gáldonyi, 1970

consolidated; no exchanges were made with non-members in order to establish continuous tracts of collective land.

At its foundation the Verseny was a collective of the first type (see p. 53), not of the third type like the Új Élet. Its members did not engage in working the collective each day, but only on the occasion of specific seasonal tasks such as the harvest and the vintage. Since holdings were scattered, members continued to cultivate their own land as they had done previously, with virtually no change. The collective came into action mainly when making purchases, collecting produce and meeting the quota of compulsory deliveries.

Members shared out the produce among themselves in proportion to the land they had contributed and cultivated throughout the year, not by means of calculating work units. Decisions were made by the assembly of members at regular meetings and there was also a chairman who did the bookkeeping and was in charge of the administration. His sphere of action was, however, ill-defined and limited, a problem which will be considered in more detail later.

In the first two years the chairman of the Verseny was a smallholder from Nagy, Sándor Kósa. Still alive today, he is a man of keen intelligence and interested and involved in community affairs. He had been a member of the informal co-operative groups in the pre-war period and was among the few who from the first believed in the greater economic scope and efficiency of collectives compared with individual traditional farming.

The Verseny was reorganized in 1953 into a full collective of the third artyel type, along similar lines to the Új Élet. At this stage Sándor Kósa was replaced as chairman by another smallholder from Nagypécsely, Sándor Pákozdi. He too is a man of intelligence and ability, but more conservative and more attached to traditional individual small farming.

After its reorganization the Verseny consolidated its holdings so that collective working would be practicable. There were some experiments with different crops in attempting to rationalize production, but efforts were not yet concentrated on the vinegrowing which later proved so successful. The system of compulsory production, quotas and deliveries prevented specialization at this time. Nevertheless the Verseny is reputed to have been more successful economically than the Új Élet partly because it was better equipped, its lands were of better quality, and its manpower matched its holdings. The farming experience of its members as well as the homegeneity of membership were also favourable factors.

The motivations surrounding the foundation of the Verseny were not so clearly economic as were those behind the Új Élet - which had attracted people experiencing serious difficulties in subsisting on inadequate plots and for whom the gaining of control over the 300-odd holds held by the State was a great incentive. The members of the Verseny were in a far more settled and favourable economic condition on their smallholdings, which were large enough for subsistence but not burdened by taxes and high delivery quotas to the same extent as those of larger landowners. The Verseny was founded in a period in the early 1950s when collectivization was pushed by the Rákosi-Gerő leadership of the Party, and in this effort: 'the voluntary principle of forming collectives could not be upheld' (Berend, 1979:102). This certainly applied to the recruitment of members to the Verseny. The smallholders had by this time come to expect strong outside interference and control over production and property relations. The land reform already foreshadowed the extent of potential interference, and the enforced production and collection of crops was operated through a tight control network operated by agents and officials in the village and outside authorities. Through this network pressure was being continuously applied on the villagers by measures varying in their severity and directness, which pushed them towards collectivization. In this Pécsely was not alone; coercive methods were employed all over the country (Márkus, 1967).[2]

In founding a collective of the first, elementary type, members of the Verseny hoped to retain control over their farming and keep their system of production and life-style as unchanged as possible while at the same time giving in to the pressure to form a collective. The Verseny therefore

avoided the adoption of more unfamiliar features, such as
collective labour on a daily basis and the work unit system.
Cooperation between smallholders of approximately similar
status and resources, with participation in proportion to
the lands contributed, was not so alien to the members of
the Verseny and there was a strong desire to retain this
system. However this was a hope dashed by the countrywide
drive by the government to bring collectives into line as
regards organizational structure. In becoming a collective
of the third type, the Verseny underwent radical reorganization: daily collective labour in work brigades was imposed, as well as remuneration calculated by the work unit
system on the basis of the labour input of members rather
than in proportion to the lands contributed. The acceptance
of landless as members was also imposed, a step hitherto resisted by the Verseny's members.

Above all, the organization of collective production
alters the peasant's scope in decision-making. The independent small farmer gazda makes his decisions regarding day-
to-day farming routines and long-range production strategies. Each gazda has his own idiosyncratic way of respond-
ing to conditions, and has a particular style of looking
after his crops and animals. Decisions must be made continuously on the order and timing of the phases of labour.
Small discrepancies and peculiarities characterize each
gazda's farming: what is planted, where, in what order,
when the vintage and the harvest are started. All these
have to be decided on a daily, weekly or yearly basis. The
gazda also coordinates the labour of the members of his
household, who form an independent family unit of production. Gazdas with approximately similar sized farms and
work force achieve different levels of production according
to their particular farming strategies. Even on the remaining household plots in Pécsely today the importance of such
individual decision-making may be observed. In the household plots and vineyards the timing of each phase of labour
is fairly individual and considerably affects the end product. Much of the regular daily communication between villagers revolves around the subject of individual farming
strategies and timings.

In the collective, members do not make decisions in the
same way as they used to on their individual farms, and
decision-making within the members' assembly bears little
resemblance to the individual gazdas' daily deliberations.
Collective decision-making had little precedent within the
traditional farming system. Either the gazda managed his
own farm individually or the hired labourers followed the

directives of their employer or his delegate. The new forms of decision-making in the collectives were a major source of problems. Some of these may be related to the complexities of the principle of ownership upon which collectives were based. Collective ownership is not an expression of some sort of homogeneous, undifferentiated 'group' property. This question may best be approached by asking: who has the rights of disposal and decision-making in relation to the affairs of the collective? A. Hegedüs (1977:92) distinguishes at least three different forms of disposal that obtain in collectives:

1. The right of disposal of State; these refer to credit, administrative control and regulations of general validity.
2. The right of disposal of the administrative apparatus of the collectives, considered as an enterprise. This refers primarily to the chairman and his close associates.
3. The right of supervision and control exercised by the body of members over the management of the means of production and the distribution of surplus value. This may be in part direct (i.e. through the assemblies) or indirect (through appointed committees) democratic forms.

In the 1950s rights of disposal and decision-making were exercised overwhelmingly by State agencies, to the extent that 'cooperative property really had a character of State property' (Hegedüs, 1977:92). Chapter 10 will show in more detail how the State controlled the collectives.

The role of the chairman in relation to the members of a cooperative was exceedingly ambiguous. In principle, the chairman was elected from among the members, by the members, but in the 1950s the practice was otherwise; chairmen in the newly-formed collectives were appointed by district authorities, on the basis of political attributes, without regard for the members' wishes. Even if the chairman happened to enjoy the members' esteem, as for example did the first two chairmen of the Verseny, the fact that he was appointed in this way served to weaken his authority. Indeed, it may even be suspected that this was not unwelcome to the district authorities, who would perhaps have been averse to a strongly-backed chairman; in this way State agencies could have better control over the collectives. Another problem in relation to management was that the chairman's social status and farming expertise were no better than that of the other members of the collective. The former gazdas were not prepared to be 'ordered about' (dirigálva) by some-one whose authority was not beyond dispute. The chairman was also dealing with his equals, in the sense that collect-ive members had equal rights regardless of their function and the chairman was neither an employer nor a landlord. The scope of action related to the chairman's office itself was unclear, so that in these early collectives there appears to have a been a vacuum regarding leadership. Only after 1961 in the larger collectives is the authority and position of the office of chairman strengthened decisively. The various informants who held office in these years remem-ber the lack of authority and clear-cut responsibilities as the greatest difficulties encountered in their position as chairman.

The rank and file of membership had difficulties of their own. In the collective, age-old discriminations and animosities were rekindled. Different social groups mingled uneasily and reluctantly - or even refused cooperation alto-gether.

For example, where landless members were in the majori-ty, as in the Új Élet in Kispécsely, smallholders and middle peasants were not accepted as members. One middle peasant in Nagy who sought membership in the Új Élet, because he was anxious to prove that he was not a kulák, was briefly accep-ted but was expelled shortly afterwards amidst great upheav-al. On the other hand, in the Verseny there was resistance against accepting the landless, but after 1953 they were prohibited from rejecting landless members. Such landless members were, however, often reminded that they had contri-buted nothing and were made to feel very uncomfortable. Many left the Verseny after a short time and went into in-dustry to get out of this difficult position.

In the Verseny, both before and after 1951, the prob-lems of internal organization remained prominent, in spite of the relative economic stability achieved. The problem of integrating independent-minded gazdas into collective work brigades was unsolved; de jure decision-making rights had shifted from individual members to the members' assembly but de facto even these much-reduced rights could not be proper-ly exercised. Nor was the leadership vested with sufficient authority to control the membership and to implement decis-ions unambiguously.

The Új Élet experienced somewhat similar difficulties of leadership and internal organization, aggravated by econ-omic failure, and in spite of the fact that most of its mem-bers had previously been landless labourers and more used to working under orders than the gazdas of the Verseny. This partly accounts for the yearly change of chairman, in contrast to the collective after 1961 when one chairman held office for 20 years.

In 1953 State policies in relation to agriculture were eased as a result of top-level crises in Party leadership. Some of the most oppressive measures were cancelled, outstanding obligations regarding delivery quotas were waived and yearly assessments were made of the productive capacity of farms and collectives, so that producers were informed in advance of the delivery quotas they would be called to fulfil in the coming year. Prices paid by the State for products were increased slightly to a more realistic level nearer their true market value. Collectives were allowed to be dissolved and members could claim back the land they contributed, or its equivalent. The motion allowing members to leave the collectives resulted in a sharp drop in membership - by as much as 39% in the whole country. Both the Verseny and the Új Élet held out, however, even though they lost about one third of their membership.

Temporarily, with these more relaxed conditions, individual farms gained in strength at the expense of the collectives. Attachment to individual farming was still very strong and it was considered, not without justification, to be more profitable and secure than farming on the collectives. In the latter there was a shortage of cash and members were paid mainly in kind, part of which they could claim during the year, subject to adjustment on the occasion of the yearly balance. The uncertain outcome of the collectives' yearly balance was not only caused by the weather and other natural hazards but was primarily due to the very high delivery quotas and taxes, which creamed off most of the profits (see pp. 57-58). These circumstances encouraged members to concentrate their efforts on the household plots which they farmed individually; as a result household plot farming prospered and some of the products were sold on the black market. Indeed, the majority of members worked only a minimum or not at all in the collective work brigades and devoted all their energy to plot farming - which was a far better and safer source of income than the collective.

Movement in and out of the collectives was common and at the same time large numbers of peasants were abandoning agriculture altogether. In 1950 alone, 11,000 farmers in Hungary left their land and went into industry (Fazekas, 1976:70).

Agricultural production was lagging behind government targets and the yearly plans. The gap widened between productivity demands and investment in agriculture that would enable these demands to be met. Administrative pressure was exercised to raise production, without providing the appropriate material support.

During the political upheaval of 1956, which may be attributed largely to the severity of the conditions throughout the country, the Új Élet and the Verseny were dispersed definitively. Each member was given back the land he had contributed to the collective and resumed independent cultivation; for a brief period early in 1957 there were no collectives in Pécsely.

In 1957, the conditions in agriculture were to some extent eased. A free system of marketing agricultural products was re-established; that is, the obligatory deliveries of goods to the State at fixed prices were discontinued. Prices for agricultural products were increased, and land up to 5 holds (about 2.8 ha) could be bought and sold freely. Such an easing-up was favourable both to the collectives and to individual peasants, but more so for the latter who could better adapt their production to market demands. The landless, however, who had been collective members up to 1956, found themselves in the same predicament as they had been in 1949; they were unable to make a living, as the local gazdas were impoverished and so unable to employ them. These landless and smallholders favoured starting up another collective when, by the end of 1957, the pressure to collectivize was resumed. By this time, the State apparatus had recovered from the turmoil of 1956 and took up the campaign once more. In order to press members back into the collectives, they were, for example, asked to pay a proportion of the debts of the collectives they had left, which had been abandoned in 1956. Those who had been active in the events of 1956 were punished and prosecuted; this brought home once more the heavy hand of State control. On the positive side, there was the attraction of recovering control over the reserve lands which had reverted to the State when the Új Élet was dispersed.

In the autumn of 1957 the third collective was founded, the Új Tavasz Termelőszövetkezet, that is, New Spring Collective of Production. It was centred on the puszta of Kispécsely, and the 300 holds were recovered from the State Farm of Tihany.

Membership comprised members of both the Új Élet and Verseny, and members with very small holdings were in the majority. As its centre was in the puszta, it was considered a revival of the Új Élet. The more prosperous members of the Verseny resumed individual cultivation, encouraged by

Table 4.3
Holdings of the Új Tavasz Tsz in 1957

153 holds	grain fields
116 holds	woods
44 holds	pastures
67 holds	meadows
10 holds	vineyards
4 holds	orchards
7 holds	marshes

401 holds (about 228 ha) = 11% of all village land

From Gáldonyi, 1970

the improvement of conditions in agriculture, and disappointed by their experience in the Verseny. Furthermore, they were reluctant to associate themselves with the 'puszta people' of the Új Tavasz.

The holdings of the Új Tavasz were constituted as shown in Table 4.3. Of this territory, 118 holds had been contributed by members, a mean of 3.5 holds per member; the remainder had been provided by the State. The collective recovered the animal stocks built up by the Új Élet: eight horses, thirty-five head of cattle, eight pigs and three hundred sheep.

The first two chairmen of this collective had already held office in the Új Élet. Both were formerly landless. Sándor Kósa, first chairman of the Verseny, reappeared here as treasurer, book-keeper and chief organizer, and it seems that he controlled the collective to a greater extent than either of the two chairmen.

The Új Tavasz already intended to redirect its methods of production towards a more rational programme, but its efforts were, as yet, modest. The members established a pig-rearing unit, and planted 5 holds of excellent new vineyards. Nevertheless the Új Tavasz remained economically weak, as shown by the value of its work unit which decreased each year: 1958: 40 forints; 1959: 27 forints; 1960: 20 forints (Gáldonyi, 1970:20).

The value of the work units was halved in two years. Villagers remember this collective as very unsuccessful and as being unable to ensure adequate subsistence for its members, comparing unfavourably with the results obtained by individual farming. The problems of management and discipline remained much the same as in the previous collectives, although members now had the experience of past years to draw on, and collectives as such began to be considered a permanent feature. As it was possible to join or leave a collective quite easily, there was a rapid turnover of membership: some joined when they found it difficult to sustain small farming; others, disenchanted, opted out. As one of the chairmen remembers: 'People used the collective as a thoroughfare.' Such fluctuation of manpower posed a grave problem for management and planning.

Yet by 1958, in spite of these difficulties, collectives achieved a certain stability countrywide (Donáth, 1977). State investments were more forthcoming and machinery stations were more numerous and better equipped. Until 1960, a collective was not allowed to invest in larger combines - even if it had the means to do so. It was therefore forced to remain dependent on the machinery stations. As the compulsory prescriptions were less detailed, though still applying to essential products (e.g. grains), the collectives could plan their production more freely, giving greater attention to the specific qualities of the collectives' land. But production methods were still largely traditional, unmechanized and unspecialized, so that the advantages afforded by the joint resources and collective manpower could not be fully exploited.

In the collectives operating until 1956, there were still genuine collective self-management features: the groups were small, composition of membership was homogenous, that is, included people of the same class background and often related by networks of kinship and friendship. This in itself however did little to further economic and organizational success. Personality conflicts were common and problems with management and division of labour were aggravated rather than helped by the fact that the relations between the members were intimately personal and lacked a well defined hierarchy of authority. On the other hand, the successive chairmen, chosen from the members' own numbers, were committed to the collective rather than to the external authorities - as was later to be the case; hence the collective could to some extent protect itself against the worst pressures (taxes, quotas, etc), for example by leaving assets undeclared.

But a major question was still open: how would collectivization be continued in Hungary? Would it remain relatively insignificant (as in Poland for example), or would it be brought to completion and become the dominant form of

agricultural production? The question had a certain immediacy for the villagers and, as informants recall, by this
time they already had a foreboding that full collectivization was inevitable. Most, however, still hoped for a
gradual, long-term reorganization. This was also a major
problem for the higher Party leadership: some factions were
pressing for radical change; others advocated a more gradual course, fearing the destructive resistance of the peasantry. At this point, we reach what may be called the second phase in the course of collectivization in Hungary.

NOTES

1. Work unit: <u>trudoden</u> in Russia - yet another element
following the Soviet model in those years.
2. Assessment of the early phases of collectivization
remains cautious in Hungary even today and, although the
'mistakes' of the 1950s are often acknowledged, we can still
read: '... the former manorial labourers, rural agrarian
proletariat and dwarf-holders desired to work within collectives ...' (Nagy L. and László F. <u>A Mezőgazdasági Termelő</u>
<u>szövetkezetak Korszerű Vezetese</u>, 1974:10). This paragraph
firmly places the beginning of the collectivization movement
as a public initiative, rather than a government one; this
book is aimed at the managerial class in the collectives
today.

5

The Second Phase
of Collectivization

Between 1957 and 1958, the central issue relating to agriculture was how collectivization should proceed; these were years of transition and of searching for new ways.

The problems and contradictions of policies, both economic and social, of the first half of the 1950s, culminated in the uprising of 1956. Steps were taken to ease the most constricting aspects of agricultural policies already in November of that year. A new line of policies was soon taking shape which, although still committed to the development of heavy industry, gave greater priority to the improvement of standards of living and support of agriculture. The new agrarian policies, worked out in the summer of 1957, made the increasing development and modernization of agriculture major aims, breaking with the hitherto prevailing policies of maximal extraction with minimum inputs and investment. A new series of regulations were passed, such as the limitation of central directives on agricultural production, cancellation of compulsory production plans (veteskényszer), adjustment of prices for agricultural products, allowance of free sale of lands up to 5 holds and relaxation of limitations on the lease of land. State investment in agriculture was increased. The beneficial results of these measures were immediate, although central planning and control remained significant and the basic problems associated with it were unsolved (Berend, 1979; Donáth, 1976).

Opinions in the Party leadership were divided on the issue of how collectivization should proceed. Essentially, the problem was how to avoid agricultural production falling back while collectivization was being implemented.

It was foreseen that the peasants would resist collectivization, and could react in ways that were damaging to overall agricultural production. Various strategies were envisaged: some favoured the strengthening of the individual farms and the postponement of collectivization until agriculture was in better shape; others, on the contrary, favoured increasing pressure on individual farmers leaving collectivization as the only course to follow.[1] The final decision was worked out by the leadership of the Magyar Szocialista Munkáspárt - MSZMP for short - (Hungarian Socialist Workers' Party) in 1958.[2]

In a memorandum released in December of that year it was stated that 'although the preconditions for immediate changes are still incomplete, these could be realized in the near future' (Berend, 1979:135). In effect, the massively coordinated countrywide campaign of collectivization had been decided upon and was set into motion in early 1959. This was to have a greater impact on property relations and modes of production than either the land reform of 1945 or the previous collectivization campaigns.

In devising strategies to be followed it was necessary to take into account that this was the third attempt to carry collectivization through, so that the dynamism of innovation may have already been spent. On the other hand, collectivization had been a possibility for almost a decade, and this would have allowed the peasantry to become familiarized with - if not converted to - the idea. By 1959, in fact, most peasants were aware of the possibility of a massive campaign. A central issue for the Party leadership was that of the voluntary principle in recruitment. The MSZMP was reluctant to make recruitment to the collectives compulsory but nevertheless the pressure to join had to be irresistible. In a certain sense, the swift and successful completion of collectivization in 1959 to 1960 came as a relief to many peasants, putting an end to years of uncertainty.

A large number of people (initially around 1,500) were recruited from Party members, workers, teachers, and so on, who started campaigning concertedly, with the assistance of workers from local factories, throughout all rural communities. These agitators did not always stop at verbal argument and mental pressure; any abuses, however, were publicly disowned and condemned by the authorities. Nevertheless, agitators proceeded with unbending intent as quantitative results were necessary to weaken further grounds of resistance. Collectivization was completed in several waves between 1959 and 1960. In the Transdanubian region it was carried through in the first wave, being virtually completed by the end of 1959. Pécsely was collectivized in the first wave.

The previous collectivization campaigns hitherto had

been aimed principally at the landless and the owners of small farms. Middle peasants and kuláks were not approached and indeed were often prevented from joining. From 1959, all sections of the peasantry were sought and indeed middle and wealthy peasants were the most encouraged in order to strengthen the collective system. This new policy ensured that the divisive trends were mitigated and that the agricultural population as a whole was brought together for common interest and association.

In Pécsely, collectivization was started in March 1959, through the local council and Party cell. These met with no response whatsoever, for those who had decided in favour had already joined the Új Tavasz, while those who had not, had been discouraged by this collective's poor record in previous years. In April busloads of workers from nearby factories came to Pécsely and groups went from house to house to convince people to sign up as members. The landless and poorer villagers were visited first, since they, having little to lose, had the least motivation to resist.[3]

Resistance was strongest among landowners, who could look back to the two previous years of less oppressive control over their farming, which had raised their hopes. The former members of the Verseny were just as reluctant to join as the other landowners who had never before been members of a collective. The pressure exerted upon the villagers during these months remains a vivid memory. As one member put it: 'It was not obligatory to join, just unavoidable.' Many villagers retired to the hills and took to their cellars, expecting to stay in hiding until the agitators departed, but few were successful. After about a week only around twenty of the larger landowners had not yet signed. One of them, incidentally the chairman of one of the previous collectives, went up to the council, inspected the list of those who had already signed and saw that the majority of his fellow villagers had joined. He believed that the chances of holding out in individual cultivation were poor, as he knew from experience that extensive land consolidation would follow, and non-members would be compelled to accept outlying land of poor quality in exchange for good land in a central position. He therefore called together his fellow gazdas and they all filed in to sign up.

Villagers determined not to join the collectives abandoned agriculture altogether, with the exception of four smallholders of whom only one is still farming individually today. Countrywide there was a drop of 16% between 1960 and 1963 in those employed in agriculture (Berend, 1979:141). In Pécsely about thirty men sought non-agricultural employment in 1960-61 alone. Whereas in 1949 83.4% of the villagers were still in agriculture, in 1961 this had dropped to 58%. In some instances the wife joined the collective and the husband left agriculture, which was advantageous because it entitled the member to a household plot, while the husband's job provided the security of a monthly wage. In previous collectives the uncertain and irregular income had been one of the most depressing features of membership. A new type of rural family was emerging and was fast becoming the dominant type: the 'heterogeneous' families wherein some members hold non-agricultural jobs outside the village while others remain in the collective (see p. 207).

This phase of collectivization was followed by more propitious conditions than the previous one. One advantage was that, after 1960, the collective became the dominant type of agricultural production countrywide, not just one of several alternative types of agricultural activity. Collectives were extended over 77% of the country's agricultural land and included 68% of its animal stock (Berend, 1979: 136). It was possible to streamline State policy in relation to agriculture and to focus it on the consolidation of the new collective system.

Investments were increased to encourage the establishment of large-scale production and loans and subsidies were made available. From the newly-recruited members' point of view conditions were more attractive than they had been previously; their right to standard-sized household plots was secured, annuities due after the lands that had been brought into the collective were ensured and the internal organizational structure of the collective was regulated, defining more clearly the members' rights.

Regulations were revised to free collectives from the direct interference of non-local agencies; these allowed greater independence for collectives and wider scope for decision-making in matters of management and production. This somewhat resolved the contradiction aptly formulated by one Hungarian economist that, before 1960, '... the State organs exercised ownership rights in the collectives through prescriptions and orders, while the risks of production and farming were shouldered by the members.' (Donáth, 1976:29).

NOTES

1. For the decision on the campaign of collectiviz-ation in 1959 see Berend, 1979; Donáth, 1980; Fazekas, 1976.

2. Until 1956, the Party in Hungary was called Magyar Dolgozok Pártja (Hungarian Workers' Party). When it was re-formed after 1956 it re-emerged under the name Magyar Socia-list Munkás Párt' (Hungarian Socialist Workers' Party) i.e. MSZMP, which will be used henceforth.

3. The way in which informants of Pécsely remember the campaign is somewhat different from reports elsewhere in Hungary. Both Márkus (1967) and Donáth (1977) assert that the policy was to approach the middle-rich peasants first, win them over and then approach the landless. I cannot account for this discrepancy; procedures were probably less uniform in practice.

6

The Three Collectives
of Pécsely

Collectivization in Pécsely finally took shape according to the officially redundant tripartite division into Nagy, Nemes and Kis Pécsely. Against strong recommendation of the district authorities, three collectives were formed instead of one.[1]

The first was the already existing Új Tavasz, in the puszta, with 459 holds. In Nagy Pécsely the Rákoczi Termelőszövetkezet[2] (Rákoczi Collective of Production) was founded with 55 members and 514 holds (9.3 holds per member). In Nemes, the largest of the three was formed under the name Petőfi Termelőszövetkezet[3] (Petőfi Collective of Production) with 75 members on 592 holds (7.8 holds per member).

The two newly founded collectives did not receive additional land from the State; all they had was that brought in by the members. For three years the three collectives shared the village lands. They were all collectives of the artyel type and a great deal of land consolidation was initiated to form continuous tracts of fields. However, little transformation was made to the structure of production and farming.

The new collectives in Nagy and Nemes, unlike the Új Tavasz, did not have a centre as such; the headquarters were the chairmen's kitchens, where brigade leaders congregated to discuss daily schedules, and from which the chairmen conducted organization. The animals and implements were dispersed in the stables and farm buildings of the richer members.

The chairman of the Rákoczi of Nagypécsely was Sándor Pákozdi, who already had some experience, having been the Verseny's chairman for three years. In Nemespécsely's, Petőfi, a very prestigious and respected gazda, Gábor Tóth, was elected chairman. This was the first collective operating in Nemes.

In the first years of their operation the three small collectives were beset by difficulties, arising on the one hand from the attitude of newly-recruited members towards collectivization, and on the other from problems related to the organizational structure of the collective itself. Inherent problems appear to have been related mainly to the principle of collective ownership, especially in the way this was understood by members, and to the position of the chairman and leaders, which has already been mentioned in relation to the previous collectives (pp. 62-64).

The pressure exerted on the peasantry in the course of the mass collectivization campaign in 1959 has not so far been comprehensively assessed by Hungarian sociography, although the repercussions were considerable - not only in relation to the development of the collectives themselves but also beyond this, in that the pressure triggered the massive abandonment of agriculture by the rural population.

The pre-1959 collectives in Pécsely did not succeed in altering the prevalent opinion that individual farming was superior in efficiency to collectivized production; expectations concerning collectives in general remained low. In Pécsely the dominant opinion in 1959 was that the newly-founded collectives would not even last a year. To the majority of members this was a comforting thought but it did not significantly relieve the sense of loss[4] that the majority of landowners experienced:

P.S. from Nagy: 'We were confused. Hitherto we put all our energy into increasing our lands. I got that beautiful stretch of woods just a few years previously. It was heartbreaking to part with it.'

T.G. from Nemes: 'To have land was to have security. In signing it over we felt uncertain; what would become of us?'

K.S. from Nagy: 'People were afraid of the collective - they imagined the coming of mess-time communal feeding (csajkarendszer).'

Cs.S. from Nagy: 'I had a very special vineyard, with a grape establishment that was unique in the region. What would become of it in the collective? I had taken such special care of it. It had been established by my father.'

K.S. from Nemes: 'We always saved our money to buy some
more land, that was the most important, to have land to
leave it to our children.'

The difficulty the former landowner gazdas experienced
in adapting to the collectives' work brigades did not however arise exclusively from the unease which most experienced at the loss of their lands. As has already been indicated (p. 62) with the discontinuation of individual farming
the deliberative functions related to management ceased. For
the newly recruited members daily labour became less varied,
more specialized and monotonous, a process which increased
with every step taken towards mechanization and modernization of agrarian techniques. The greater part of the members' working day was taken up with tasks in relation to
which decision-making was not required, for decisions were
exercised firstly by outside authorities and secondly by the
chairman and brigade leader, and only to a lesser extent by
the members' assembly. The problem of decision-making as
exercised by the members' assembly had already emerged as
problematic in the Verseny and the Új Élet on two counts:
firstly, the lack of significant precedents in traditional
farming; secondly, the limitation imposed on the scope of
decision-making by outside authorities. In the collectives
after 1959, this problem persisted, with the added aggrava-
tion that membership was larger and of a less homogeneous
composition. In the Új Élet and the Verseny membership had
been constituted mainly of people from the same stratum:
landless in the former and smallholders in the latter. In
the collectives formed after 1959 recruitment was based on
locality - Nemes, Nagy and Kispécsely. In the Petőfi, based
in Nemes, the core of the membership was formed by a group
of about twenty wealthier gazdas and a smaller proportion of
smallholders and landless. In the Rákoczi of Nagy the majority were smallholders and only eight were former wealthier
gazdas. In the Új Tavasz the majority of members were landless, but not all.

Although collectivization made the concept of land ownership as an index of status and wealth redundant, awareness
of how much land each member had contributed remained vivid
for a long time. Arguably it persists to the present day.
Older members had, and still have, fairly precise knowledge
of pre-collectivization patterns of land ownership in the
village. Soon after the foundation of the collectives, members followed attentively the use to which 'their' land was
put by the collective. When the first tractor was bought
jointly by the Rákoczi and the Petőfi in 1961, some of the

older, weaker animals were put down. There was turmoil in the village: 'Why are they destroying my horse and not his horse?' Some of the vineyards were high on the hillside and the collective decided against continuing their cultivation, causing grief and resentment for the previous member-owners.

In the attitude of members towards collective labour, the way in which collective ownership was understood appears significant. In principle, collective members have vested interests in the efficiency and outcome of their joint efforts. In practice, however, this was not experienced by them. They did not deliberate individually and responsibility was shared and hence dispersed among members. The right of deliberation and disposal, as exercised by the members' assembly, was of a different order from the individual decision-making exercised by the gazda on his holding. In the members' assembly the issues brought up related more to general planning: for example, what proportion of the lands should be allocated to different crops? In what way should brigades of workers be constituted? What larger investments should be made? On a day-to-day basis, however, the chairman and brigade leaders coordinated the execution of the production plan, decided on the next task at hand and allocated them to the workers' brigades. At the level of day-to-day interaction and labour, members thus could not exercise deliberative rights.

The assembly's voice in management was also curtailed in practice by the subordinate and dependent status of the collectives themselves in relation to the district and country authorities and, ultimately, to central government. Even after 1959, the main decisions in relation to the collectives' production were made by external authorities who did not have full knowledge and expertise in local conditions and who were committed not to the interests of these collectives but rather to 'higher,' regional or national level interests. State departments broke down programmes of production, assigning parts of this plan to be fulfilled by individual collectives. Year by year, the structure of production, investment and marketing of collectives was decided by external authorities. Until 1956, as was seen earlier (pp. 57-58) a closed system of control over collectives was exercised by means of the production plans and delivery quotas, as well as through control over machinery, grants and loans. Although after 1956 collectives were claimed to be independent, changes were formal rather than substantive and essential elements of control remained. Local councils were still responsible politically for the achievement of the part of the plan assigned to their community. Their own material and moral rewards were dependent on fulfilling the plan, which gave them an incentive to force the collective to abide by the 'directives' issued to them and these effectively had the strength of commands. The councils had effective means of persuasion: they allocated loans and grants and provided essential resources for production. Although after 1959 the collectives no longer received compulsory production orders, except on basic products such as wheat, loans and grants were attached to obligations to produce a quota of specific products such as meat or industrial crops. On the other hand the marketing agencies, who had a monopoly in their field, were issued with orders to buy up certain quotas of products, so that collectives wishing to find a market for their products had to meet these demands. The collectives did not have direct contact with the marketing agencies, but only through the mediation of the local council. Such indirect contact between the producers and the buyers was unwieldy and complex, allowing the councils inordinate power over the collectives.

Prices for agricultural products were fixed centrally and continued to serve as a means to draw away resources from agriculture. They were not indicative of costs of production or of market value, but were set as much as a third lower (Donáth, 1977). Collectives were not able consequently to accumulate capital and become independent from State grants and loans.

Controls remained extensive, in spite of the changes from 1959; as many as forty to fifty different State departments could still interfere in the affairs of a collective. To illustrate the bureaucratic complexity involved, Donáth mentions that in 1964 about 339 different reports had to be filled in by each collective, supplying answers to thousands of questions (Donáth, 1977:213). Only from the mid-1960s onwards were these restrictions gradually eased; for example from 1965 the collectives were allowed to negotiate directly with the marketing agencies. Significant change occurred in 1968 when the New Economic Mechanism was introduced (see pp. 93-94), but even today the true scope of the collectives' economic and entrepreneurial independence is debatable (see Chapter 10).

Thus, at this stage, the principle of collective ownership, which is central to the structure of collectives, was called into question externally, through the intervention of, and control by, State agencies, and internally, through the difficulty of making this principle manifest at ground level, in day-to-day interaction.

Many anecdotes circulate about the interpretation of

collective ownership and point to the difficulty of acting
according to its ideal interpretation. The contradiction of
de jure ownership rights but absence of individual rights of
disposal over that property, is well illustrated by this
often quoted anecdote:

> ... When the brigade leader found that the collective's
> shepherd was neglecting his charges, he pleaded with
> him: 'Look after them well, after all they are your
> own ...' to which the shepherd responded by placing
> his knife at the throat of one of the beasts saying:
> 'If they are my own, I will have this one for dinner.'

For the members, the central question was: '<u>In what way am
I the owner</u>?' The standard answer was that if the collective prospered, its work units would be worth more, hence the
revenue of each member would be higher. However, the relationship between the collective members' income and the
profits of the collective was not direct, for there was the
intervening deduction of the considerable dues and taxes (p.
57); secondly, the collectives' prosperity, or lack of it,
was far more influenced by the quality of its holdings, the
marketable value of its products, its level of mechanization, and the ability of the management, than by the quality
of the individual members' labour. Members were aware of
the indirect relationship between their labour and the
achievement of the collective, and their interest in the
work they performed diminished accordingly.

In collectives all over the country many members - estimated at about 20% to 25% (Donáth, 1977:200) - did not work
in the collective at all, despite their membership, and this
was common to Pécsely too. The members who did work concentrated on achieving as many work units as possible with the
minimum effort, or even falsifying their records with the
tacit agreement of the management, for whom it made no difference at all how the profits that remained after all dues
had been met were divided.

In the work brigades the style and standard of each
member's labour was not uniform and adjustments had to be
made towards uniformity. In these years this had the effect
of reducing rather than increasing efficiency. <u>Gazdas</u> who
used to strive towards maximal efficiency on their farms
often found themselves out of step in the work brigades;
previously known for their impeccable work-style, they adopted a listless, careless way of going through the motions of
labour in the collective. As one brigade leader remembers:
'It was a miracle that the vineyards survived that kind of

treatment.' This problem was so general that labour in the collectives became synonymous with shoddy labour, while high quality labour is described as being 'as if one works in one's own small farm.'

The chairman could do little to remedy this. It proved of little effect to plead, 'It is your own,' because, as has been seen (pp. 62-63), the principle of joint ownership did not travel well from the level of theory to the level of practice:

> I did not know how to discipline a fellow gazda. I knew when one was at fault, but I could not say it directly without creating offence. So I pretended I did not know who had been responsible for a piece of sloppy work and just went around saying, 'Look, whoever has done the dressing of these vine stems, does not know his job ...' Everyone knew who had done it so he was shamed, but could not take offence openly ... there was no other way.

The position of chairman was to be strengthened only in later years at the expense of the members' assembly, after greater independence was allowed to the collectives. In these initial years, however, whatever authority the chairman had was derived not from the office he held, but from his status within the cooperative community. In the Petőfi of Nemes, the chairman was a leading gazda in his own right, as was the chairman of the Rákoczi in Nagy. This allowed them to exercise the office of chairman with some degree of authority and success, even if they did not quite meet the demands of the office.

As landholding ceased to be a valid criterion of status and rank, uncertainty prevailed about appropriate forms of behaviour; new situations arose and new patterns had to be worked out. This was even more pressing as there was increased daily interaction between members within the collectives. The problem of 'social equality' came up in several contexts. For example, in the collective of Nemespécsely, a highly complex and artificial work system was adopted in an effort to grapple with this rather unwieldy concept, a standard term of party propaganda. Within the labour brigades members agreed to adopt a uniform pace of labour, regardless of individual variations in ability, strength or capacity. In this way, if one member finished planting or hoeing one row he had to wait until all other brigade members caught up with him before he could start on the next. It was reckoned that all brigade members should achieve the same number of work units and thus earn the same income. This system was highly counter-productive and production declined to the level of the brigades' weakest members, while more agile members were prevented from achieving their best. In the Rákoczi of Nagy, however, no such enforcement of equality of achievement was practised; members knew in advance how many work units a task was worth and they were free to achieve as much or as little as they wanted. Scope was left for stronger members to be more successful.

Such a difference in work methods was only temporary, as members of the Petőfi soon renounced it, but this small example is a good illustration of the uncertainties of these years when the villagers had to cope with a series of unfamiliar concepts - another being 'collective ownership' - which were not easily translatable into day-to-day action. The smallholders who formed the bulk of the membership of the Rákoczi of Nagy displayed a more relaxed attitude to the management of their collective. This was partly because they had already had the benefit of experience of a collective through the Verseny, experience that was lacking in Nemes.

Nevertheless, there was acute sensitivity to 'injustice.' In defining the work unit value of each task, for example, there was wide scope for disagreement: should hoeing for one day be equivalent to tending a team of horses for one day? It was difficult to translate widely different tasks in terms of a uniform code of values to everyone's satisfaction. This remained a sore point with many members, particularly those whose function was specialized, such as shepherds and team drivers. Beyond that, the quality of labour could not be defined quantitatively by means of the work unit system; a poorly hoed row of vines counted for the same number of work units as one done impeccably. The collective accounted both as of equal value, but the members remained painfully aware of the difference. Response took various forms, depending on individual temperament: some left the collective altogether; others adopted the lowest standard of labour which they could get away with; while yet others continued to work impeccably but nursed a grievance. No matter how aware the management was of such problems it could do little to alleviate them. These problems were not confined to Pécsely. Elsewhere, complex measures were adopted to make members more committed and efficient, such as, for example, giving tracts of land to the exclusive care of one member (and his family), who could keep the surplus yield above a predetermined quota to himself (Féja, 1961:10; Donáth,1977). This, of course, is nothing more than share-cropping and, as such, was often resisted by Party supervisors on ideological grounds in the collectives. Such a system was not adopted in Pécsely at this time although it was tried later.

In spite of such difficulties, the close, daily interaction fostered a certain amount of group solidarity, encouraged by the healthy competition that developed between the three collectives. Each was eager to show that their collective was better than the next. By this time (1960), because of the extension of collectivization throughout the country, the possibility of reversal back towards individual farming had receded and this also encouraged members to make the best of their common enterprise.

From 1959 to 1961 little change was made to the production systems of the three collectives. Investments, such as those made in buildings, implements and improvement of the soil, did not result in greater productivity but merely replaced outdated structures or adapted them to the needs of collective farming. Only the establishment of new vines represented a real gain. Production techniques continued to be traditional, and the collectives had great difficulty in making ends meet. A negative factor was that the price system was based on low purchase prices for agricultural products and high prices for the items required for cultivation, such as fertilizers and pesticides. After 1959 this system worked against the collectives, because they required greater capital inputs than individual farms did. Adjustment of these discrepancies was not made until 1964, with further reform in 1967, so the collectives' first years were the most difficult. To offset deficits, the State handed out loans and grants, which increased bureaucratic complexity to unmanageable proportions. The debts were partly cancelled in 1965, but the collectives in Pécsely did not profit from this as much as they could have done because they had made it a point of honour to take up as few loans as possible.

Collective members relied heavily on their household plots - which provided more than half of the family's revenue. To ensure the minimum needed for the family's subsistence, it was vitally necessary to concentrate on the household plots rather than rely on what the collective could supply.

The average number of work units achieved by active members ranged between 250 and 350 per year. The value of each work unit in the three collectives is shown in Table 6.1. Only the Rákoczi of Nagy showed a substantial improvement by the second year; the others declined. The maximum yearly income could be around 11,900 forints per year for a

Table 6.1
Value of each work unit (in forints)

	Rakoczi Tsz	Petőfi Tsz	Új Tavasz Tsz
1959	25 fr.	26 fr.	27 fr.
1960	34 fr.	23 fr.	20 fr.

Gáldonyi, 1970:26

member of the Rákoczi who put in a maximum number of work units. In practice, however, members did not achieve even half of the maximum number of work units, and about a quarter of members did not do any work at all in the collective. The members' interest was entirely focussed on their household plots and, in view of the problems just outlined, the Rákoczi could not make members interested. Economically, collectives held little attraction as they were short of cash and the quarterly advances for members were uncertain and insufficient. Clearly, the small collectives were incapable of development as separate entities and a merger was imminent.

The families in the village were forced to begin to assess how they could employ their labour capacity to the best advantage and to diversify, for clearly the collectives had failed to engage their full allegiance or to ensure their livelihood. Non-agricultural labour started to become attractive and the small household plots were elevated to a great significance, in view both of the essential income they could provide and the satisfaction of allowing the type of labour to which the villagers had been accustomed. These two factors will be examined in greater detail in subsequent chapters, the aim here having been to outline essential steps of the transformation that was taking place: firstly, the alteration of the villagers' relationship to labour, following the change in the system of land ownership; secondly, the differences and similarities in the attitudes of different groups in terms of locality and former status. This chapter has also tried to show the divergence between the de jure and de facto situations within the collectives, as regards leadership, rights of ownership and participation.

We will now turn to the circumstances of the creation
of the single collective which included members from Nagy,
Nemes and Kispécsely.

NOTES

1. Pécsely was not exceptional in this respect; the
tendency elsewhere in the country was for the formation of
several small collectives in each village (Erdei, 1959:99;
Bell, 1979).

2. Ferenc Rákoczi 1676-1735, Hungarian patriotic leader of the kuruc uprising.

3. Sándor Petőfi 1823-1849, patriotic revolutionary
poet. His poetry and personality remain symbols of national
freedom.

4. Collectivization is not invariably presented as
hardship by Hungarian analysts. For example, Sárkány (1978:
127) writes: '... the large agricultural enterprises ensured
that the peasants of Varsány, liberated from the means of
production ... could change their way of life and consciousness and prosper.' It is an unfortunate wording that implies that the peasants wished to be freed from the ownership of their lands and collectivization came to the rescue
in this aim - which is far from having been the case.

7

The First Merger

Following mass collectivization in 1959 and 1960, the collectives formed did not necessarily follow the logic of economic optimal size. Separate small collectives in villages, such as in Pécsely, were formed on the basis of social, rather than economic considerations. Formation of larger units were initiated in 1960, on the argument of the advantages of 'economies of scale' (Donáth, 1980:407). The first mergers initiated aimed at better exploitation of machinery, buildings and equipment and better cost effectiveness of large scale production. These mergers were to some extent economically justified. That mergers did not stop but gathered momentum in the next decades, well beyond the pace justified by mechanical and technical progress, is another question to which we shall return in later chapters. But in the 1960s the merger of the three collectives into one in Pécsely was, on the initiative of external authorities, aimed at optimal collective farm size. This does not seem to have been the case with the later mergers (Chapter 9).

In the course of the mass collectivization campaign in 1959, the district council in charge of collectivization in Pécsely had put before the villagers the recommendation that a single collective be founded instead of three; this advice had been disregarded. A year later, a general meeting of the three collectives was convened and a merger proposed. The members of the Rákoczi of Nagy were not prepared even to discuss the possibility and walked out. Of the three, their collective was in the best shape. Nevertheless, there were already many members who believed that the joining of resources and manpower could represent a substantial economic advantage, and so in 1960 the Rákoczi and Petőfi collectives jointly purchased a tractor.

Resistance to the merger was on social rather than economic grounds. The strong sense of local identity of Nagy,
Nemes and Kis-Pécsely, described in Chapter 1, still prevailed, even though they had constituted a single village
since 1940. The members of the three small collectives also
felt intimidated by the prospect of a larger membership,
where members would not necessarily be so well known to each
other as they were while the collectives were still separate. Even in the present situation, forms of social interaction within the collective work-brigades were strained,
and having to cope with an even larger body of fellow members was a daunting prospect. While the collectives were
small, members expected to be able to exercise control in an
individual, direct manner, to understand better the problems
of production and to participate in the running of the collective through the members' assembly. The small membership
size of the three collectives ensured that routine interaction took place within a relatively small, familiar social
field. Fellow work-brigade members were neighbours, kin and
komas. In the event of a merger, such routine interaction
would necessarily extend over a much wider social field and
would bring together people who were not as tightly bound by
long-standing social ties. As it was, there had been long-
standing rivalry and strife between the residents of Nagy
and Nemes and the puszta-people of Kis were looked down on
by both.

However, the decreasing value of the work unit was
alarming and indicated that these three small collectives
were merely removing the advantages of individual farming
without allowing the benefits of large-scale agricultural
production. Thus, by the third year of relentless pressure,
the district authorities had their way and the merger took
place.

The merger of 1961 in fact opened the way for a new
phase of economic development, and the possibility of more
rationalized, large-scale production came within reach.

The new Rákóczi collective began with 178 members on a
territory of 1,455 holds (about 829 hectares). By 1969 active membership increased to 185; 117 men and 68 women. In
addition there were 68 retired members, some of whom worked
part-time.

The decade which opens with this merger represents the
most successful and dynamic period for the collective of
Pécsely. There were still problems of internal organization
and management but, after two or three years, economic development was so significant that these problems were pushed
to the background.

After 1961 the new Rákoczi progressed irreversibly beyond the format best described as 'kitchen collective' - with the chairman's kitchen being the focal point of the previous three small collectives (p. 77). Increased manpower and territory allowed the new Rákoczi to start more specialized production, for which its territory was best suited, although in the first years emphasis was on the distribution of maximal income - that is maximal calculation of work unit values - rather than re-investing a part of the profits in production. Members demanded the maximal income because the erratic and low quarterly payments had been one of the most depressing aspects of collectivization in earlier years.

State help to the collective was mainly in the form of loans, but other social services were introduced which improved the villagers' general standard of living. For example, supplementary benefits were paid to large families, nursery facilities and services for the elderly were improved. A medical centre was established in Pécsely in 1960, with a doctor in residence; previously a doctor had called on a weekly basis only.

It has been shown previously (p. 81) that before 1965 the collective's products were marketed through the intermediary of the council, which was both a complex and bureaucratic body; this subjected the collectives to a large measure of control by the council, and it also involved them in a system of centralized planning of production which discouraged specialization. Nevertheless, from the beginning the new Rákoczi collective managed to start orienting its production towards quality wine-growing. As the villagers put it: 'In the Pécsely basin three products are important: grape, grape and grape.' Henceforth, the Rákoczi's production plans took this into accunt.

The vineyards of the Pécsely valley were mainly located across the hillsides and they were fragmented, individual plots, difficult to work collectively or with machinery. The first initiative of the new Rákoczi collective was to establish high quality grape over 60 holds of flat ground, as well as 20 holds to be used as small farms cultivated by individual members. These new establishments were planted not in the traditional way but in a more modern 'cordoned system.' With this, the rows of vines are planted about 9 feet apart, and the vine stems trained to run over wires extended parallel to the rows, about 6 feet above the ground. Cordoned vineyards produce a greater yield because the vine stems can grow longer, unlike those in traditional establishments where the vine stems are trained up 3-foot

Table 7.1
Grape production in the Rákoczi collective, 1961-1969

Year	1961	1969
Total production	973 quintals	3,706 quintals
Average production by hold	12 quintals	28 quintals
Size of vineyards	81 holds	132 holds

Gáldonyi, 1970:32   (1 hold = 0.57 ha)

poles planted by each vine. The cordoned establishments can be worked mechanically, since machines can proceed between the widely-spaced rows; in the traditional establishments, on the other hand, the rows are spaced only about 2 feet apart. The disadvantage of the cordoned system is that the vines are exhausted more quickly and need to be replaced after about 20-30 years, whereas the traditional vines may go on producing for as long as 60-80 years. Between 1961 and 1969, the grape production in the Rákoczi increased as shown in Table 7.1.

The single, most decisive alteration in the Rákoczi's agricultural production was the increase of vine-producing territory and the improvement of the yield through the use of fertilizers and pesticides.

The new Rákoczi also established an animal farming centre, as well as a pig-fattening unit and a dairy, but these were set up to comply with council directives rather than in an expectation of profit. A smaller range of crops was grown: wheat, as prescribed by the State, as well as rape, corn and alfalfa. The Rákoczi had a small, local distillery, mainly for the benefit of members, a small tavern in a nearby village where the collective's wine was sold, and a gravel quarry in the Pécsely basin. By 1969 the animal farming centre was equipped for 100 head of beef cattle. A large area of swamp was drained and brought under cultivation; this alone cost 70,000 forints. The collectives were not allowed to purchase heavy machinery until 1960; after this restriction was lifted, however, they were able to build up their own machinery centres. The Rákoczi had acquired ten tractors and three lorries during the first ten years of its existence, as well as a number of small specialized machines. In this way the collective made itself independent of the State-run machinery stations. These investments were financed largely by subsidies and loans.

In the first ten years the Rákoczi invested in building essential structures, such as grain stores, machine sheds and sheep folds, which allowed it to do away with the ad hoc arrangements which had prevailed hitherto. A house in the village was bought for the administrative centre. Electricity was installed in the Merza manor, which became the animal farming centre. Members looking after the animals were housed in the manorial buildings and the manor house itself. A cellar of 500 hectolitre capacity was erected. These investments were made with considerable State aid but nevertheless the cautious management kept loans to a minimum; in retrospect this can be seen to be an unfortunate caution in view of the cancellation of such debts in 1965.

Mechanization, which replaced manpower and draught animals, was one of the most significant steps for modernization. The animals used on the fields consumed a great deal of feed, which was saved when draught animals were reduced. However, the disposal of cattle and horses was carried out to a greater extent than was warranted, rendering impracticable the cultivation of awkward stretches of hillside plots; these were therefore abandoned. Chemicals and industrial compounds were increasingly employed, and high yield cereals and crops were adopted. The collective also developed subsidiary branches of non-agricultural activity such as building (mainly for the collective itself), transport and processing.

In 1968, a series of reforms known as 'New Economic Mechanism' (NEM) were introduced. This had a decisive impact on the subsequent development of the economy in general and collectives in particular. In essence, the NEM aimed to strengthen the collectives as independent enterprises and to relieve them of some of the control exercised over them by State departments. The price of agricultural products was increased by 9% in 1968, and by 10% in 1970. The debts of the collectives were cancelled once more in 1967. The collectives were de jure made equal in rights to State marketing agencies but, of course, the State Bank monopoly remained in vigour and the marketing agencies are even today better able to dictate their terms than the collectives. A National Council of Collectives was founded in 1968 to represent the interests of the collectives and put forward propositions to State departments, although the latter are under no obligation to implement them. In order to regulate the internal organization of collectives, the rights and duties of management and membership were formulated and put into law. The secret ballot was introduced for the election of chairmen, but nevertheless outside agencies' control has remained (pp. 116-117). In the collectives, Committees of Control (Ellenőrző Bizotság) were formed, comprising members who formally have the right to supervise management and administration, and to relay information to the main body of members. The working of this committee remains doubtful, however, for the majority of members do not have the ability to oversee management, and there are not adequate safeguards to avoid the management exercising influence over this committee.

An essential result of the NEM was that collectives acquired greater financial independence and control over their funds. Thus collectives now have amortization capital, funds to cover a minimum pay for members, production capital for expenses of the yearly production cycle, development funds for future investments, and finally, social and cultural funds. Each collective may freely decide on the amounts allocated for each of these purposes. The pay of members is guaranteed to be met before obligations to the State, representing a major departure from the previous system of 'surplus distribution' (see p. 57). Basically, the remuneration of members has been divided into two parts; one major part is paid monthly in cash, which represents 80-90% of the estimated total, and the remainder is paid at the end of the year, depending on the profits that have been made. If the year closes with losses the collective can have recourse to its reserve funds, but of course, if a collective is consistently running at a loss, it runs out of reserves. On the other hand, very prosperous collectives have to pay progressively increasing rates of taxes on their profits. By 1968 collectives began to show wide discrepancies in their progress, so this system of taxation serves to even out such differentials; the taxes from the stronger collectives are used to subsidize the weaker ones. To some extent the incomes of members of different collectives are equalized, but this, of course, diminishes the stronger collectives' incentives to reach higher levels of profits (Donáth, 1980).

As a prelude to the NEM, which was aimed at industry as well as agriculture, the collectives' rights in relation to the holdings they worked were regulated. This was a point of the greatest significance. The holdings of the collectives were constituted from land originating from three sources: members, the State, and non-member third parties.

Non-members technically owned about 23% of the land in the control of the collectives, although they had no means to claim control over it. This came about for two main reasons: first, members joining the collective brought in lands which they were leasing rather than owning; second, ownership rights could pass to non-member inheritors after a member's death. A further 28% of the collective's holdings was derived from the State's reserve lands. Only the remainder, that is 49%, was property of the members themselves. In order to bring all lands controlled by the collective into corporate ownership, the State lands were made redeemable for a token sum. Third parties were compensated by five times the sum of the annuity to which they had been hitherto entitled, and these lands, too, became corporate property. Members were also encouraged to give up their nominal ownership rights and, in effect, to sell their lands to the collective cheaply, but few in Pécsely availed themselves of this opportunity. Nevertheless, the situation was greatly simplified, since henceforth only the collectives and the members had property rights over the holdings of the collective. The fact that no member can take land out from collective corporate ownership - even if he gives up membership or the collective liquidates - and no third parties can own such holdings, ensures that gradually all land in collective use will be incorporated into the collective property block. As most young people who inherit land from parents who were members tend not to join the collective, they too must renounce their ownership for a token sum.

The establishment of the collectives as landowning corporations not only allowed their economic stabilization but also the planning of long term production programmes. The individual fields which formed the collective have been fused irreversibly into a single indivisible estate.

By 1968, manpower too had been consolidated, with fewer members leaving. However, many founding members reached retirement age, and to compensate for this loss less labour-intensive techniques had to be introduced and non-member workers had to be employed to work alongside members.

The input of members' labour into the collective greatly improved, the majority of active male members achieving 258 working days of 10 hours per year. Women worked considerably less: about 200 8-hour days.

In less than ten years the Rákoczi accumulated a strong reserve fund and non-distributable capital, as will be seen from Table 7.2. The value of the work units increased, and as a consequence so did the members' income, as is shown in Table 7.3.

Table 7.2
Assets of the Rákoczi collective, 1961-1969
(in thousand forints)

	1961	1969
Non-distributable capital	541	6,668
Production capital	432	2,084

Gáldonyi, 1970:32

Table 7.3
Value of the work unit in the Rákoczi, 1961-1969

Year	Work unit value	Av. yearly income
1961	35 (forints)	11,550 (forints)
1964	54	17,820
1965	38	12,540
1970	55	18,150

Gáldonyi, 1970:33

Until the mid-sixties it still appeared to be a realistic prospect that some peasant-production features could be perpetuated within the collectives, albeit in an updated form: through the devolution of stretches of land to members' care on a sharecropping basis and through the work unit system, for example. In this way, to use Erdei's terminology, a 'bourgeois-peasant' stratum could emerge (cf. Kolosi, 1980:46). This did not in fact turn out to be the case, as large-scale rationalization of production gathered momentum. The collective members did not remain involved in collective farming as a family, echoing the traditional peasant system, where the household is the main unit of production. The women who were not themselves members of the collective did not participate in work on the collective's fields. Several times in Pécsely there were campaigns to allocate, for example, cornplots to members to be worked by

the family as a whole, in return for a quota of the yield.
These were not successful: the corn fields remained neglected and eventually a work brigade of members had to be
called in to work them. The household plots in Pēcsely were
so much more profitable, that sharecropping for the collective held little attraction by comparison.

Production processes proved more determinant in shaping
the collectives' development than features of collective
ownership, and the enterprise features of collectives became
predominant. The members' relationship to collectives increasingly became of an employer-employee type, similar to
that of non-agricultural workers. Members related to collectives individually, and for the collectives the disadvantage of this was that commitment to the collectives' affairs
remained very low, to the detriment of the quality of labour. In conjunction with other features, this contributed
to the absorption of the peasantry into the worker stratum -
as we shall show in the chapters to follow.

8

Internal Organization in the New *Rákoczi* Collective

In the new <u>Rákoczi</u> collective the major problem of internal organization was that certain groups of members refused to work together. The great divide was between the Nagy and Nemes members. As the chairman remembers:

It was not possible to put members from Nagy and Nemes in the same work brigades. They each had separate brigades. It was no problem to put former landowner <u>gazdas</u> with former poorer members of the landless. The problem was the locality ...

And a member from Nagy Pécsely recounted with feeling:

Those were a proud lot. They did not want to work with us; they even had their meals together in the fields when the brigades had to work side by side ...

This member here alludes to the assumed superiority of the <u>gazda</u> of Nemes, which reaches back to the pre-1848 <u>nemes/</u> <u>serf</u> division, as well as to the greater landholding wealth of most of Nemes' inhabitants - as opposed to the poorer non-nemes inhabitants of Nagy Pécsely (Chapter 1). This opposition ceased to have any practical significance after 1848, but it survived to some extent as a locality-based sense of distinct identity, and was extended to all inhabitants of each locality, regardless of wealth or <u>nemes</u> descent. This locality-based sense of identity and pride did not override other considerations of individual ranking, of course, where landownership was determinant, but when it was instead a question of the inhabitants of each village as a group, then rivalry, competition, and a strong sense of identity were expressed, and the inhabitants of Nemes were accused of haughtiness and pride.

In the new Rákoczi members from Nagy controlled most offices. The chairman, Lajos Hőbe, was elected unanimously and so could not decline the office, although he was not keen to have it. He had previously been a prestigious gazda who had played only a small role in the previous collectives, even though he had been a member of the Verseny. He had good connections with Nemes through his wife, who is a member of the most prestigious, rich, formerly nemes families of Nemes - the Kántors. The choice of Hobe for chairman indicated the tacit agreement of members that a new man should hold the office rather than one who had been chairman in one of the three small collectives at the time of the merger. If the latter course had been taken, it would have implied that one of the three had somehow 'overcome' the other two.

The election of Hőbe for chairman proved fortunate; he remained in office unchallenged until the next round of mergers, when he assumed vice-chairmanship. There is no doubt that continuity and stability of leadership had been a bonus for the Rákoczi. In the previous collectives, frequent changes of chairman, preceded by contest and uncertainty, were always unsettling. Hőbe's character may have contributed to the stability of his tenure. He is acknowledged to be a good farmer, keeps himself to himself and is rather withdrawn, all of which may have helped him weather the difficult years, when he was trying to conciliate the various groups in the collective.

The merger of the three collectives brought about an enterprise on a different scale, as has been shown previously (Chapter 7). This meant departures from traditional farming techniques and, concurrently, the internal structure of the collective underwent important changes.

First, there were changes in the position of leadership and management. In the three small collectives there had been problems regarding the legitimacy of the chairman's authority since, for the members, the chairman remained very much 'one of us.' In the Rákoczi some distance developed between the management and members. There was a growing administrative body, starting with an accountant and a secretary, building up to eight office workers by 1968. The chairman, burdened with an increasing administrative workload, no longer took his place in the fields to work alongside ordinary members, as had happened in the smaller collectives. He did most of his work from his office, coping with paper work, negotiating with the council, and so on, while the brigade leaders were delegated to supervise the work in the fields. Management, acting within a broader scope and surrounded by a team of administrators, started to attract power to itself, and its authority could no longer be traced directly to the members' assembly from whence it ultimately derived.

The character of the members' assembly also underwent some degree of change. It was one thing to speak up in a gathering of 30-70 members, most of whom were quite well known to each other, but quite another to speak up in an assembly of 180 or so which included members from all three localities of Pécsely. The territory of the new Rákoczi was larger and the problems of cultivation were of a different order. Decisions to be made were not 'like those on the small farms, only larger' - they concerned agricultural tactics of a different kind. The range of production had become narrower and more specialized than it had been on the peasant farms. The first years also coincided with the introduction of new agrarian techniques which employed new types of chemical fertilizers, pesticides, soil analysis, high-yielding crop varieties and machinery. This made collective production far removed from the methods with which the members were familiar; it devalued their expertise and it also tended to limit their ability to exercise rights of participation in the decision-making process through the members' assemblies. The scope of members' participation decreased in proportion to the increase of the management's scope for decision-making.

On the other hand, the formalization of the collective structure and establishment of the management's authority improved discipline among the members. Disagreements between management and members, or among members themselves, were resolved through formal channels rather than ad hoc ones. The chairman no longer went round at daybreak from house to house, pleading with members to come and attend to some pressing task, as had been common before. However, work discipline improvements were not due to the success of 'ideological education' but, in the view of the contemporary observers, to the more direct relationship between the collective's profits and members' income (cf. Donáth, 1977).

In the first years of the new Rákoczi there was very little occupational differentiation. The brigade leaders, for example, worked alongside the ordinary members, even though they also had the task of overseeing the brigade's labour. Former gazdas had greater chances of being promoted to brigade leadership on account of their acknowledged expertise and social prestige; the kulák discrimination had ceased. The position of teamster was coveted; this also tended to go to former gazdas because of their proven ability with horses and oxen and the fact that they had brought draught animal teams into the collective. The traditional prestige value of well-groomed horses as markers of status was, in a sense, carried into the collective, and ensured the continued prominence of respected gazdas in the collective (Kunszabó, 1970:65-66). Former gazdas were in a better position to secure the best positions for themselves not only on account of their acknowledged farming ability - in Pécsely, as elsewhere, the richer gazdas were reputed to be the best farmers (cf. Galeski, 1975) - but also because they usually had extensive networks of kinship and friendship as well as ties of patronage and mutual support. The landless and poorer members, many of the Catholic newcomers, as yet had not built up dense networks of relations in the village and were thus at a disadvantage in securing the better positions for themselves. This is not to suggest that the oppressive pre-war divisions and distributions of advantages according to landownership continued; these were, in fact, gone for good. The firmly held concept of landownership as being the determinant of status, privileges and social relations had lost its relevance within the framework of socialist production, but nevertheless indirectly certain attitudes held over from the traditional system continued to be held on to for a while.

Even within the relatively undifferentiated occupational system of the Rákoczi there were major differences in the completion of work units; hence income levels varied significantly. Table 8.1 shows the number of members and the income they earned in 1964 (Bodosi, 1966).

Table 8.1
Incomes in the Rákoczi collective, 1965

Above 20,000 fr.	49 members
20,000 - 15,000 fr.	22 members
15,000 - 12,000 fr.	16 members
12,000 - 8,000 fr.	17 members
8,000 - 5,000 fr.	14 members
below 5,000 fr.	24 members
nothing	39 members
Total	181 members

According to this chart, more than half of the members earned less than 12,000 forints in the year, and sixty-three members earned below 5,000 forints or nothing. Comparing these earnings with wages in industry at the time, it is found that the 72 members in the top earning brackets in the collective earned as much or more than could be earned, for example, in the Füred ship factory, where the average yearly income for an unskilled or semi-skilled worker was around 20,000 forints; in the building trade, average income was about 18,000 forints.

The income differentials within the collective were, as a rule, compounded by the incomes generated by the household plots, as the members who achieved the greatest number of work units or who occupied the highest paid positions, that is foremen and teamsters, were also the strongest members who would work hardest on their plots. Those who achieved more work units, or who had higher pay, had rights to more fodder and grain as part of their remuneration and could put these to good use: for example, to feed their own animals. The members who achieved fewer work units were usually the weaker, older members or the former landless, who did less work on their plots because of their diminished strength or, in the case of the former landless, because of the poorer quality of their household plots (see Chapter 16). These inherent advantages and disadvantages contributed to the development of wealth differentials, in spite of the equalizing structure of the collective. The crucial resource has, however, by this time become capacity for labour, not ownership of land.

Until 1973 the new Rákoczi remained very much a village affair, and the villagers were proud of the excellent economic progress of their enterprise. It was a village enterprise in a very real sense: all members, including the management, came from the village, and administrative and production processes took place entirely within the village boundaries. The collective was continuous with the village - even though both politically and economically it was still closely monitored by outside agencies.

Over the ten year period of common interests, collective labour and intensive day-to-day interaction among members, the local sense of identity of the residents of Nagy, Nemes and Kis, which had remained so strong in the years before mass collectivization and the first merger in 1961, started to lose its divisive edge. The work brigades increasingly contained members from all three localities, and reference to locality of origin and residence gradually lost its competitive meaning. This is not to say that rivalry ceased altogether. For example, the building of a new collective administration centre in 1969 was still the occasion for a fierce struggle over its location: Nagy and Nemes both claimed that it should be built on their side of the village. Eventually, Nagypécsely won. A similar dispute took place in connection with the building of the new medical centre in 1965, but on that occasion a compromise was reached and the new building was erected exactly between the two locations, at an equal distance from each.

This period came to an end in 1973 when a new wave of mergers was engineered and the Rákoczi collective was merged with the collectives of the neighbouring village of Szőllős and the nearest small town, Füred. From 1973 onwards the Pécsely collective is merely part of a larger unit and its centre shifts away from the village.

9

The *Jókai* Collective

The new merger in 1973 was brought about by the district council of Füred as part of a countrywide series of
mergers to increase the economic potential of smaller collectives and, in particular to strengthen those that were
not economically viable.

The partners for the merger were determined by the fact
that they had neighbouring fields and a common production
profile. The structure of the collectives operating separately was reckoned to be too narrow and limited to accommodate the adoption of new techniques and more modern high-
powered machinery that came into use in the early 1970s.

The Jókai Termelőszővetkezet[1] of Füred was, like the
Rákoczi, the result of a series of previous mergers, as is
shown in Figure 9.1.

By 1973 the Rákoczi had an excellent record of progress
and a very stable, consolidated management, although it was
still a very small enterprise. The present chairman of the
Jókai emphasizes that the new merger was sought by all
parties and was not the result of pressure from the district
council, but this claim cannot be accepted without some
qualification as far as the Pécsely members are concerned.
As the Rákoczi accountant summed up:

> In 1973 we merged with Füred regretfully, led by ratio-
> nal considerations which were explained to us, but emo-
> tionally we cannot accept it, though we all know that
> the future belongs to the larger collectives ...

Such feelings were echoed throughout the village and
there can be little doubt that the members' assembly of
Pécsely needed a great deal of persuasion before agreeing to
the merger.[2]

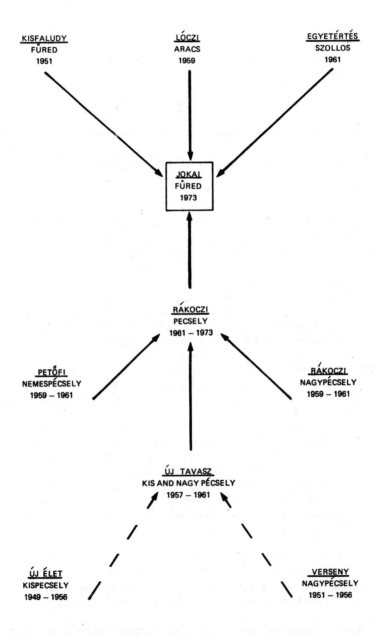

Figure 9.1   The sequence of mergers to form the
Jókai collective

Strategically, Füred proved to be the stronger partner. It is a small and developing town, and the seat of the district council to which Pécsely belongs, conveniently located for transport and other services. It therefore enjoys a distinct advantage over its village partners. For Füred, an important consideration in seeking a merger with Pécsely and Szöllős was that it had run out of good land for further vine establishments and the two villages had plenty; the merger allowed Füred to establish a further 160 holds of quality vines.

After 1973 the newly-built administrative centre of Pécsely lost its importance, both symbolically and practically, for the Jókai headquarters was moved to Füred. The Jókai chairman is a man from Füred; Lajos Hőbe took the second place as vice-chairman. Collective chairmen have been required to hold higher educational qualifications since the early 1970s; the former gazda chairmen could not remain in office and the era of the 'farmer-chairmanship'[3] came to an end.

The collective, of which Pécsely is now only a small part, covers a territory greater than the area of each of its member-communities; the membership includes people from each partner community. There are 367 members, of whom 173 are active; the other 194 are pensioned or are not active workers. There are also 73 non-member regular employees. The holdings of the Jókai are shown in Table 9.1.

Although the merger did not essentially alter the programme of production, it did expand its potential, especially as regards mechanization and the refinement of vine-

Table 9.1
Holdings of the Jókai collective (in hectares)

808 ha	ploughed fields
227 ha	vineyards
334 ha	meadows
414 ha	grazing fields
942 ha	woods
27 ha	orchards
58 ha	not cultivated

2,810 ha total
2,767 ha in cultivation

growing techniques. Production specializes in grapes; 31% of the total revenue comes from this crop and the Jókai is among the best of this type of collective in producing quality wine. As regards its size, it can be classified as a collective of medium size in relation to national averages; as regards productivity and profits it also qualifies for a decent middle position, according to officials in Füred.

The main crops grown are autumn wheat, rape, lucerne, corn and fodder; these represent about 28% of the total production. Livestock is also reared: there are about 180 dairy cows, 800 beef cattle and 5,000 pigs. Livestock farming in the Jókai has now virtually reached its limits; it cannot be expanded much further without breaking regulations of environment protection enforced in the Balaton area. Grain production is continued mainly because it is precribed by the government, regardless of whether it is profitable or not. Meat farming allows the collective to claim grants.

In 1973 the work unit system of remuneration was abandoned in favour of a guaranteed monthly wage packet for members supplemented by a yearly premium and adjusted to the profits of the collective in the following year; that is, if the profits fall short of plan, wages are readjusted downward in the following year. So far however, adjustments have invariably been upward, as the Jókai has made very good progress and profits. The monthly pay is scaled according to the type of division in which the members work and the capacity in which they are employed, as well as according to the number of working days they are bound to fulfil. This form of remuneration does not differ in essence from that of employees of the State Farms, except for the yearly bonuses and the yearly readjustments of pay scale according to the profit margin.

The average income of members in 1976-1979 is shown in Table 9.2. By Hungarian standards these incomes are fairly high; to each would be added the yearly premium, which usually amounts to about one month's wage.

Occupational differentiation, which already started to develop in the days of the Rákoczi (although, as has been seen, it remained fairly elementary), gathered momentum in the Jókai, keeping pace with modernization of production.

The chairman, vice-chairman, chief agronomist and accountant constitute the top level of management. They work in close conjunction and consult regularly, assisted by a large staff of administrators and book-keepers. The agronomist is one of the most important holders of office; he plans the annual production quotas and coordinates the various branches of the cooperative taking into account both

Table 9.2
Incomes in the Jókai collective, 1976-1979

Year	Av. monthly income per active member in forints	Av. yearly income per active member in forints
1976	3,317	39,808
1977	3,448	41,376
1978	3,825	45,897
1979	3,924	47,085

Számadási Tájekoztató, 1979, Jókai Tsz.

internal resources and external directives on production. In the Jókai, the chief agronomist, from Füred, is assisted by branch production agronomists, one for viticulture and another for crops. The branch production agronomist for crops is a young man from Nagypécsely. He is from a Protestant landowner family established in Nagy since 1779; he knows all the members and the határ in which he works, and is very well-liked by the villagers. The branch production specialist in viticulture is also a young man from Nagy, married to the daughter of Pécsely's council president. Other members of management and administration are mainly from Füred: for example, the chief accountant and chief agronomist who work in the headquarters in Füred assisted by junior staff.

In the Jókai there are three main branches of production: animal raising, crop farming and viticulture, which are complemented by the subsidiary branches of transport, building, gravel-mining and machinery maintenance. Different labour brigades are employed in each branch of production.

The agricultural branches, composed of viticulture and crop farming, are worked by several men's brigades and one women's brigade. Agricultural and viticultural labour brigades may be brought together or separated, according to seasonal demands for labour. The animal-raising brigades are quite separate and do not work in the agricultural sectors. Dairy cows and beef cattle are concentrated in the manor of Kis, while the pig-raising unit is based in Szőllős.

The members employed in the machinery maintenance, transport, tractor and truck driving brigade form a class of their own. The smith, carpenter and wheelwright of the village are employed in these sectors, together with those (mainly younger) members who are qualified mechanics or tractor drivers.

A brigade leader and branch production leader is responsible for each brigade. The machinery maintenance brigade works in close conjunction with the other branches of production, as most of the agricultural labour phases are mechanized. In relation to the stock-raising branch, the members are mainly involved in transport.

The major line of occupational differentiation divides the management and leadership from the ordinary workers. This is expressed both in the wage differentials and in the scope of responsibility, expertise and performance of manual labour. They are paid up to three times as much as the average unskilled labourer.

In Pécsely the superior education and urban background of the present chairman mean that he cannot be evaluated in the same way as ordinary local members. He is in a class of his own, unlike the chairman of the Rákoczi who had formerly been a village gazda and did not have an undisputed specialized qualification to justify his position. This is both an asset and a liability. It demonstrates the more impartial, rational criteria used for selection for the office, but also emphasizes the separation of the collective from the village.

The agronomists are acknowledged to hold their position on account of their professional qualifications, although older members sometimes resent the use of modern agricultural techniques with which they are not familiar and of which they do not approve. Incidents when some modern technique has failed are recounted with relish, laced with cynical remarks such as, 'Agronomists should be given gumboots instead of motor cars ... ' meaning that they do not know the particular properties of the határ as well as the old gazdas, and their high pay is therefore undeserved. But, apart from such occasional suspicions, villagers on the whole accept that their expertise is valid, and in practice they have taken on many modern techniques pioneered in collective farming, and used these on their plot farms.

The brigade leaders or foremen are villagers and do not hold significantly higher qualifications than ordinary members. In fact, it appears that these coveted jobs go to people who have some additional social assets such as party membership or close kinship connection with council officials to support them. They receive higher pay than ordinary members and seldom do manual labour. Through their position

they have access to resources which they can use for their
own benefit of make available within their circle of kin and
friends: for example, the allocation of contracts for sideline of vine-stem grafting, which are highly paid. Most
villagers are expert in this, particularly the older people;
nevertheless the foremen and their circle seem able to secure the large contracts for themselves. However, ordinary
members appear to overestimate the advantages of being brigade leaders, and these have to put up with a great deal of
pressure from their kin, friends and neighbours, all of whom
expect to be included in the dimly-perceived inner sanctum
of privilege.

There are no women in the leadership circle of the
Jókai; the women are either members of the agricultural
labourers' brigade, or work in the lower echelons of administration. The women in the better administrative positions
are often the wives of foremen or agronomists. The women's
labour brigade is dwindling: at present there are only
twelve women who are regular members, although more participate on a seasonal basis. The main reason for this decline
is that the older women who had no qualifications at all
have now retired, and younger women, who all learn some
skill such as typing or accounting, do not take up the stre-
nuous outdoor work of the women's agricultural brigade. The
women usually work fewer hours than men and are lower paid.
For women, the advantages of working in the collective are:
the right to a household plot, work in the village itself,
and a flexible work schedule which allows women to attend to
household chores as well as plot farming.

For the men the best jobs are considered to be the ones
that require some technical skill, such as mechanics. Tractor driving is well paid, but the older tractors in particular were very uncomfortable and the shaking was injurious to
health in the long run. Truck drivers are also in a good
position: they have a varied occupation, and they may use
the vehicles occasionally for private errands.

Animal keepers are among the highest paid, but their
jobs are hard and demanding. Many of them live in the isolated and inadequate buildings in the manor, and in spite of
the material advantages there is no competition for positions in that branch. Several older members have asked to be
transferred to the animal-raising branch in the years just
before retirement, for the higher pay of these years establishes the rate of their pensions.

The allocation of work in the various branches of
production is determined by ability and qualifications, as
well as other more vague criteria which smack of nepotism;

nevertheless, more objective selection criteria appear to be gaining ground as specialization increases. The collective is, however, not only a factory-type enterprise but also a social institution concerned with the welfare of its members in a broader sense: requests for specific jobs whether on health grounds or to earn a higher income for a larger family, for instance, are sympathetically considered.

In the <u>Jókai</u> the level of members' education is significantly higher than it was in the earlier collectives: there are nine members with university education, twenty-five with higher technical school education and thirty-four skilled workers. These figures include members from Füred and Szöllös; if Pécsely members are considered separately the picture is less favourable, with no one with university level education, ten with technical school education and only sixteen skilled workers.

Active membership among founding members has diminished greatly with retirement age being reached and replenished from among the young has not compensated for the loss. Serious manpower problems have developed; vinegrowing is very labour-intensive and many phases of production cannot at present be carried out mechanically. This made it inevitable that employees would be engaged. The collective's workforce is therefore mixed, with members working alongside employees. From several points of view the position of employees is more attractive than that of members. Due to a countrywide labour shortage, the wage paid to employees is marginally higher than that of members, in order to attract manpower. Employees are seldom attracted to joining collectives as members, a move which does not provide any benefits. Although employees are not entitled to a household plot proper, they may nevertheless lease a plot for a token sum.

The members of the collective earn a slightly lower income than that of industrial workers but, as will be seen in Chapter 12, they can recover the difference through their household plots. The industrial workers have better working conditions, paid holidays in special resorts and subsidized meals at their workplace, but these differences are slowly being reduced as conditions in the collectives improve.

NOTES

1. <u>Jókai Mór</u>, 1825-1904, Hungarian novelist of great renown.

2. In other Hungarian villages, too, there was great resistance against the mergers. For example, in Varsány in 1965, signatures were collected and all villagers gathered in front of the Church to present their protest against the contemplated merger, but the crowd was summarily dispersed by the police (Tagányi Z. 1978).

3. Cf. Kunszabó Ferenc, <u>Elnöktipusok a szövetkezetben</u> (Chairman-types in the Collectives) 1974.

10

The Collectives' Dependence
and Independence

Vulnerability to centralized State control appears deeply woven into the structure of collectives and into the principles and practice of their operation. Since 1967, significant reforms have been made to extricate collectives from precisely this vulnerability, and their autonomy and independent self-management have been central aims of post-1967 agricultural policies in Hungary. Yet even in 1978 the Central Committee of the MSZMP was dealing extensively with the problem of excessive interference in the collectives' affairs and the need to enforce cooperative democracy. The question is raised by Donáth (1980, 487-488) as to why it is that the Government is regularly compelled to stand up for the enforcement of principles laid down in the legal provisions, and why these cannot become effective. As Donáth rightly points out, this is one of the central problems that needs to be understood in relation to socialist systems, and one that is rooted as much in the social as in the economic context.

The historical circumstances under which collectives were formed and the subsequent phases of development undoubtedly need to be included among the determinants, since it was through them that the villagers set their attitudes towards collectives and formed their strategies in allocating family labour, income and production. Concurrently, the agencies of control, issuing orders from central policy makers to grass roots level, were also the product of the last thirty years and these now appear to generate 'automatisms,' that is, routine actions and attitudes hard to counteract from above.

In the 1950s, in what might be considered the first phase, there were severe limits set on collective autonomy.

These have already been discussed in Chapters 4 and 5. The question to consider here is how far the reforms since 1967 have been effective in undoing the systems of control then established.

In principle, the collectives are today defined as autonomous, self-managed enterprises: production and marketing decisions are made independently; financial issues, the yearly production plan and fund allocations need not be approved by outside authorities although guidelines according to which production plans should be drafted are predetermined and regional authorities check their fulfilment. The collective sets down its own internal organizational charter, establishes its labour requirement, and determines its members rights and access to household plots and services provided in relation to them.

In practice, the dependence or independence of collectives appears to have two distinct yet interrelated aspects: one considering the collective as a corporation and the other, contained in it, the collective's membership. Each aspect needs to be considered separately.

Collectives as corporations see their economic autonomy limited mainly because agricultural prices still remain set too low in relation to production costs. Hence collectives' chances of accumulating capital are limited, making them dependent on grants, subsidies and loans, of which the National Bank retains a monopoly. This affects their scope with regard to investment projects, which have been centrally controlled since 1971. Investment aids to projects other than those already supported (e.g. forestation, roadbuilding) have to be justified and submitted to stringent scrutiny (see Swain, 1981: 232-236).

Second, certain subsidies and grants are linked to the production of grains or livestock, which means production plans have to be directed into those areas, even if they are not very profitable for a particular collective. Third, the allocation of funds and provision of incentives to both workers and management has been regulated by decree: since 1975 an upper limit has been set for the wages of management; since 1977 the wages of all workers and members have been regulated. This is a problem for example in the Jókai of Pécsely. They would have had the means to increase the members' pay but cannot do so without incurring penalties.

As far as administration is concerned, the main interference has been caused by the pressure towards mergers throughout the 1960s and 1970s. The mergers were claimed to be justified by the potential advantages of larger enterprises and the strengthening of weaker collectives. The advantages of larger collectives as regards more cost-effective production, however, has since been questioned (Donáth, 1980:415-416) and it was not always the case that weaker collectives were the target. In Pécsely for example, the Rákoczi was not an unsuccessful collective (see Chapter 7) and the merger of 1973 was the wish of neither the local management nor the members. Donáth concludes that the mergers mainly benefited a new emerging stratum of professional managers and were pressed for mainly at the level of county and district authorities, who seem to be better able to exercise control over larger and fewer collectives. Pécsely's example confirms these observations: the merger of 1973 was the work of district authorities and indeed one official in the district administration has been made the chairman of the Jókai following the mergers.

Lastly, the autonomy of collectives is vulnerable to interference by the appointment of its management - and this is also related to the mergers. In the larger collectives local 'farmer' chairmen no longer had a place, as they lacked the formal qualifications that have been made compulsory. In many small collectives strong capable chairmen did not emerge and this was a considerable hindrance to overall efficiency; in others, however, as in Pécsely, the local chairman had proved himself a very capable man and his replacement was not essential. Replacement of 'farmer' chairmen by specialists, pre-selected by outside authorities, questions the members' right to elect their own leaders; it is also clear that a man so appointed is likely to remain more committed to carrying through policies favoured by the authorities who sponsor him, rather than those of the membership. The situation described by Hann (1980 and 1983) in Tázlár is one such example.

Having said all this, it also remains true that the collectives do have a great deal of leeway in interpreting the guidelines and directives issued, and in this respect there are wide variations from one collective to the next. The constitution of work brigades, the brigade leaders' scope of authority regarding work organization, assistance for the retired, housebuilding, and support in relation to household plots vary from collective to collective and that suggests some independence in internal organizational matters. As shown through the example of Tázlár, this specialist cooperative has been able to stall and ignore, well into the 1970s, the most specific directives of outside authorities, who desired to see the extension of the collectivized sector (Hann, 1980). M. Hollós(1983) compares the neighbouring collectives in Tiszakécske and Nagykörös, noting the differences in their internal organization which have wide-ranging repercussions regarding both economic results and members' attitudes to the collectives. For example, the allocation of household plots and help provided by the collective are crucial issues. Some collectives choose to reallocate the plots yearly - on one continuous tract reserved for that purpose - a practice that greatly reduces the use to which plots can be put. In other collectives, as in Pécsely, and Tiszakécske in Hollós' example, plots are allocated on a permanent basis, do not change hands yearly, and are allocated, as far as possible, near each member's house or where his cellar stands. Restricted (zártkert) areas, devoted entirely to plots and protected from encroachment, are a further advantageous alternative for members; these are also taken up in Pécsely and Tiszakécske. The importance of plot farming to collective members will be seen in the chapters that follow and it is clear that a collective leadership that supports the plots is giving a great bonus to its members, but as Hollós shows, not all do. She does not say, however, why the leadership of the collective of Nagykörös follows the 'hard line' it does, nor why the members' assembly and committee of representatives are not able to change matters to the members' best advantage and, for that matter, to the collective's advantage as well.

As Hollós shows, the economic results are poor in this collective, a fact not unrelated to the members' discontent and poor management. The comparative inability of the members' assembly to make decisions against the managing body seems to be the case here, and we shall return to this point later.

The character of leadership in a collective is a major determinant of its autonomy. If the leadership is local and well supported, it is also less likely to be dependent on outside officials and it may also be more willing and ready to pass on some of its autonomy to the lower levels of membership. Undoubtedly, leadership needs the support and cooperation of the members and the more its position depends on that support, the more willing it may be to further the members' interests. It is also clear that the poorer the economic results are in a collective, the greater the chances of outside intervention become, although, as the example of Pécsely's Rákoczi shows, good results are no guarantee that interference will be avoided. Vulnerability to interference seem to be the major problem: this may take different forms from one collective to the next, but no collective can be sure of being exempt. And past experience appears to confirm that interference can issue from not one but many levels: from central Government changes, such as the steep increase of taxes on plot farming income (Kulcsár, 1982: 148-149), regulation of wages (Donáth, 1980:484), or control of investments (Swain, 1980:233-236); from regional authorities' interference in the form of investigation into the collectives' affairs (Hann, 1983), or forcing a change of leadership and pressure towards mergers, as was the case until well into the mid-1970s. The management itself may follow a more centralized leadership style as reported by Hollós (1983:93-122) and may be pledged to a course favoured by external authorities (Hann, 1980). And, one might add, the above represent only the kinds of interference which have been recorded and are official; covert, unrecorded interference has not been taken into account.

The assembly of members, which in principle stands at the apex of the decision-making hierarchy in most diagrammatical renderings of the socialist collective structure (cf. Hollós, 1983:103), in Hungary as well as, for example, in the Soviet Union (Humphrey, 1983:103), de facto seems to be of very marginal significance.

In spite of the string of reforms since 1967, the active participation of members in the collectives' affairs has not been realized to the extent implied by the democratic principles upon which collectives are supposed to rest. As has been seen, collectives have become larger than the local, village enterprise format, and have grown into complex, specialized enterprises relying heavily on expert and specialized management and technical staff. The members' assembly meets half-yearly, and is not de facto a deliberative body; it is rather of purely symbolic significance. The members are presented with the production plan and an account of the previous half year, which they formally acknowledge. Ordinary members have little access to, and cannot participate in formulating management strategies, and they cannot oversee the complex marketing policies involved. Production techniques employed are far removed from the farming techniques with which members are familiar, and even if some disagreement develops and members feel compelled to query some detail, they are very disadvantaged vis-à-vis the specialists in charge. Furthermore, the management is in a good position to make information inaccessible to members. In Pécsely, both members and management agree that little effective contribution is made by members at the assembly and, as the chairman put it: 'As long as the income is good, the members leave matters of policy entirely to us.' It remains a question how far the membership is involved if the income or whatever central aspect of the management's policy is unfavourable to members; Hollós' example of Nagykőrős would suggest that the assembly of members is no more active there either.

Since the mergers of the 1970s, the functions of the assembly of members have largely been taken over by a board of members' representatives. A conference of these delegates may decide on a modification of the collective's constitution, discuss and approve the yearly plan and make decisions relating to collective property. These delegates are elected at the general assembly by a show of hands and number 5-10% of the collective's membership. Through this board, the general assembly's participation in decision-making has become even more indirect and insignificant.

The participation of members is obtained, therefore, not so much through the assembly of members as through a variety of other lesser committees which deal with specific problems that directly affect groups of members. There is the Control Committee, drawn from members, which consults with the chairman, vice-chairman, chief agronomist and accountant to discuss the yearly plans and their proposed execution. There is no effective way of checking the influence the management may have on this committee, which is constituted from members who cannot compete with management leadership in terms of expertise, influence or authority. There is a Disciplinary Committee, drawn from members, to investigate problems of discipline among members and settle disputes between management and members. There is also no effective way of checking the management's influence on this Committee. The Nominations Committee assesses the background of potential candidates for the chairmanship; in practice, however, the district council and the Party appear to have first say in the pre-selection of candidates and, in any case, as candidates are no longer selected from among people known in the village, or from the villagers themselves, their election is little more than a formality.[1]

In addition there are other committees, such as the Small Farm Committee, the Women's Committee, and the Pensioners' Committee, whose functions are to represent the interests of those particular groups in relation to specialized activities. They pass on to the management suggestions and grievances in connection with work conditions, the household plots, working hours, distribution of fodder and firewood, and so on. In more than one way the management leadership can control the activities of these subordinate committees since, although nominations for representatives of these committees take place at the general assembly, pre-selections are prepared in advance by the management and members expected to be 'difficult' may be bypassed.

In addition there are the <u>Munkahelyi Közösségek</u>, roughly translated as 'labourers' organizations,' in the various production branches, such as agricultural fieldworkers, stock-keepers and mechanics, who come together to discuss problems relating to their own sectors. Their influence, however, very much depends on the management's willingness to accede to their suggestions. Participation through lesser committees and sectional groups removes major decision-making domains from the assembly of members, thereby strengthening the members' 'worker'-type relationship to the collective: profit oriented and subaltern rather than participant and co-owner (see p. 119), as the formal charter of collective organization would suggest.

Yet the collective is more than just an employer. It plays a significant part in the villagers' life beyond just providing work for its members. The collective determines how the agricultural land of the village is put to use, not only the land under collective farming but also the plots farmed individually. The household plots to which members are entitled (to be discussed in Chapters 12-20) are allocated by the collective and the small, privately-owned plots have also been affected by the collectives' decisions during the course of the innumerable land consolidations which have taken place. Plot farming involves practically all families in the village (pp. 148-151), and to this extent almost all individuals came into contact with the collective. Beyond land allocation, the collective is involved in the small farming activity of the villagers in a wide variety of ways, as will be seen later (Chapter 14).

Beyond the domains of production and work, the collective is involved in its members' lives in less formal ways. In times of need members may ask for assistance, for example, in a family crisis, marriage, or other such events. Loans, gifts or cash may be offered to members if the need arises. In relation to housebuilding members expect assistance with materials or transport. Pensioners are helped with small services - goods, firewood, and so on - although these are not always accomplished as promptly and efficiently as expected. Before 1973, while the village was still the centre of collective farming, such personal attention was more prevalent than it has been since the last merger. This change is particularly resented by pensioners who perceive a lessening of informal support, such as prompt availability of fodder and hay for their animals, or the annual outings organized for the elderly. It is likely that the collective would be prepared to be more helpful in principle but in practice its more rational and complex structure is less able to accommodate particular community and personal concerns.

The collective is closely interlinked with other village institutions, such as the council, the consumer cooperative, and the school. The active and even intrusive part played by the council in the formation of collectives and their subsequent operations has already been examined (p. 58). Although the dependence of the collective on the local council has weakened since the last merger and the reforms of 1967, both collective and council are subordinate to the same higher official departments and are bound by the same central and regional policies, giving them common ground. The school, Culture House, and other village institutions may count on financial contributions from the local collective which, more often than not, has more funds for the purpose than the council itself.

The question of the autonomy of collectives and the degree of member participation cannot be viewed only in terms of how far the autonomy falls short of declared aims and the formal charters. The State's role has not been only restrictive: the concentrated and rapid implementation of modernization programmes for agriculture could hardly have been achieved otherwise. Once the commitment to full collectivization of agriculture was made, the requirements of large-scale agricultural production gathered momentum, favouring, for example, the emergence of a strong, technologically oriented managerial élite and at the same time exposing the irrelevance of the principle of collective decision-making and ownership. And this process was foreseen by the members themselves: in fact, they were arguably the first to perceive the likelihood of this course of events, if we consider the attitude of members throughout the successive phases of collectivization. The strategy of agricultural families in planning the allocation of their labour has been fairly consistent throughout the country since the 1950s, with the engagement in industry of some family members and dynamic development of the small farm by others. Hence, the family members who do remain in the collective relate to it in ways that shield them to a considerable extent from the de facto limitations they encounter as members. For example, the extent to which collectives have or lack autonomy, or the extent of the true scope of deliberative rights of the general assembly, concerns the members far less than one might assume.

NOTES

1. See C. Hann for an account of how outside authorities can influence the election of chairman for a collective (1980:132-136).

11

Relationship of Members to the Collective

By definition, peasant production implies the unity of the production enterprise (farm) and the domestic economy of the family (Galeski, 1972:11). Commonly, peasants are credited with attachment to the patrimony (land) and to the value they put on the ownership or control of that land. Without denying the significance of such attachment to values and assets inherited from the previous generations, the waves of mass peasant migration from village to town in Europe since the last century should alert us to the danger of overestimating that factor.

The processes that have taken place in Hungary since World War II include modernization of agricultural production, through the drive of ideologies which '... have an ultimacy of commitment in the name of which a wide range of sacrifices are demanded and procured' (Smelser, 1967:37). In relation to collectivization, as was seen in previous chapters, the sacrifices demanded were great indeed, and the peasantry has been pushed towards rapid changes in attitudes and values, and abandoning age-old habits and life-styles. Yet, '... the sting of change lies not in change itself but in change that is devoid of social meaning' (Frankel, 1955: 27). It is a matter of definition and, ultimately, of arbitrary judgement, to assess changes to be devoid of 'social meaning' but, at this point, Frankel's words sum up well the problems with which the present study is concerned. Undoubtedly, the crucial problem facing the villagers after the war was that of shedding traditional ways of production, labour and community interaction and adapting to an entirely new system. But this adaptation was not one-sided. The collective system itself was altered by the manner in which peasant families engaged their labour in the collectives.

In the early phases not only was their commitment reluctant and half-hearted, but it was also paralleled by part of the family manpower being engaged in other sectors: non-agricultural employment and household plots which were dynamically developed into a major economic sector. The relationship of the villagers to the various sectors is well exemplified by the difference between 'peasant' and 'worker' attitudes to work.

The traditional peasant way of life involves complete cycles of production, in which all phases are interrelated. Family, household and production forms an integrated whole and disengagement of these spheres was, in Hungary, the burden of one generation. The worker, in assuming that status, separates work from household and, as a corollary, from many other aspects of the peasant lifestyle and attitudes. As is shown by Jávor (1983:280-282), in relation to changes in Varsány as long ago as the early 1900s, scarcity of land set in motion the development of the 'worker' type. Differences between the peasant orientation and that of the landless forced to seek employment outside agriculture, have been reflected clearly in attitudes to labour. The peasant orientation implies attachment to land, self-sufficiency and independence, an individual rhythm of work without set hours and with short breaks, but stretching from dawn to dusk. Working in groups, under orders, in jobs which involve only parts of the production cycle, is alien to these men. On the other hand, the worker or worker-peasant (cf. Jávor, 1983: 280) has already adjusted to working by the clock, under orders, in larger groups and for set wages; self-sufficiency and independence are already less valued than the security afforded by the monthly wages.

In the collectives, neither 'group ownership' principles nor the traditional peasant orientation to work has received expression. Members came nearest to retaining aspects of the peasant orientation in the Verseny of Nagy in the 1950s, but were defeated partly by the lack of previous experience in realizing its full potential within a collective framework and partly by external intervention that could not be resisted.

In Pécsely, land scarcity was not pressing before 1945 (p. 35), and employment in industry was neither sought nor desired. Only by the 1960s, in response to the anti-peasant policies of the previous decade, did non-agricultural labour come to be considered a realistic and desirable alternative (p. 195). But the 'worker'-type conditions of labour were to come to the village unsought, through the collectives. Every step taken towards mechanization, modernization, and expansion of collectives through successive mergers has been a step towards it. 'Worker'-type conditions of labour were also furthered by specific organizational changes, such as, for example, the introduction of monthly payments in lieu of the work unit system, specialization of management, and inclusion of employees alongside the members.

In the early years, while the collectives still represented a half-way house between peasant production and agricultural enterprise, not quite living up to good standards in either, the major problem was what Hegedüs (1977) described as 'organized irresponsibility.' It has been seen how difficulties with discipline and quality of work affected the early phases of collectivization (pp. 82-83) and this has been a problem throughout Hungary. As the collectives assumed a more entrepreneurial character, strengthened their organization and specialized the system of production, the 'worker' orientation has undoubtedly become dominant, resulting in a better integration of members into the collectives' work system. Not that irresponsibility and lack of commitment have been eradicated completely, but they have certainly become a less urgent problem since the 1970s. It is also clear that this cannot be attributed to the success of ideological education, the development of socialist consciousness or commitment to the social good, rather to both the economic incentives and adaptation of the overall family strategies to the new systems which include collectives, non-agricultural employment of some family members and plot farming. Hence the attitudes to collectives and the form of members' engagement is only partly understandable in terms of the individual members' link to the collective; it is rather the family's strategy of labour allocation that is more indicative of the role collectives play in the villagers' life. And this role relationship furthers the 'worker' orientation, as it disengages the workplace from family and household, the interests of which are instead recentralized through common interest in the plots and engagement in other, non-agricultural sectors.

In the development of relating to collectives in this way, failure to realize the principle of group ownership appears to be a major factor. Indeed, collectivization is often viewed as no more than a transition from private landownership to State ownership.

In Pécsely, there are apparent discontinuities between, for example, the Verseny in the 1950s and the Jókai today. The difference is not merely that the Jókai is larger, more prosperous and uses more machinery. Other significant changes took place through successive phases and mergers, such as the separation of management from the body of members, the increasing inability of members to secure participation through the assembly, and the inclusion of employees along- side members. These developments render the distinction between State Farms (which are State owned and worked en- tirely by employees) and collectives redundant. Ending the difference between these two forms of enterprise is consid- ered by many in Hungary and elsewhere in Eastern Europe as not only desirable (Galeski, 1975) but inevitable (Donáth, 1976). Undoubtedly, in both collectives and State Farms, it is the corporate enterprise element that is relevant and not the principle of ownership upon which they are based. Access to control over disposal is more significant for both than the principle of ownership (Kolosi, 1980:39). In the weakening of the relevance of the principles of ownership, the modernization of agricultural production has been em- phasised (Donáth, 1976) yet, as has been seen, even in the 1950s the principle of collective ownership received little expression as far as the members were concerned. The delib- erative rights of the members' assembly were made question- able from the outset by external control and, later, by the strengthening of the collectives' management, whose author- ity has grown at the expense of the members' assembly.

In this light, the discontinuity between the collect- ives' structure then and now appears less pronounced, sug- gesting that the economic development of the collectives did no more than bring to completion elements that have been present all along. This proposition may appear to be of purely academic relevance; certainly for the members it was more. Collectivization campaigns between 1949-1959 were conducted under the slogan that members would remain owners of the land they contributed and, once inside the collect- ive, the commitment of members to the collective was encour- aged through the promise: 'It is your own.' Although such statements carried little conviction, members nevertheless made weak attempts to see these principles realized. The fact that, since 1967, few members have given up their pure- ly theoretical rights of ownership over the lands they have contributed (see p. 95) appears to indicate that some still cling to the notion that they 'own' that land; a barren hope for, as has been seen, it is the control over resources that is crucial and not any right of ownership. The way in which campaigns were conducted, the arguments used to per- suade members to join and the experience of the validity or otherwise of these arguments cannot be ignored as determin- ant factors shaping the relationship of members to the col- lectives. Bearing these points in mind, how can we define the relationship of members to the collective in Pécsely?

In spite of individual variations of particular members' relationship to the collective, arising from their different temperaments and outlook, certain general types of relationship can be distinguished.

There are those who are completely detached and have no expectations at all from collectives in general. These are usually the older members, particularly those who were formerly owners of self-sufficient farms. They come mainly from Nagy and Nemespécsely, and they tend to retreat to their plots, which are of the best quality. One typical member of this type is KS of Nemespécsely. He is now 70, Protestant and of nemes descent, a former middle peasant. He is still considered to be one of the best gazdas and his prestige is high. He was branded a kulák in the 1950s, an experience that left him a bitter man. He joined the Petőfi collective in 1959 reluctantly but was a conscientious member, although he focussed his attention on his household plot and livestock. None of his children joined the collective and all three left the village. KS never accepted any leading position in the collective, such as brigade leadership, although it was offered to him. He is uninterested in the Jókai's affairs and in collectives in general.

Not all older members reject the general ideal of collectives; there are many who have specific grievances against only the local collective, these grievances being mainly that they feel they cannot have their say. The older gazdas think they would have a great deal of advice to offer on the basis of their intimate knowledge of local conditions and they feel that their traditional expertise has been devalued. Such is PI, a former smallholder of Nagypécsely, who played an active part in the organization of the Verseny but resents the independence of the specialist management of the Jókai. Although he admits: 'Collectives are the future ...' he adds with less enthusiasm: '... they are unavoidable.' He is an intelligent man and feels his advice is never sought or taken and feels that speaking up in the assembly is useless. He is full of ideas about how things should be run, and blames the management of the Jókai, for example, for letting large tracts of valuable hillside vineyards go to waste.

In spite of such attitudes, not even the older members want the old system of traditional farming to be restored. Their physical strength is just about enough to cope with their household plots, and they are aware that the younger generation would not continue independent farming - neither would they wish them to do so, for their aspiration for their children is to see them rise out of agricultural status and occupation. Their own membership in the collective is of a detached, distant kind, and their families' social and material welfare is sought through dynamic plot farming and encouraging children into non-agricultural employment.

For members who have not been landowners before collectivization, and for younger members in particular, relationship to the collective is less problematic than for the former landowners and older members. The former's interest is limited to the income, the household plot benefits, and work conditions, and they relate to the collective as they would to any other employment. The seven young villagers in the mechanics brigade well exemplify this type. Their qualifications would allow them employment in industries nearby, but they chose to join the Jókai because they have adequate housing locally and are also engaged in profitable plot farming. They consider the local collective to be a good one, and the household plot derived from membership excellent, but they are not concerned about participation in the collective's management. This kind of relationship is undoubtedly on the increase, as more elderly members retire and demand for skilled workers increases.

Finally, there are those who have identified with the aims of the collective and have developed a 'this is ours' attitude to it. It is a very small minority, mainly those who are Party members and/or have a leading position, for example, as branch production manager or brigade leader. Their feeling for the 'common property' (közös) is more pronounced, partly out of ideological commitment and partly because their position allows them greater control and participation in the collective's affairs. SzI of Nagypécsely, a former landless man, is one example of this type. In the 1950s he was a leading member of the local Party cell and organizer of the Új Élet and Új Tavasz. He was brigade leader and is now branch production manager in the stockfarming centre. He is committed to collectives in general and to the Jókai in particular, and is a man respected in the village for his ability and character. Yet neither of his two sons has joined the collective; one is a builder who moved away from Pécsely and the other is the storekeeper of the grocery shop in the village.

A final point may be made about the relationships between the members themselves. In the 1960s the common problems affecting the villagers, as well as their daily interaction in the work brigades, certainly brought them together, though not always in ways they desired; as has been seen (p. 99), there was great resistance to members from the

different localities and with different former status. Although by now much of the former divisiveness has been ero-
ded by time, nevertheless there is little evidence of strong
group or brigade consciousness developing in its place among
co-members. The members mingle with each other during work
hours and join the worker-association of their branch, but
they seldom meet socially at other times. After work hours,
the ties of kinship, neighbourhood and age-old connections
between families retain their hold. In other words, individuals whose families have been connected socially or by kinship, independently from the collective, keep these ties up
as members, but membership by itself does not seem to draw
members together. In this, it is of no small significance
that individual attitudes to events such as collectivization, the anti-<u>kulák</u> system and the uprising of 1956 varied
considerably. The lack of certainty as to where others'
sympathies and interests lay predisposed people to turn towards the closest and, at times, safest circle, that of the
close family.

It is misleading to consider collectives and social
relations within them solely on the strength of collective
labour: the existence of the complementary sector of plot
farming has marked consequences on the way in which members
relate to the collectives and to one another. Social relations within the village, the household economy and income
differentials are only partly determined by the members'
work in the collective, and the villagers' approval of the
status quo is not based solely on the existence of collectives, but on the system as a whole, which of course includes
also plot farming. While the collective has grown away from
the village and has developed into an independent enterprise
with little or no village character, plot farming has remained an essentially village affair. It mobilizes and involves more villagers than the collective, not individually
but as families and households, and perpetuates traditional
techniques of production as well as forms of interaction,
mutual help and reciprocity, as will be seen in Part 3.

Beyond the Collective

12

Plot Farming:
The 'Second Economy'

Plot farming is commonly classified as part of the 'second economy' that thrives parallel to the primary socialized economic sector of Hungary.

Definition of activities constituting the second economy is open to debate. A broad definition includes plot farming, small private enterprises and services, as well as additional incomes gained illicitly through the socialist sector itself through using common resources to private ends. Bribes, tips and gifts also come under this heading, as well as the undertaking of private jobs during work-hours or the use of equipment in the place of employment for private purposes. Letting accommodation, or exchanging council-owned accommodation privately, and private loans may be classified within the second economy. Overtime work and secondary jobs are marginally second economy activities too.

A narrow definition of the second economy includes income raising and production activities which are not organized by the State and which fall outside the socialized sectors of production, and which provide incomes over and above wages from main employment but are not illegal. In this definition, the second economy is the domain where a secondary distribution of resources takes place, and whereby the socially organized primary distribution-pattern is modified. It is distinguished from the first economy, not in terms of legality but of legitimacy. The distinction is essential. 'Legal' means that which does not contradict formal laws or statutory provisions. 'Legitimate,' in the Hungarian context, means that which is politically and ideologically acceptable; but of course, the boundary between illegitimacy and illegality is neither always clear nor unchanging. A wide range of activities are legal yet not legitimate or of doubtful legitimacy, and that ambivalent status is characteristic of second economy activities in Hungary.

The particular sense in which 'first' and 'second' economy is used in relation to socialist societies has been a matter of controversy. It has been argued that only illegal activities of an income-generating kind belong to the second economy, making it comparable and equivalent to the same category of activities in non-socialist countries (cf. Marresse, 1980; Holzman, 1981). The proposition that only illegal activities belong to the second economy implies that the private sector is fully integrated in the country's formal economic organization and is not in opposition to it. To argue that the private sector is part of the second economy emphasizes the irregularity of this sector, and this is not a view that many sociologists and economists in Hungary today wish to promote, to avoid eventual suppressive policies that might follow. I will argue that the second economy in socialist countries cannot be equated with its counterparts in non-socialist countries, since it is not the legality or otherwise of the second economy that is at issue in Hungary today, but its legitimacy, and the fact that the fundamental principles of operation of the private sector are different from those of the first economy. The structure of the second economy as it appears in socialist countries is specific because socialist systems have a level of theoretical and ideological models in terms of which the economy and society are regulated, which is lacking in non-socialist systems (cf. Humphrey, 1983:74). In the chapters that follow the second economy is examined in terms of its differences to the socialized sector and the first economy.

The second economy - of which plot farming is commonly assumed to be a part - importantly modifies the distribution of incomes and resources of the socialized sector, within which income differentials are relatively narrow. The secondary distribution operates through its own dynamic. This dynamic appears to have so far eluded definition, but recently some interesting propositions have been put forward, which, abandoning the starting point that the second economy arises merely out of the incomplete or inefficient application of control throughout the socialist economy, suggest instead that it emerges from inherent structural characteristics of the primary economy itself. This approach considers the second economy as structurally bound up with the primary economy and attempts to identify mechanisms of the latter which stimulate or give rise to secondary distribution.

Chronic house shortages and an economy riddled by scarce resources have been identified as objective economic conditions which stimulate secondary distribution (Ferge, 1978; Erdélyi, 1979). Over-employment and lack of material incentives within the socialist sector is emphasized by Gábor (1979:22). In a brief but suggestive paper, Bogár (1980:38) links the development of a strong second economy to the manner in which the socialist mode of production has been established. He suggests that the socialization of the means of production has been carried through in Hungary with excessive speed and to an excessive extent, so that a social 'immune reaction' has been triggered. This reaction became manifest in areas of economic and social life which governmental social control could not quite reach and harness. By this he means that independent economic sectors and areas where individual initiative could be exercised have been compressed within narrow limits; in consequence these areas became overactive and, in a certain sense, 'overheated.' The strength of this view is that it is not limited to just the consideration of the principles and content of the socialist mode of production but also reflects upon the social field in which the socialist mode of production has been applied, considering this 'receiving end' to be capable of reactions which may modify, counteract or even cancel the intent of central planning.

This argument may be of relevance when considering plot farming. It has been an all too common assumption that directives handed down from higher echelons of government will be realized unchanged and will fulfil precisely those aims for which they were designed. Yet the massive discrepancies between plan and actual results showed that even if central directives are carried out formally, their substance may be modified in unforeseen ways by the social field in which they are applied. This has been proved to be particularly true in relation to household plots.

Plot farming is not always unambiguously classified as part of the second economy, and many authors hesitate to consider it alongside the less integrated and less legitimate sectors as it is neither illegal nor conducive to gain without labour. Nevertheless, the fact that plot farming may give rise to greater income differentials than the socialized sector allows, and that it is essentially a private, individual undertaking, qualifies house plot farming as a part of the second economy.

It is characteristic of the second economy as a whole that its units of common interest are small, based on the individual, family, the household, neighbourhood, workmates, colleagues and local networks. The experience of collectivization has shown that the attempt to create a sense of collective ownership and commitment to the közös (communal property) by compulsion and ideological education has been unsuccessful. In fact, individuals became so alienated from collective property that any common interest and responsibility were rejected (see p. 258). Mistakes in planning and massive bureaucracy have further exacerbated this sense of alienation. This situation appears to have enhanced the importance of private, personal interest groups and networks based on local, occupational and kinship relationships, a state described by E.R. Wolf (1968:2):

> ... the formal network of economic and political power exists alongside and intermingled with various other kinds of informal structures which are interstitial, supplementary and parallel to it ... [because] ... the formal table of organization is elegant indeed but fails to work unless informal mechanisms are found in direct contravention.

While it is useful to introduce the concept of second economy, it is nevertheless to some extent misleading. There is close contact between the first and second economies and the activities of both overlap considerably; as far as the individual is concerned, there is a single economic field with a variety of alternatives - some in the socialized sectors, others outside it. These may complement or oppose one another, accommodate different types of relationships and attitudes to work and income, and affect social and economic relations in a variety of ways. The individual is often not even aware in which field he or she is operating, and neither is that important to him or her. It is, however, certain that through the second economy, however narrowly or broadly one defines it, a substantial element of flexibility and versatility is introduced into a system that is otherwise rigid and unwieldy.

Although collectivization in Hungary contributed decisively to the modernization of agriculture as a whole, in the early phases it failed to supply sufficient agricultural products to cover the needs of the members themselves. During the 1950s this was attributed to the lack of large-scale agricultural techniques and machinery, insufficient production capital, the half-hearted attitude of members as well as sabotage by the kuláks. Since that time, and particularly from the mid-1960s onwards, however, significant economic progress has been made and the collectives have greatly improved production, strengthened their organization and accumulated capital - without being able, however, to fulfil the country's need for agricultural products. The supply from family plots is as vital today as it was in the 1950s, and it is likely to remain so for the foreseeable future.

Family plots in Hungary followed the model of that in Soviet Russia and their position within the socialist economy has been riddled with similar contradictions and ambiguities (cf. Lewin, 1980). Essentially, the problem presented by household plots has been that, while they have been the most efficient sector of agricultural production within the economy, their existence has only tenuous legitimacy in terms of socialist ideology and dogma, and has been considered to be motivated by the peasants' wish for private gain and obsolete traditional ways of thinking.

In spite of the plots' economic significance for both the national economy and the producers themselves, there were regularly recurring campaigns in Hungary to restrict or suppress them, through limitations on their size and livestock, high taxation and limitation of access to essential goods necessary for their production (fertilizers, implements etc). Such restrictions were, however, invariably followed by a decline of production on the plots, which worsened the country's food supply situation and compelled the government to revise its policies.

When the first collectives were formed in Hungary in 1949, there were no hard and fast restrictions on the size of the plots that could be retained in private use and countrywide their size averaged 4 holds, which meant that the largest part of members' land remained as plots, as members of the collectives at this time came mainly from the lower strata of landowners (Hegedüs, 1977:468). However, alerted to the 'entrepreneurial' quality of plots, in 1951, the government limited their size to below 1 hold, and the average size of plots throughout the country was reduced to 0.6 holds in 1951 and 0.7 in 1952. Delivery quotas on plot production were increased, resulting in the prompt reduction of their output which caused severe shortages. In consequence the government was forced to ease restrictions and this was done by cancelling compulsory delivery quotas on wine and milk. These were nevertheless minimal concessions which had little effect in increasing plot production.

The plots' economic function was twofold: first, they were essential for the producers' subsistence, which could not be met by the collectives alone; second, they were meant to ease the transition from private to collective farming. The first economic function was duly met by the plot; otherwise, collective members would have starved.

However the second function was not fulfilled. Collective members were constantly aware of the vulnerability of their plots which could be, and often were, further restricted, charged with taxes or otherwise interfered with at a moment's notice. Furthermore, as will be seen below, the continuous need for production on plots and the problematic relationship of members to the collectives endowed plot farming with a significance much greater than simply that of a means to ease transition.

In 1953 agrarian problems were reassessed by the government, but no changes were made to policies regarding the plots. The main concern at this time was for the collectives, in relation to which plots were regarded very unfavourably. The weakness of the collectives was blamed on the careless, uncaring attitudes of members towards collective property and labour, which stood in sharp contrast to the dedicated attitudes of these same members to their plots. Hence the conclusion was drawn that the plots were the cause of the weakness of the collectives (Juhász, 1980:28).

In 1954, while the basic restrictions on plot farming remained, more supportive opinions were voiced (Erdei, 1954: 684). The plots were still tolerated, mainly as a means of subsistence for the producers and their families, though in fact significant proportions of plot products reached the market.

In 1957, the matter of agrarian policies was very much to the fore and the Theses of Agrarian Politics, which dealt mainly with the problems of the collectives, was issued by the Central Committee of the MSZMP. The problem of the plots was not mentioned, except that the right of members to a plot was reiterated. It was clear that in this case the plots were considered from the point of view of making the collectives more attractive, rather than as problems in their own right. Thus the previous restrictions on plot size and on livestock that could be kept remained in force. In the period after 1956 the subject of plots received even less official attention than previously; they were not supported but neither were they further attacked. At this point it was the local leadership of the collectives that had to grapple with the problem of the difference in members' attitudes to their plots and their collectives which remained a continuing irritant.

In 1960 the matter of the plots was raised by the Central Committee of the MSZMP, which declared the need to support them to produce more for the market; this was the first time it had been officially acknowledged that the plots were not just to provide food for household consumption. However while concluding that the plots required more support, no positive initiatives were taken; the 'support' was only that they were not curtailed.

The plots continued to be considered as temporary and, even in 1963, the MSZMP's textbook of political economy states: '... in the beginning of building socialism the plots provide substantial products for the national economy ... but in the later phase their role declines.' (Dankovits, 1963, quoted by Juhász, 1980).

The main problems plot farmers encountered were the lack of security of tenure, lack of fodder, feed, fertilizers, implements and machinery, unorganized and limited possibilities for marketing, and high taxes.

The first positive official encouragement of plot farming occurred in 1967, when standard-sized houshold plots were allocated to individuals rather than to family units. Thus, if there were several members of a family in the collective, each member would have the right to a plot; this could add up to a fair sized small farm if several of the family were members. The right to the plots' existence and their complementarity to the collectives was acknowledged at this point. To halt the continuing decline of plot production a series of rulings was passed between 1969 and 1970, mainly organizing the supply of fodder and feed as well as marketing the plot products. The main reason for this more supportive stand was that it was by then clear that the collectives were in no position to assume the production supplied by the plots, nor could they do so in the foreseeable future. Of course this had always been known to be the case but only by 1970 was the political situation such that some official acknowledgement could be granted to the plots, and policies be revised accordingly.

This more supportive policy brought immediate results in stimulating plot farming, but it did not in itself prove sufficient. Livestock, for example, continued to decline. Small stock, pig and vegetable production increased but slumped again in 1975, with a 12% decrease in milk production and a 30% decrease in pork production. The plots were very sensitive to marketing conditions and prices, as well as to the availability of animal feeds, and problems in this respect were directly reflected in decreased output. The policies on plot farming were still ambiguous in the 1970s: alongside the acknowledgement of their vital functions, the taxation system was tightened to check their assumed excessive profits. The producers responded by promptly withholding production.

In 1976 the supportive statements of 1967 were repeated

and reinforced. There was further development in that private plots (i.e. those that were not derived from membership of a collective) were declared to have equal rights of support from collectives with those of the household plots proper. Since 1967 the government has aimed not only to halt the decline of plot farming, but to increase it.

After 1960 the ideological evaluation of plot farming changed and its complementarity to the collectives emphasized, with the plots being represented as quasi-integral parts of collectives. For example, one of Hungary's leading economists, F. Donáth, has argued that, since members may renounce their share of plot lands and claim compensation in cash instead, plots are nothing but 'a part of the members' pay in kind.' He thus enlarges the concept of collective farming to include plot farming as well, in an attempt to play down the ideological incompatibility between the two. This interpretation appears rather laboured, stretching the meaning of payment in kind too far, for, in the case of plots, this 'payment in kind' is no more than an opportunity for collective members to work after hours. Such interpretation does not alter the fact that it is a question of two types of relation to production which are fundamentally different in kind and effectively opposing each other: large-scale industrialized agriculture on the one hand and small-scale individual enterprises on the other.[1] It would appear that the present tendency to view plots merely as branches of collective farming serves to justify their continued tolerance and support but, as one contemporary author writes: 'a campaign to integrate collective farming and plot farming would harm our collectivist policies' (Juhász, 1980:115) - although subsequently Juhász concedes that a closer integration of the two sectors would be desirable and that at the moment integration is far from complete. The development of this debate is by no means of academic interest only, for it determines the way in which government policies in relation to both collectives and plots unfold.

Although government policies undoubtedly shifted towards tolerance and encouragement of plot farming, the way in which this policy was implemented stood in the way of realizing those aims de facto. For example, numbers are not often quoted to demonstrate government support of plot farming: in 1983, 12,000 large-stock, 160,000 pigs and 180,000 rabbits were supplied to plot farmers; the large enterprises produced 22% of the fodder used on small farms, sold 450,000 tons of fertilizers, 60,000 million forints worth of pesticide to plot farmers and so on. Such numbers would indeed confirm that support given by the socialized sector to

small farms has been prodigious, and the small farmer ac-
knowledges that despite increased prices, he has been supplied with the necessary means of production on the plots.
However, as has been pointed out (Gonda, 1984), this does
not need to be described as 'support' or 'help.' Help is
given to the needy for free; to get things for money is not
help but merely a mutually advantageous transaction. Desc-
ribing the process of making available the means necessary
for production for money as 'support' means that it has been
made available for something that does not have full legitimacy: here, the term 'support' does not refer to the transactions themselves but to the uncertain status of plot farming itself. If plots were to be fully and completely legitimized, to supply the necessities for production through
regular economic channels would not need to be referred to
as support.

The complexity of government measures in relation to
plots makes it almost impossible to assess how far they are
advantageous to plot farmers. When prices for plot products
fall, as was the case in 1983 for wine, for instance, the
disadvantage is clear, but when prices are increased the advantage is not. For example, the government announced that
from January 1984, milk prices were to be increased by 0.55
forints per litre and pork by 1.42 per kg. However, at the
same time it was announced that prices of fertilizers were
to be increased by 16%, small machinery by 12-13%, protein
feeds by 8% and so on. At the same time social security
payments payable by plot farmers was increased from 700 to
850 forints. Unannounced, the prices of spades, fuel and
foil tents were also increased.

Weight and quality categorizations change frequently
and when this happens the advantages are not easily apparent
to the small farmers. It is good that pork prices per kg
increased by 1.40 forints, but at the same time, the 3
forint export benefit ceased, and the price increase only
applies to animals weighing between 95-105 kg. So the plot
farmer finds it very difficult to assess how changes might
affect him. He may have to resort to the simplest arithme-
tic to do so: how much can I buy today from the net profit
of the farm compared with the previous year? That the reckoning is not consistently to his advantage is shown perhaps
by diminishing production on plots; for example, in 1982
there were 203,000 cows on small plots as opposed to 338,000
in 1970 (Gonda, 1984:86).

Dependence on government agencies and collectives remains, and since essential supplies are available mainly
through them, supplies to small farms may be controlled -

withheld or rationed at will. In marketing contracts changes may be made after contracts have been agreed, for example, the buyers may refuse to provide transport to collect
livestock or change their quality grading. The plot farmers
are not in position to protect themselves since they do not
have any organization representing their interests. The
small farmer with his problems stands alone in relation to
the socialized sector and the government agencies. Not having self-managed autonomous voluntary groups representing
their interests, they rely on individual networks and 'pat-
rons' to solve their problems (see p. 282).

The unpredictability of measures in relation to small
farms is another hazard. For example, just before vintage
in 1983, the announcement that marketing agencies would pay
10-20% less for the wine already contracted and taken in was
not known or agreed in advance. Back-dated tax investiga-
tions or changes in the water rates retrospectively may hit
the small farmer at any point. Neither does the small farmer know in advance the proposed community plans and these
may encroach on his farm. Stretches of land may be re-
assigned for housebuilding purposes and plots summarily
ceased.

At present the most important consideration for plot
farmers at the local level is to know how the local collective relates to their activity. In Chapter 10 it was seen
how collectives are effectively in control of most land in
the village, and their support is crucial to plot farmers.
Yet it is not in the interest of collective management to
support plots as they receive little credit for results
achieved in that sector; official praise and grants are
mainly awarded for successes in the collective sector.[2]
Second, the large-scale agro-techniques and organization of
the present collectives are not suitable for farming on
small plots, which have different requirements. In order to
be of real assistance, the collectives need to set up a separate and complex network of services to deal with the plots
and not all collectives are willing or able to do this. Finally, the collectives' management are wary of the members'
plot farming activities, for these tie down their interest
and energy to the detriment of their performance during work
hours in the collective. This problem is much less acute
today than it was in the past, when collectives were less
mechanized, more vulnerable and dependent on local labour,
but certain rivalry and suspicions remain nevertheless.

The importance of plot farming for the national economy
is acknowledged by the government today, but the plot farming sector is firmly held in a state of dependence from the

socialized sector. Dependence in practice means one year's fodder is not available - as was the case in Pécsely in 1978, which resulted in a drastic reduction of cows on the plots. It also means that pastures may become unavailable from one year to the next, that rabbits or doves are no longer marketable through the local collective, that maize and barley are in short supply, that the quality of feed changes unpredictably.

It is generally acknowledged that production on plots is cheaper than on the large-scale enterprises but it is not clear how much cheaper. Assessment of the profitability of collectives is almost impossible, since there are too many intervening elements. As well as costs of labour and materials, depreciation of equipment, administrative charges and so on, grants, loans, and subsidies have to be considered. In collectives some products are heavily subsidized; for the establishment of stables in collectives grants are given, thereafter each additional cow is rewarded by 20,000 forints and calves by 5,000 forints. Price supplements are given for each litre of milk and meat stocks get quality supplements, even if the animal concerned has been farmed out to a private small farmer most of the time. The price paid for beef cattle from a collective is 27,000 per head, while only 24,000 forints is paid for a similar animal from a small farm. So the price obtained for products is not only determined by quality, but by where it has been produced (Gonda, 1984). However, the tax system in relation to collectives is different and more complex than it is for small farmers. The very complexity of the system stands in the way of clearly assessing prices and costs, and leaves lingering suspicions on the part of both the small farmer and the collective that each is disadvantaged compared to the other. This fact in itself is a barrier to the integration of the two sectors, but nevertheless it has not stood in the way of the dynamic development of the small farming sector, as will be shown.

146

1.   It is essential to distinguish two different
aspects of the relation between the two sectors as Tepicht
has done (1972:80). From the socio-economic point of view,
plot farming and collective are undoubtedly opposite. But
from a technical point of view they may be complementary and
technical integration may be advantageous to both, but complementarity must be understood here mainly with reference to
the   allocation of different branches of production to each
(for example, stock raising to plot farming and grain and
fodder production to collective) and the provision of marketing contracts for plot farming products by the collective.   On the production-technique side, as will be seen in
later chapters, the organizational structure of the collectives is of diminishing use to the plots, because the two
types of production are of such a different scale of magnitude.
2.   The management of collectives is entitled to bonuses on the plot farm products marketed through the collective, but this is of such small amounts and so seldom applied
for as to be of minimal consequence for how the collectives'
management relates to plot farming of the collectives' members.

13

The Small Giant:
Form and Function of Plot Farming

In addition to the collectively-farmed fields which occupy the greater part of Pécsely's agricultural territory, about 126 hectares remain in individual cultivation. The area is small, perhaps one tenth of the collectively-farmed land, but its significance is far greater than its size would suggest.

The plots were formed on residual agricultural land, mainly on that which could not be usefully fitted into the collective's production programme. Plot lands are nonetheless often of very high quality in Pécsely, the majority being scattered on the hillsides where the best land for vines is located, but where mechanized cultivation is not practicable.

Officially, justifications for the plots were the following:

1. to enable members of the collective to produce food for their own consumption so that the collective could concentrate on commodity production;
2. to ease the transition from individual farming to collective farming;
3. to exploit existing facilities of peasant production which could not be usefully employed by the collective;
4. to supplement the incomes of members which initially were not sufficient for their subsistence, and thus to check mass abandonment of agriculture;
5. so that assets specific to both small and collective farming would complement and mutually benefit each other (Fazekas, 1976:55).

These justifications emphasized the temporary nature of plot farming within the socialist agricultural system, and

Table 13.1
Plots in Pécsely, 1972

Household plots of collective members			Complementary plots not derived from collective			
under 0.5 ha	over 0.5 ha	all	under 0.5 ha	0.5-3 ha	over 3 ha	all
36	99	135	22	17	2	41

From: Általános Mezőgazdasági Statisztikai Kötetek, 1972, p. 162.

were formulated with the assumption that when collective
farming had been firmly established, plot farming would
wither of its own accord. Since 1959, however, the plot
farming system has assumed a far greater role than had been
ideologically designed for it. Although the plots occupy
only 15% of the country's agricultural land, they provide
almost one third of the gross agricultural output nationally; in 1978 26.3% of crops and 45.8% of livestock has
been produced by the plots.

The plot farming system is versatile and flexible. In
the context of the present-day Hungarian economic structure
that is a distinct advantage. The collectivized sector
cannot produce either the quantity or variety of agricultural products to satisfy the market and so the plots fill a
vital role in the economy. Plot farming therefore needs to
be assessed within the context of collectivized agriculture
and not independently from it, even though the plot farming
sector is essentially a 'private' sector in terms of initiative, control and profits.

In spite of their relative territorial insignificance,
plot farms in Pécsely are of considerable importance to the
villagers; they provide large revenues, tie down significant labour power, and occupy a central position in the
villagers' affective interest in a way that the collective
does not.

The majority of households in the village control at
least one plot, through one or other household member.
These plots are 'household plots' (háztáji) - that is, land
allotments to which all members of the collective are entitled. Their standard size is of 0.57 hectares, about half
of which may be vineyard. In 1972 there were 176 plots in
Pécsely (Table 13.1). Household plots are allotted to members of the collective for life, and may be inherited or
sold provided they are located in the closed garden areas
which are designated for plots only.

The conditions attached to household allocation vary
from collective to collective. In some, for example, in the
village of Kislapos, household plots are re-allocated annually by lot, so that members cultivate a different stretch
of land every year (Bell, 1979:110). The plots of Kislapos
are used for growing corn, potatoes or fodder, and such a
system of household plot allocation does not encourage investment or innovative development. Not surprisingly, the
majority of members (65%) opt to take their plot shares in
kind or cash in lieu of the land itself. In Pécsely, however, the household plots are allocated definitively and do
not change hands annually. In a vinegrowing area, where

plots include vineyards of considerable value and not just bare land, permanent holding is essential. Furthermore, vineyard plots are usually furnished with cellars which are owned individually. In Pécsely, the majority of vineyard plots are controlled by the same people who owned them before collectivization. The consolidation of holdings farmed collectively affected the vineyards on the hillsides least. The collective's vineyards are mainly recent establishments on flat ground; the need, therefore, to take hold of the traditional hillside vineyards least amenable to mechanical farming did not arise.

In addition to the household plots, there are forty-one so-called 'complementary plots' (see Table 13.1) which have not been allocated by the collective but have been obtained by purchase, inheritance or lease. In other words many plots are not derived from membership in the collective, or families may control both household plots and complementary plots (Table 13.2). Thus, while not all villagers are entitled to a household plot, not themselves being members in

Table 13.2
Villagers engaged in plot farming, by occupation

Sector	Occupation	No.
Collective member	manual	93
	non-manual	7
Collective employee	manual	9
	non-manual	-
Agricultural	independent	5
Non-agricultural	manual	90
	non-manual	22
	independent	5
Retired	agricultural	77
	non-agricultural	34
All		342

From: Altalános Mezőgazdasági Statisztika OSH, Budapest, p. 162.

the collective, in practice the majority of villagers are involved in plot farming.

Table 13.3 shows that out of a total population of 595, there are 534 villagers living in households that have a plot under their control. Only 31 households do not have plots of any description; these usually consist of elderly people enjoying a pension who are too weak or ill to undertake physical labour, although they are not necessarily the oldest villagers, for there are a number of villagers, both men and women, well into their seventies or eighties, who still work and control a plot.

Immediately following mass collectivization in the early 1960s the tendency was for the maximum amount of land to be incorporated into the collective farm but, by the 1970s it had become apparent that not all fields were suitable for collective farming. Awkward stretches, mainly in the hillsides, were therefore left uncultivated; in order to restore them to use, a system of long leases was adopted in the mid-1970s, on very advantageous terms, for up to 50 years. In this way, those wishing to occupy themselves with plot farming can easily engage in it, even if they have no means of acquiring land. In practice, therefore, there is no shortage of land for plot farming; on the contrary, it is rather the amount of wasted vineyards that constitutes a problem.

The plots in Pécsely are valuable, because a standard size collective plot vineyard of about 0.3 hectares may net as much as 20 to 30 thousand forints a year. Many families work plots two or even three times that size, made up from allotments of several members or complemented by privately purchased stretches. Production expenses are kept low, in spite of commercial sprays and fertilizers that are used, because most plot farmers have all the equipment they need and the family supplies the bulk of the labour. In 1979, the highest income from plot farming in Pécsely was in the region of 100,000 forints, but incomes vary greatly between households. Exact figures for incomes are hard to compile systematically as people are reluctant to disclose precise figures, but it is generally estimated by informants that, on average, incomes from plots amount to about half a family's total income. This is consistent with national averages (cf. Enyedi, 1979:79).[1]

There is a close correlation between overall family wealth and the scale of plot farming. The wealthiest families - judged by their housing conditions and assets such as cars - are those who have the largest and best plots, <u>in addition</u> to the employment of one or two members in the

Table 13.3
Number of household members in households with plots

	Number of household members					
	Collective household plots		Complementary plots not derived from collective			All
	under 0.5 ha	over 0.5 ha	under 0.5 ha	0.5-3 ha	over 3 ha	
	85	340	65	40	5	535

From: Általános Mezőgazdasági Statisztika OHS, Budapest, p. 162.

collective or industry. Those few families however who make a living exclusively from small farming are among the relatively poor. Versatility in form and function are important new features of plot farming; plots may be traditional or innovative, market-oriented or for household consumption, and may be specialized to a greater or lesser extent. The purpose plots fulfil considerably influences their form - plots which serve mainly to satisfy the elderly gazda's emotional attachment to traditional farming are quite different from the plots established in order to fulfil specific material goals.

Engagement in plot farming falls into distinct types, even in Pécsely where specialization in vine-growing is predominant.

The older, former small and middle peasants in Pécsely characteristically produce for the market but retain traditional techniques and branches of production, for which they have the means, equipment, and local network of relations. They re-invest a certain percentage of their production capital year after year, but investments in modern farming methods are limited to the purchase of small mechanical implements or the conversion of vineyards to the cordoned system (see p. 91). Although attentive to market demands, these people avoid branches of production which, although perhaps more profitable, are less prestigious in terms of traditional evaluation - such as for example, pig fattening. Plot farming profits are generally destined to some pre-set purpose - house renovation, building, or the purchase of a car. The independence gained by plot farming and emotional attachment to the land are very important and material gains play a secondary role. Older people still have low consumer habits and the main beneficiaries of plot farming are their children. Few plot farmers of this type make exact calculations in terms of investment-return; a vague sense of 'it is worth it' is more typical - which, of course, determines how much physical labour they are ready to devote to their plots. For many, the main benefits of plot farming are in the farming itself.

The former landless are likely to find less satisfaction in farming for its own sake; they do not aspire to the reputation of good gazda and the purpose of their plot farming is beyond farming itself. They convert the material benefits of plot farming into general improvements of lifestyle, mainly ensuring their homes are better equipped with modern comforts.

The younger plot farmers, now in their thirties and forties, are often skilled workers, who engage in plot

farming more out of a calculated choice, having carefully
assessed how profits compare with earnings from other
sources and having adjusted the plot's production to the
market. All the young plot farmers in Pécsely have some
other employment and one that is often chosen to help the
requirements of plot farming; it is often a job that allows
flexible work hours or allows access to facilities that can
be put to use on the plot. These young men are more likely
to innovate, to engage in new areas of production which do
not have local tradition or are not traditionally considered
to be prestigious: pig-fattening or sheep farming for instance. They are more interested in modern techniques - for
example automatic feeding machines - than the older gazdas.
For them, plot farming is a means towards a goal - to achieve an ideal of modern life-style - and, as such, engagement in plot farming is considered to be temporary until
those goals are reached. How temporary or otherwise their
engagement in plot farming really proves to be remains to be
seen.

These various types of engagement which have been outlined will be examined in greater detail in the following
chapters, but one aspect of plot farming needs to be considered first: it is not, as a sector, independent. Plots do
not fulfil the purpose of providing subsistence for the
producers and their families; the majority of plot farmers
have regular incomes from their employment or pensions, thus
plot farming is both dependent on and integrated with other
economic sectors, the extent of which is examined in the
next chapter.

NOTES

1. Donáth (1977) quotes the following ratio of incomes
from the plot and collectives (averages nationwide):

	1958	1961	1964
Collectives	56.9%	45.6%	47.7%
Plots	43.1%	54.4%	52.3%

14

The Integration of the Plots and the Collective

While plots are independently cultivated and are part of the private, as opposed to the collectivized sector, there is substantial contact between both sectors.

Most plots (76% in Pécsely) are derived from membership in the collective, which organizes plot allotment to members. Household plot allotments in Pécsely are permanent and most members have occupied the same plot since 1961. The collective was, and is, in overall control of the village's agricultural land - directly for lands within the collective sector, less directly for those outside it. For example, the collective designates the areas for the 'closed gardens' exclusively devoted to plot farming, it leases land for prospective plot farmers, and it may compel a plot farmer to relinquish his plot if it stands in the way of consolidation. In practice, local agricultural land is almost entirely under the collective's control. The collective influences the use to which plot lands are put, and the plots' output is brought into line with overall production plans. For example, the collective encourages vine-growing by establishing new vineyards at great expense - the cost of establishing 0.57 hectares of vine is 100,000 forints - and allocates them to members. The last new vineyards were established in 1969 on 23 hectares of land. They were distributed to members whose old vineyards were exhausted, and to those who did not have vines on their plots. There was little competition for these new establishments as the existing stocks absorbed most of the available labour.

Collective members are entitled to a variety of services in relation to their plots - such as transport or purchase of fodder, fertilizers, pesticides - at reduced rates. Levels of production on plots could certainly not be maintained without such services.

Services in relation to stock raising branches of plot farming are also substantial. Chicks, ducklings and geese are provided by the collective, and contracts for pig raising and sheep farming may be negotiated. The collective provides the piglets, for example, checks their health, provides feed, and guarantees to take them at pre-negotiated prices.

Plot products may be marketed through the collective and, in effect, 80% of all plot farm produce in Pécsley is so marketed. In 1978, 18 head of cattle, 887 quintals of grape and 595 hectolitres of wine, worth almost two million forints, were marketed through the collective.

The agronomists of the collective are available for consultation and advice, and the Small Farm Committee protects the interests of the plot farmers - although, in fact, the effectiveness of such committees is by no means certain (see p. 120).

Cooperation between the collective and the plot farmer is not always ideal. Since the Rákoczi merged with the collective of Füred in 1973, its facilities and equipment have been adapted to large-scale agriculture and cannot be usefully employed on plots. Plot farmers have consequently been encouraged to invest to some extent in modernizing their methods of cultivation, for example, by buying small machinery or by switching to the cordoned system of vines (p. 91). Such investments in modernization are in fact limited, first because few can raise the necessary capital, and second because there is uncertainty about the future of plot farming as a result of frequent and unpredictable policy changes in the past (Chapter 12). Lack of help from the collective also triggered the re-adoption of more traditional means: for example, taking advantage of the recent re-establishment of the right to keep horses, several plot farmers have bought horses and make good profits hiring their services to fellow villagers.

As well as official cooperative links, there are also informal contacts, whereby members make use of facilities belonging to the collective inasmuch as they have access to these. It is difficult to assess the true extent of such activity as much of it is not admitted publicly, but sometimes it can be seen to be taking place. For example, collective trucks and cars are used for private deliveries in the course of a member's housebuilding, or for carrying swill for the privately owned pigs, and so on. People even occasionally admit to such practices, but they assume that 'others' do it to a much greater extent than they do themselves (see also Chapter 18).

In assessing the relationship between collectives and household plots, it must be borne in mind that the plots are no longer units of production and consumption, but are specialized commodity production enterprises. Formerly, peasant farms integrated different sectors which complemented one another; these have now been separated so that one part, mainly grain production, which is amenable to industrial mechanized production, has been taken over by the collectives. The other part, which is highly labour-intensive and less easily adaptable to industrialized farming methods, such as livestock rearing and vine growing, has remained largely in the control of plot farmers. But, as is often pointed out by Hungarian economists, for plots to be able to focus on specialized, labour-intensive branches of production, it is essential that the production of grain, fodder and so on, be carried out by the mechanized system of collective farming. It is on this basis that J. Tepicht has proposed that the sectoral integration of peasant production, previously achieved at the family farm level, is now organized on a national scale through the complementary relationship between the collectives and the small plots (Tepicht, 1973:15-45; see also Hann, 1980:94-97).

In Pécsely, the complementarity of the two sectors is also apparent from the manner in which families' incomes, which derive from them, are allocated within the household economy.

15

Household Economy and Small Farming

Most plots are cultivated in a labour-intensive, traditional way, with minimal mechanization and investment; this accounts for their relatively high profit margins.

In the majority of households, wages of family members are allocated to routine living expenses, while the income from the plots is saved towards larger investments: home improvements, construction, purchase of a car. Such budgeting follows from the fact that income from the vines is received in one sum and may vary greatly from one year to the next, while wages can be accurately calculated to cover routine expenses. The necessity of accumulating some capital arises from the chronic shortage of housing which prevails both countrywide and locally.

The importance of housing conditions and the housing market in the village in relation to household economy cannot be over-emphasized. In Pécsely, most houses were, or still are, in need of major improvements to adapt to a higher standard of living. The traditional peasant houses were not damp-proofed, and their thatched roofs require regular renewal or replacement by tiled roofing. In most houses there was no sanitation or running water. Living space was cramped, with whole families occupying one or two rooms. Since the war, such conditions are no longer considered suitable, especially by the younger generation. Young people aspire to brick-built houses with proper sanitation, central heating and all modern amenities; they are no longer content to occupy one room in the parental home.

Housing conditions present more pressing problems for the young whose parents were landless or poorer landowners before the war, because the parental homes in such cases were from the outset of poorer quality. Those who were richer landowners had better quality houses initially, and

159

their children have less need to build new houses, although here, too, the ideal for the young is to set up a home apart from their parents.

Many are driven to leave the village simply because housing is so inadequate and the nearby town of Füred offers better chances of finding modern accommodation. Several possibilities are open to them: they may sign up to purchase a flat in a complex erected by the building cooperative or apply for council housing. Either way they have to wait for several years before a flat becomes available; the usual waiting period is about 4-5 years, but may be longer. The flats acquired in this way are usually very small, comprising two to three rooms. Prospective house buyers may team up and build a 4-flat complex, in which case they are eligible for greater bank loans than builders of individual houses. In 1977-1979 eight young couples chose this option. They teamed up with kin and friends, as well as non-villagers in the same predicament, and built such 4-flat buildings together. In Füred in 1978 a flat could be obtained for between 300 and 350 thousand forints, and 450 to 500 thousand forints by 1985.

For those who decide to settle in Pécsely, the prospects are worse. If they build, it must be an individual house which is much more expensive than a flat. Help from within the village is, however, available; family and friends give a hand with building, and professional builders are called in for the jobs which require special tools and expertise. When finished, such village houses are of a higher standard of comfort than the small flats of Füred, but the expenses are higher too, and bank loans are less easily available. In the past few years inflation has pushed up house prices steeply; the total price may run to 500,000 forints and loans are given to cover only about one-third of that sum. Houses in relatively good condition do not often come up for sale in Pécsely itself, but when they do they offer the best solution for young couples determined to settle in the village. The price is usually lower than that for building a new house, and renovation can be completed just as and when required. One such house came up for sale in 1981, during my stay; it was sold for 350,000 forints, but a further 100,000 were required for essential renovation.

Wages alone cannot finance the building or buying of a house, and it is here that the income from plot farming is essential.

Parents and grandparents are important contributors to setting up young people while they themselves often continue to dwell in old, thatched houses. House-building as a major investment has acquired such prestige as the material expression of status that the young are encouraged to aim for the best - which is usually well above their means. The efforts made are great, straining and absorbing family manpower for many years. In order to achieve the ideal house - which includes all modern amenities right down to the tiled bathroom and washing machine - the plots have to be exploited to the maximum extent and fellow villagers have to help in the building of the house. When it is complete, the work of fellow villagers who have helped has to be reciprocated. A good illustration of the prestige value of housing in Pécsely is a case where the only son of elderly parents had no intention of marrying or even of settling in the village, but the parents nevertheless insisted on buying a site in the middle of the village - beating several eager, prospective buyers -and building a house, which stood empty for several years. This is, however, only an isolated example; generally housing remains an acute problem and new buildings meet a very real need.

Young people wishing to build or to buy a house may want to diversify the plot farming beyond the vine-growing to accumulate the capital required. The most current, and easiest, option is to take up pig-fattening contracts with the collective. Most houses have the necessary outbuildings and very little capital investment is needed. Pig rearing is quite compatible with other employment and is not labour-intensive, although it requires regular attention. There are four to five young families in Pécsely engaged in pig-rearing contracts and they deliver between thirty and a hundred pigs per year to the collective. In the opinion of most villagers the work is quite messy and unattractive when such large numbers are involved, and it is usually done only for as long as the proceeds are needed. No one in Pécsely admits to being permanently committed to this in the same way as to vine-growing, although as the price the collective pays is in the region of 2,000 forints per head, profits are high. People engaged in pig fattening have worked out advantageous ways of acquiring swill and feed - usually through informal channels - and so their expenses are kept to a minimum.

Further possibilities are offered by sheep farming, on contract to the collective, and on a more modest scale rabbits may be raised at home; they also find a ready market. Rabbit breeding is favoured by older pensioners, as it demands a great deal of attention, yet little physical effort. Versatile exploitation of plot farming is well exemplified

by the following account of one young couple of Nagy. PL,
the husband, is aged about thirty, his father was a shep-
herd, who is now retired from the collective. He has two
young children and works as a driver in the Jókai. His wife
is trained in viticulture but chose to take advantage of the
three years' paid leave (see p. 197). She contracted to
raise between sixty and a hundred pigs per year, grossing
about 200,000 forints, with expenses reducing the profits by
about one half. PL keeps a team of horses and a hundred
sheep, grazed on leased land and shepherded by an old
villager. In addition they have a standard-sized vineyard.
The object of this expansive small farm activity is the
building of a five-roomed house in the village, to replace
the one-roomed dwelling in which they now live, sharing a
courtyard with parents with whom they do not get on well.
PL has informal access to a variety of collective resources,
for example obtaining feed and transporting it home daily.
Both husband and wife consider such exhaustive small farming
temporary and hope to reduce it when the house is completed
and furnished - which may take several years - and the wife
plans 'to read and go to the theatre more often.' However,
they appear to enjoy farming life, and the husband is particularly interested in animal farming, perhaps continuing in
some ways the vocation of his father.

Completion of the building of a new house does not necessarily lead to a reduction of small farming; the Jókai's
young branch agronomist has already completed what is probably the most attractive new house in Pécsely and he also
has a car. Nevertheless, he continues to farm his excellent
vineyard and has set up a small pig-rearing compound, equi-
ipped with an automatic feeding device, to take about forty
pigs. Such small farming units are more likely to be permanent, rather than oriented specifically towards achieving
set material goals.

On a smaller scale, but to a significant extent, vegetable plots contribute in kind to the village households.
Not everyone markets plot produce, but nobody in Pécsely
produces exclusively for the market, not even the two households described above. Households invariably have a vegetable plot, and often corn and potato fields as well as an
orchard. To some extent this perpetuates features of the
traditional peasant life-style and provides important
supplies not readily available elsewhere in Pécsely. Vegetables and meat are only rarely on sale in the local shops.
Household production of eggs, vegetables, fruit and meat
represent a very substantial and steady contribution towards
daily needs and allows cash economies to be made. In almost

every courtyard there are chickens, ducks and geese. About half the households fatten at least one pig, and generally two, each year. In practice more than half of all households benefit from the pork produced, as it is standard practice for the parents to raise the pigs owned by their children together with their own, making use of the existing sheds which the modern villas lack. Corn produced on the plots is used to feed the small stock and pigs and is not usually marketed.

Until 1973 there were restrictions on the number of large stock that could be kept, resulting in severe depletion of animal stocks countrywide. In Pécsely in 1975 there were still a hundred cows, but only thirty-three in 1978 and seventeen in 1979. The main reason for such rapid decline, in spite of restrictions being lifted on stock ownership, is that young women are not willing to take over the care of animals from the older age group. Another difficulty has been the acquisition of fodder from the collective. When delay and problems of supply occurred, as they often did, the temptation to give up was great and, once the cow was sold, there could be no going back; this particularly demanding area of farming would not be resumed.

Horses are a different matter; there are several villagers who, after many years, recently purchased one or two. There are about ten horses in Pécsely and they are used on the small farms of the owners or contracted out to help other villagers. In the village there are a further thirty horses which form part of a riding school (see p. 280), but this establishment is quite removed from village life and small farming.

These activities do not ensure the self-sufficiency of the household; indeed, self-sufficiency is no longer an ideal, nevertheless the contribution made is significant and it satisfies objective needs.

16

Plot Farming and Development of Income Differentials

The problem of assessing differentials of income and wealth hinges upon the definition of 'narrow' and 'wide' differentials. Income distribution in Hungary is reckoned to be narrow, within a range of one to ten. The minimum set monthly wage is about 1,200 forints and the maximum is between 12,000 and 14,000 forints (Ferge, 1978:28). With this range of incomes Hungary rates among the countries with the smallest income differentials (Paukert, 1973:2-3).

Undoubtedly the income distribution of the socialized sectors is modified through the second economy, but it is difficult to assess the extent to which this occurs because of the 'hidden' nature of the latter. In a socialist economy, re-investment of profits and capitalization are restricted, so that surplus incomes are directed towards consumption (Ferge, 1978:28) which, by socialist standards, is often claimed to be 'prodigal' although it would not be considered as such in Western Europe.

In Pécsely, income over and above what is strictly required for subsistence is directed towards obtaining adequate housing, cars and durable goods which conform to the present ideal of a modern life-style. Differentiation among villagers ranges from those who have more or less attained that ideal to those who have done so only partially or not at all.

To define wealth differentials the following indices, proposed by Hegedűs (1977:124), are the most useful:

1. quantity and quality of equipment, housing and durables;
2. possibilities of further accumulation;
3. level of day-to-day consumption.

Wages - in agriculture, industry or in different occupational positions (unskilled, skilled, professional) - cannot fully account for the observable range of differences in material prosperity between the villagers. In Pécsely, the highest wages are those of the collective's management: about eight to ten thousand forints in 1983, compared with three to four thousand forints monthly wage of ordinary workers.[1] But a man's place in the occupational ladder in the the collective (or industry) is a poor indication of his true assets. One finds that ordinary members of the collective may live in conditions comparable to the collective's agronomist. On the other hand, a brigade leader may live in comparatively modest conditions. Of course, wages count - but not as much as one would expect. Other variables are also significant.

The first variable that cannot be ignored is the starting point of families in terms of wealth, when collectivization was completed and landownership lost its significance.[2] In spite of the equalizing effects of removing virtually all land from private ownership, the former landowners carried distinct advantages over other villagers; they had better houses, more equipment, cellars, livestock and, significantly, the lifelong attachment to, and the expertise and habit of farming for themselves. Vineyards became a crucial asset in plot farming; the former landowning gazdas found it easier to focus their attention and expertise on that sector than the landless who had not formerly owned vineyards. Former landowners, better equipped and better housed, did not need to acquire so much in the way of equipment or housing. Second, within the collectives the former gazdas were in a better position to obtain the better paid jobs, for example, as team drivers (pp. 101-102). Indeed, the former landowning families seized their initial advantages and have remained among the most prosperous in Pécsely. Considering, for example, families who were on the kulák list in the 1950s (p. 50), one finds that, of the seventeen who are still living in Pécsely today, twelve are among the richest in the village. The remaining five are retired and their children have moved away. Of the prosperous former gazdas, TG of Nemes is one example. He was chairman of the Petöfi between 1959 and 1961. He and his wife come from formerly wealthy families. At present, they live with their son, who is a driver for a transport company, and his family. The TG family has an imposing and renovated old house, a car, a motorcycle and small machinery to work their vineyard. Their cellar on the plot is spacious and a room has been added to it so that it can serve as a weekend house - an unnecessary luxury since the plot is a few hundred yards from their house in the village. Old TG has retired from the collective and his pension is average (about 2,000 forints); his wife is also pensioned. His son earns a monthly 4,000 forints, and his wife is not employed. Clearly the wages alone do not account for their prosperity. They are, as a family, very involved in plot farming. Old TG is one of the most highly regarded gazdas; his wines are exceptional and his vineyards among the best. His plot is larger than the average, comprising about one-and-a-half holds. In order to pay for the possessions they have acquired, one may estimate that the net yearly income from the plots has to be in the range of 60,000 to 80,000 forints.

The initial advantage of former landowning gazdas is, however, not the only determining factor of wealth differentials. Many examples of former landowning families can be found who do not display similar material progress as the TG family described, and conversely, excellent material progress has been achieved by formerly landless families. There is a row of fourteen newly-built houses in Pécsely: of these, twelve belong to young families who were landless before 1945. For example, SS is a formerly landless man, a labourer, now in his seventies. In the land reform he received 3 holds (1.74 ha), mainly vineyards. Both he and his wife joined the collective in 1949 and remained members until their retirement. They had a good standard vineyard which was without a cellar and not exceptionally well equipped, yet over the years it procured them enough profits to allow them to contribute substantially to the building of a two-storey villa for their daughter and her husband. They themselves continue to live in a dilapidated thatched house, former labourer quarters.

The poor in the village are fairly easily identifiable, although it is impossible to pinpoint criteria for this. In Pécsely there are about thirty households which have a standard of living significantly below the average although they manage better than the landless labourers of the pre-War period. These households mainly comprise old-age pensioners who have no family left in the village. In most cases illness, solitude, alcoholism and a low cultural level may be identified as the main hindrances to improving their lot. Some receive social assistance from the council (five in 1978), and some are in the course of applying for places in old people's homes.

Alcoholism is an important debilitating factor in Pécsely and there are four or five young families where it is the main cause of very poor living conditions, in spite of average earnings. None of these families is, however, engaged in plot farming. The problem of alcoholism is not only limited to such families; there are others where one or other member of a family is affected. The local doctor puts the number of more serious cases at around thirty-five.

In general, the level of material prosperity in Pécsely appears to be relatively high on account of its exceptional resources for plot farming and relative proximity to several economically prosperous centres, namely Füred, Veszprém, and Lake Balaton.

The problems of housing, particularly for young people, have already been seen, but there has been an enormous improvement in the housing stock of the village; of the total 192 dwellings, 72 are either newly built (i.e. built in the last ten years) or have been thoroughly renovated. All houses have electricity but only one-quarter (55) have running water. Bathrooms and internal plumbing are lacking in the majority of houses, and central heating is found in only the newest (33). In recent house-building 'luxury' fixtures are increasingly featured with each owner aiming to outdo others by adding wrought-iron gates, chalet-style roofing, porches, and so on. As for domestic appliances, the majority of houses in Pécsely have electric stoves, refrigerators and (less often) washing machines. All families have radio - there are 245 in the village for 192 households - and the majority have television - at present 152 sets. Cars are less common, but found in a fair number; there are forty-two in the village, and five families have two cars. Motorcycles, of which there are forty-eight, are popular. As regards food consumption, no one in the village is less than adequately supplied, and there are no significant differences in this respect between the poorer villagers and the better off. By and large, the same applies to clothing. Older people wear the simpler and more austere-looking black or blue traditional frocks, but they do so out of habit, not of need. Younger people are indistinguishable from their urban counterparts in their style of clothing, and special emphasis is laid on the clothing of small children.

The level of prosperity enjoyed by the villagers in Pécsely, in particular in relation to the acquisition of durables, cars and modern housing, requires considerable outlays. It has been seen (p. 166) that the former status of villagers does determine to some extent their material circumstances today. Apart from a family's starting point - its former status - another factor of great significance was at what point in its domestic cycle a family was in the 1960s. The greatest advantage could be reaped from the dual arrangement of collective membership and plot farming in the improved political and economic climate of the 1960s and 1970s. Hence families where the household head and his wife were in their forties during the 1960s had a distinct advantage over others: they were still in the prime of their strength yet had some experience in traditional farming. With the help of their teenage children they could establish good small plots adapting to new opportunities, store up enough working years in the collective to qualify for good pensions and accumulate savings to set up their children.

Less advantaged were the villagers who were older in the 1960s, that is over fifty or sixty. They could not accumulate enough working years to qualify for an adequate pension and many no longer had the energy to exploit plot farming to the full. The children of this generation of villagers have in many cases left the village to settle in town and have found employment in industry; consequently they are the least likely to have helped their elders in plot farming. A family's ability to exploit the dual system of collective and plot farming is very much determined by the availability of manpower within the household - which brings us to the question of the division of labour and the daily schedule of Pécsely families.

In Pécsely in 1978 about 51% of active collective members worked an average of 280 ten-hour days in the year and, in addition, two to two-and-a-half hours each day of the year on the plots, an average similar to those found by surveys countrywide.[3] The plots mobilize significant after hours labour and the yearly, weekly and daily work of the villagers has been restructured to accommodate the full exploitation of the plots. The major difference between the present work schedule and the pre-collectivization one is that all active working villagers have set working hours and are not free to determine how to spend them. On the traditional farms, the gazda rose at dawn and scheduled his daily tasks as best suited him. The days were long with relentless work until sunset but at a personalized, irregular pace. Today, after working hours, the villagers hurry along to their plots and put in a further couple of hours work. Sunday was traditionally a day of rest, religious service and family gatherings. With the present work schedule, Sundays, as well as other public holidays, have acquired a special importance as working days entirely devoted to the plots. The paid yearly holidays are likewise not used for the purpose for which they were designed - that is, taking proper rest - but are taken piecemeal as the plots demand, not only for active working of the land but for the organization, purchasing of implements, and other errands which arise in connection with the plots. The working of plots is rarely an individual affair, but usually involves family units composed of various members and not necessarily only those living in the same household. Women and elderly parents play a great part in plot farming; their labour would otherwise not be usefully employed. The plots can be worked on a flexible work schedule, which can be fitted in with household chores, or the pace may be adapted to the declining strength of the elderly.

Labour division in plot farming conforms in some ways to the traditional labour division of individual precollectivization farms. There is commonly one main worker, acting essentially like the gazda; such a worker keeps a constant watch over the plot and is the main worker and decision-maker. In relation to vine-growing, in particular, there is ample scope for decision-making in relation to work phases and timing. Women however may be in full charge of a plot and vineyards; this runs counter to traditional ways, according to which women seldom worked in the cellar. In the vineyards, too, they had only specific tasks. There is no such restriction today and a woman may be acknowledged to be as good a vine-grower as her male counterpart - although the best wines are still thought to come from plots where a male gazda is in charge. The women who run plots by themselves are usually widowed or (less often) divorced. Their children are grown up and live outside the village and come in to help with the vintage and the harder chores, such as spraying pesticides, which invariably remain male jobs. Those women who do not have children who are prepared to come and help, use hired labour. There are some instances of women living in households with several family members, who are nevertheless in charge of substantial plots; in such cases one finds that there is no man in the right age group to assume the role of gazda. For example, in the TS household in Nemes, there is an aged father and a young son, but it is the divorcee mother in her fifties who is in charge of a substantial vineyard comprising four standard size allotments from the collective.

Around every individual in charge of a plot there is a 'ring' of various helpers. The degree and scope of help varies considerably, ranging from regular, daily help to once-yearly help during the vintage season. Members who help regularly are recruited from among the immediate family: wife, parents and children. A number of sons and daughters retain such a link with the parental household, even though they no longer live in Pécsely (Chapter 19). If sons and daughters live in separate households in the village itself they may have their own plot, in which case the two households will help each other on a reciprocal basis, as the need arises. It is common, however, for the elderly parents to be in almost sole charge of a plot while the rest of the family - who either live in Pécsely or away from it - come to help only with the larger tasks.

To sum up, plot farming employs the following types of labour:

1. the main person in charge (gazda) who is the principal decision-maker;
2. a first ring of helpers from the immediate family, who directly benefit from the income of the plot;
3. a second ring of helpers who may have a separate plot of their own and who do not benefit from the income of the plot on which they help out, but either receive reciprocal help or are paid for it.

The network of reciprocal help on the plot is dense and an important ground for interaction between villagers. Help is not only required in the form of labour at peak times or for specialized tasks, but also for borrowing implements, transport and so on. More distant relatives may give occasional help on the plots, but never on a regular basis; strict reciprocity is always required. Extended family groups, including, for example, married brothers and sisters do not, as a rule, work plots jointly, as the household members do. Joint working of one plot, by members of more than one household, is however common, pairing elderly parents and their married children (see p. 210), in addition to help from kinsmen, friends as well as fellow villagers, and hired labour is generally used.

Ownership right over a plot does not determine the way in which it is managed and worked. For example, in the TS family (p. 80) the mother controls and manages a plot of which she 'owns' only a quarter; the other portions of the plot come from the collective membership of her parents and son. In other cases the vineyard may derive from the collective membership of a son or daughter but may be worked principally by an old and energetic parent, or the son may work the household plot of his enfeebled parent, a collective pensioner.

The income derived from the small plots, as has been shown, is often used for building a house or purchasing a car within the close family circle. It does not seem to matter who actually does most of the work on the plot or whose collective membership makes it available. In many cases, the elderly but active parent who is in full charge of the plot concerned benefits the least from the income that is forthcoming. One very characteristic 'type' to be found in Pécsely today is the old pensioner couple or widow with no children living in the village, who carry on plot farming well into old age. There are about twenty-five such pensioners, who receive between 850 and 2,000 forints pension a month, depending on the number of years they worked before retirement. Such a pension is about half the average monthly collective income. The consumer habits of these older people remain traditional; that is, their subsistence needs are modest and their pension just about covers them. They work with remarkable vigour and tenacity nevertheless, as long as their health permits, and quite possibly even beyond. They usually sell most of the grapes or wine they produce, keeping only a minimal amount for personal consumption. As long as they work the vineyard their income from it may be quite substantial; they do not use it for themselves, but either deposit it in a savings account which will benefit their children after their death or give it to their children straight away to contribute towards their housebuilding or their more expensive urban-style consumer needs. The main feature of this type of smallfarming then, is that the income generated does not go towards the producer's own subsistence. For these older people, plot farming appears to satisfy a need other than that of their own comfort. It ensures the continuity of a life-style which the older gazdas could not quite renounce. The tenacity of their attachment is expressed by relentless self exploitation, and even those who can no longer work full-time continue as best they can, eventually resorting to some hired help, but even so journeying daily to the hills to inspect the vineyards. In Pécsely, the former landowner gazdas remain the most conspicuously vigorous small farmers, well into old age.

Retired people in Pécsely have ample opportunities to find work other than on their plots. They may work part-time in the collective or contract for daily labour on the plots. There is a great demand for such occasional daily labour and the going rates are high - about 200-300 forints per day. Even the oldest, weakest pensioners are in demand at the peak season of work, but in fact such daily labour is undertaken only by villagers who had not been independent landowner gazdas before collectivization. The former landowner gazdas do help out on plots belonging to fellow villagers of similar background, but they are reciprocated in kind, that is by return help, rather than in cash.

There is a pool of about twenty-five to thirty villagers, all over fifty, who regularly undertake paid daily labour. The terms of employment are now quite different from the pre-war era, and the bargaining positions have changed. Alongside the cash transaction involved, long-term ties of cooperation exist in all such cases and the employer has to nurture these ties with care. Many such relationships date back to the pre-collectivization period, when the same people were cseléd-s, that is, labourers of the people who employ them today. Naturally, not all former cseléd-s continue with such work; some make a point of honour not to do so. The employed are not usually in desperate need of the cash they earn in this way, for they all have pensions. It can be said, therefore, that hired labour within the village has a more complex meanig and is not limited to a simple cash transaction. In some respects it is related to other forms of reciprocal exchanges of help (visszasegités) which do not involve cash. Nevertheless, the villagers consider the reciprocal help in kind or labour as a symmetrical exchange, where the parties are on an equal social footing, while in a cash transaction for labour, the exchange is asymmetrical, the employer assuming a superior position. This is why gazdas do not engage in paid transactions among themselves.

Finally, the limitations of plot farming should be considered. The main practical limitation to the expansion of plot farming by any family is the availablility of labour power, rather than land. Family labour is, by its nature, limited, vulnerable to loss of members through death, their moving away or their refusal to do the hard, physical labour involved. It is in the nature of plot farming that such losses are irreplaceable. Hiring labour, as was shown above, is not only expensive in the long run, but is also dependent on existing long-standing ties and is not on free offer. Some families have expanded plot farming to its limits, fully exploiting family labour and land allotments, but such expanded effort remains very vulnerable. In one recent example, in a family living in Nemes, the son was drafted into the army and the aged father died; consequently the mother had to reduce her small farm, since small machinery could not compensate for the loss. This particular feature of plot farming - its vulnerability to loss of family manpower - holds the key to the entire sector's future developement. Of somewhat lesser significance, but still important as regards plot farming, are the networks of reciprocal help beyond the family, which will be examined in the following chapter.

NOTES

1. It is difficult to translate the value of these incomes into English terms. In 1980 the rate of exchange was
about 70 forints to the pound. In the 1960s the prices in
Hungary were much lower than today, as inflation has been
catching up with Hungary as well. By Hungarian standards
the quoted incomes are fairly high and have a greater purchase value than their equivalent sum in pounds in this
country.   An acceptable pension is around 1,500 to 2,000
forints per month. The cheapest car can be bought for about
90,000 forints.
2.   Connection between former status and present scale
of plot farming has been shown by Juhász, 1980:46-48. The
former wealthy and middle peasants are more likely to be
engaged in plot farming (only 5-6% in 1972) while from the
former landless as many as 17% are not engaged in plot farming.   The former landowner peasants led by a significant
margin over the former landless in producing greater value
through plot farming.
3.   Orosz-Schindele, 1977:8-9, Időmérleg a háztáji
gazda - ságokban (Work schedule in plot farming).

17

Networks of Reciprocity

In one recent publication it has been noted that: 'The traditional neighbourhood ties, based on exchange labour and mutual assistance, have disappeared. Neighbours often choose to work together in the cooperative and spend their free time together but these activities are based on free choice and are not constrained by the former type of economic necessity.' (Hollós and Maday, 1983:16) On the basis of observation in Pécsely and elsewhere (cf. Simó, 1983) this statement may have to be qualified. Networks of reciprocity remain important, not in relation to work in the collectives but to plot farming and housebuilding. As Simó shows (1983) the economic value of the reciprocal help exchanged through informal networks of kinship and friendship, is vast. Most of the houses built in rural areas (that is, 40-45% of the houses built in Hungary) are built to a large extent using informal help, which does not involve cash transactions at all but is based on reciprocity. In rural communities cash is needed to buy the houseplot and the building materials only; the building itself is largely done by friends and kinsmen. Equally, plot farming requires a fairly extensive network of reciprocal help. It is unlikely that the present level of plot farming and the solving of pressing housing problems could progress without such networks of reciprocal help. It is, however, true that this help is somewhat different from the traditional forms of cooperation existing in earlier times; before World War II the level of peasant existence was altogether much nearer to bare subsistence levels and today, the question is not: 'Will I have enough grain to see us through the year?' but: 'Will I be able to move into the new house in spring?' The questions are undoubtedly of a different order, yet they are still posed with some urgency.

In Pécsely the plot farming sector perpetuates some of the traditional peasant elements within the village today; this is the case not only as regards the actual techniques of farming, but also of forms of social interaction. Within this system the family unit is involved in a common production enterprise as well as the distribution of income. I refer here to the common form of budgeting whereby the wages or pensions of individual household members are used for the family's day-to-day expenses, while the annual profits from the plots are saved towards larger projects involving a wider family circle, for instance solving the housing problem of children or grandchildren who have already moved away from the parental household.

The women and the elderly are those most actively involved in small farming, and they conserve the more traditional community links. They remain in active interaction with fellow villagers, working alongside one another, exchanging mutual help; most importantly, they maintain constant face-to-face communication related to the plot farming in which they are engaged.

Plot farming is not an individual affair, but a family one, and reciprocal cooperation between plot farming families and households is great. Help with housebuilding can be, and often is, reciprocated by help on the plots and vice versa. It is important to note that reciprocal cooperation ties exist between families and not individuals. If, for example, the Toth son helped the Kantors in construction, this work can be reciprocated by another member of the Kantor family, not merely by the one whose house is being built. Some more organized villagers go as far as to keep a logbook of the help they have received or given so that they do not remain in debt either way. The demands of reciprocity are strong, regulated by custom, and notorious defaulters run the risk of isolation.

Acceptance of help without prospect of return to the giver is resisted. The standard phrase to decline such help is: 'nincsen rea szolgálatom,' that is, 'I have no return for it.' Establishing a relationship of reciprocal help has implications beyond the transaction itself and has other bearings on social relationships. In the course of fieldwork, I was inevitably drawn into the network, but the form it assumed was closely regulated by the relationship I had with the informant overall and, if our relationship was of a formal nature, I did not have the 'privilege' of being of assistance. When I was helping with the vintage or with transport, for example, that in itself marked a closer relationship, and inevitably I was in no position to refuse the gifts of wine, fruit and so forth offered in return.

In autumn, groups of people engaged in relationships of reciprocal help are activated; during that period all villagers are simultaneously engaged in recruiting members for their own vintage. Failure to recruit enough helpers is a drawback, for transport has to be arranged for that date and other complex arrangements, such as preparing the cellar and implements, and feeding the helpers who congregate, must be made. There is therefore great competition to secure the services of the right number of people, and care must be taken to ensure that reciprocal help can be returned. Final arrangements cannot be made far in advance, as the time for picking the grapes naturally varies.

In September and October people are busily making arrangements, allocating family labour to other families, and at the same time procuring helpers for their own vintage. Who finally turns up is always a matter of conjecture in view of the complexity of the arrangements. An added difficulty is that the collective's vintage is probably progressing simultaneously, and this of course fully occupies collective members' time. The collective solves its own problem of labour shortage by recruiting schoolchildren, university students and even army recruits to pick the grapes.

Many villagers make use of contacts outside the village to ensure the necessary numbers of helpers and, as far as they can, opt out of the intra-village network of reciprocity. Sons and daughters living in towns recruit colleagues, and friends come just for the joy of it. Nevertheless, even with such help from outside, the entire village is involved during vintage time even those who do not have vineyards.

Other occasions which require group work and reciprocal help are pig-sticking in December to January and corn picking in November, but both these are of lesser significance. These occasions involve smaller groups mainly drawn from the inner circle of family and friends. Besides these there are the day-to-day chores with which the villagers cope individually, asking help as the need arises.

The networks of reciprocal help operate within clearly defined groupings and set forms. Three types of common forms of transaction may be distinguished:

1. those taking place between kinsmen, in which case the transaction is 'symmetrical,' that is it does not imply any status difference;

2. those taking place between friends and neighbours where reciprocation is in kind or return help and again does

not imply a status difference;

3. those taking place where a cash transaction is involved and the transaction is of an employer/employee type and is asymmetrical in terms of status of the parties involved.

The vintage offered the best opportunity to examine these patterns, because it is a prime occasion on which larger groups are visibly engaged, in contrast to the more pervasive everyday interactions which are more difficult to observe.

It appears to be a common rule that the categories of helpers in numbers 2 and 3 above are recruited from one side of the village; that is, Nemes residents help in Nemes and Nagy remain in Nagy. Only kinsmen appeared to cross to the other side. This points yet again to the tenacity of the Nemes/Nagy division.

The pre-war status groups tend to interact among themselves, thus, at the vintage of one of the former larger landowners of Pécsely, one would find among the helpers the more prestigious of the village residents (such as the village doctor) alongside kinsmen and some other former gazdas. At the vintage of a former middle peasant gazda, members of families of similar standing to the hosts are found and, similarly, at a 'poor man's' vintage an entirely different set of people congregate. Paid labourers are present at all levels, in all groups. The number of helpers at a vintage is a matter of pride and status, indicating that the network of friends and relatives of the house concerned is widespread. Vintages of wealthier families are occasions of importance, and draw large crowds. The quality of the food served reflects the host's standing and the dispensing of unlimited free drinks is obligatory.

Such socially selective ties of reciprocal help indicate the existence of ongoing social relationships of which reciprocal help is only one expression, where groups are formed related by social bonds beyond the act of working together. We may compare these spontaneous groupings with the prescribed groupings of the labour brigades within the collective, where people work routinely side-by-side, but do not come together for any purpose other than work in the collective. This is, for example, very much the case with the women's working brigade of Pécsely, who always work as a group, doing similar work, arriving and leaving the village as a group. Nevertheless, in the village after work, they disperse and do not as a rule keep up informal contact after hours - unless such a relationship already exists independently of membership in the work brigade. The women in the work brigades come from both Nagy and Nemes Pécsely, from a variety of backgrounds and pre-war status groups. For their informal relationships outside work hours, villagers resume their traditional networks, which indicates the ongoing importance of age-old ties linking local families. Naturally, this does not exclude the possibility of individual friendships developing in the workplace, but the traditional groupings remain of the utmost significance in the village's social life and everyday routine.

A more elusive common interest also binds small farmers. Wine-cellar neighbours (cellars are spread over the hillside; they are not under the houses) often have a closer relationship than neighbours in the village. Cellar neighbours show a keen interest in each other's vineyards, and borrowing of implements and tools is common. They often meet during rest breaks, and in the evenings cellar neighbours may gather in a cellar to enjoy a glass of wine. These are pale reflections of the pre-war traditional custom of pinceszer - regular gatherings of men in the wine cellars for nightly discussion, drinking, singing and eating. This custom was discouraged in the troubled 1950s, when gatherings of any kind were suspect. At present the gatherings take place only rarely, which leads to an impoverishment of village life (see further, Chapter 25).

Decison-making in relation to the vineyards has an affective significance far beyond the material benefit derived from it. The greater part of communication between villagers revolves around the small farms and vineyards. As the villagers stroll down the village street and exchange greetings with fellow villagers, the topics of casual conversation are largely related to their small farm activities: how they are managing, how the current weather is affecting the grapes, and so on. Efficiency and success in a small farming plot are matters of pride; they can be seen and judged by all fellow villagers, unlike the achievements of a job outside the village. As for the success or otherwise of the individual villagers in their place of main employment, it is only possible for others to assess the material progress that results; hence the increased prestige value of items such as houses, cars and furniture (see pp. 285-287).

Those who have no plots are excluded from a wide range of community interests and interaction. In some cases it seems that older persons, who have no immediate need for the revenue from plots, and for whom continued work is an enormous physical effort, nevertheless continue to run a plot because parting with it could lessen their participation in the village's social life and would limit interaction with fellow villagers. In other words, they would be more isolated.

18

The 'Elite' of the *Széphegy*

The Pécsely basin is surrounded by a formation of gentle hills, shaped like an amphitheatre, which open towards Lake Balaton. The hillside is divided into sections, known by ancient, poetic-sounding names. The vines owned by Pécsely residents are located on the lower middle half of the belt of hills. The vineyards on the top half are owned by villagers of the surrounding villages of Vászoly, Barnag and Tothvászony, which otherwise do not have good vine-growing territories.

Not all sections of the hillside are valued and developed equally. They are classified according to their productive qualities, proximity to the village, the condition of the road and the status of the gazdas who have property there. Vineyards further away from the village are less easy to reach and are therefore less developed and less valuable; roads leading to them may be impassable at certain times of the year. The primary consideration, of course, is the quality of the soil and its orientation to the sun, and protection from frosty winds.

Formerly, the most renowned and prestigious vineyard sections lay on the Nemes side, and were carefully nurtured by the wealthier gazdas. There are still some excellent sections there but overall, the best sector at present is on the Nagy side, let's call it Széphegy (Fairhill). It covers a territory of about 20 holds (about 12 hectares), and twenty-two families, of whom only two are from outside Pécsely, own the vineyards there. In contrast with the other hillside sections, the Széphegy is covered throughout with valuable, productive vineyards, whereas the other sections are dotted about with wasted, uncultivated land. Such uncultivated wasted stretches, it appears, total as much as 300 holds (171 hectares), which is all vine that has been lost since collectivization. Half the vineyards of the Széphegy are traditional establishments; half are already cordoned ones. The area stands out as the largest fully cultivated stretch of vines.

Establishing vines is a costly and long-term commitment - to establish one hold of new vines costs in the region of 100,000 forints, and this starts to produce only after about three to four years. It repays the investment after about five to six years. Throughout the 1960s and the 1970s there have been regular re-drawings of the boundaries of small farm areas as successive consolidations have taken place. Until the mid-1970s there were no fully protected closed garden areas, and there was great uncertainty among small farmers about the fate of their vineyards. At the same time, the collective gradually drew back its cultivation to the easily accessible flatland areas while abandoning cultivation of the hillside vineyards. The villagers themselves were reluctant to renew their exhausted vineyards as well as being unable to invest capital in new establishments. The effect of all these factors added up to the loss of a staggeringly large and good vine-growing territory.

One area alone remained exempt from these conditions of uncertainty and change, instead enjoying full security; this was the Széphegy. The reason is that the vineyards of the collective president and his sons, the collective agronomist, the council president and his family, are all located in this area as well as those of some other well-positioned individuals. These people were, and still are, excellent gazdas who nurture their vineyards with great care. The other owners with vineyards in this stretch benefited from their neighbours, for they could rest assured that consolidation would not affect that particular stretch; if the collective agronomist planted a new stretch, they could confidently follow suit - and many did so. Thus the Széphegy is the jewel of the határ of Pécsely, with evenly-cultivated vineyards.

The beauty of this particular section also reveals the other, less tangible, help to which the owners had access though the collective, such as fertilizers, pesticides and transport. Ordinary members also have an equal right to these, but cannot always secure them exactly when required; in vine-growing good timing of work processes is particularly important.

To be sure, privileged official positions do not in themselves explain and fully account for the superior conditions of the Széphegy. The owners are dedicated and attentive to minutiae in the care of their vineyards; they keep constant watch over them and, as they say. 'One part of the heart and mind of the good gazda is always on his vineyard.'

To be a gazda of a Széphegy vineyard offers a certain prestige. These gazdas form a special group, and the lands there are worth up to twice the price of vineyards elsewhere. The gazdas of Széphegy are also the select group who continue the regular gatherings in the cellars for drinks and conversation.

The example of the Széphegy appears to show that plot farming was most successful where conditions remained constant and protected from changes and encroachments, and where there was a very close integration with the collectivized sector. It also points to the fact that plot farming as practised today is essentially different from individual farming before collectivization. It is not 'like before only smaller' for, by the reduction of the individual holdings, and with the concentration and restructuring of production and labour which took place, the ties with the socialized sector of production and marketing are of real significance.

Some of the 'second economy' aspects of plot farming may briefly be considered in relation to the example of the Széphegy. Here, a secondary distribution takes place through the privileged access, through their positions, of some people to goods and services, without the borders of legality being crossed. Not only do the higher management members of the Széphegy have direct or indirect means to secure goods and services for their own benefit; but also those in lesser positions - drivers, storekeepers, brigade leaders - have better access, in the form of perfectly legal help from the collective. The problem here is not that some are advantaged, but that these advantages are basic and, in the normal course of events, should be available to all producers. However, as has been seen, in the first years of collectivization such help was scarce since the collective itself was weak in both resources and organization; later, when it was gathering strength, it 'resented' the labour that members withheld from the collective but lavished on the small farms, so there was scant support for small farming. Finally, with the plots having won for themselves a respectable position and the collective having no need to fear 'competition,' and integration being the wish of both sides, the collective is restricted in its ability to help all plot farmers equally because its equipment and organization are adapted to large-scale farming.

19

The Invisible Population

In relation to rural communities in Hungary today a singular social phenomenon deserves attention which, for want of a better term, I will refer to as the 'invisible' population. Broadly, I use this term to describe categories of people who are closely involved in the economic and social life of the village but are not permanent residents:

1. sons and daughters of residents, who live outside the village but nevertheless retain important economic and social links with the village through their parental households and the small farms.
2. sons, daughters and siblings of villagers, living outside the village, who continue to farm a small plot in Pécsely, although they no longer have close family or parents living in the village.
3. newcomers, who have purchased a small plot in Pécsely and spend holidays and weekends farming - or often pretending to farm to satisfy statutory regulations.

These categories of people do not figure, as a rule, in sociological studies - hence their invisibility - although their presence is a significant feature of Hungarian villages. They deserve attention not only because of their significance in the life of the village today, but also because the way in which the village will develop in the future will depend on the role and importance that these groups will assume in the village.

The three groups coexist alongside each other but can be seen to represent successive stages of disengagement from small farming; they also show the stages of the separation between residence in the village and individual farming of its agricultural land.

Table 19.1
Parents classified by the residence
of their children over 15

Parents whose sons & daughters	Nemes	Nagy	Both
are all non-resident	25	15	40
are all resident in	21	17	38
some are resident, some not	28	19	47
Total	74	51	125

The first group, that is residents' sons and daughters
living outside the village, is at present the most significant. Table 19.1 shows the number of parents classified
according to the place of residence of their children over
fifteen.

There are altogether 161 adult sons and daughters of
parents still resident in Pécsely who are living elsewhere
with their families, and every year a few more school lea-
vers or newly-married couples join their ranks, as soon as
housing becomes available. In 1979, for example, the completion of a new residential complex in Veszprém was marked
by eight young couples from Pécsely moving there.

Although for a minority of those who leave the village,
continued relations with their parents left behind remain
only of a narrowly circumscribed personal nature, the majority continue to relate to the parental household in a more
general and active way, which justifies their consideration
as semi-integral parts of the village. First, they regularly return to Pécsely to participate in the cultivation of
the plot farms, and second, they remain direct beneficiaries
of a large portion of the plot farm products and the cash
income. Many of the plot farms are in fact run almost entirely for the material benefit of such non-resident sons and
daughters. The arrival of scores of cars and buses is a
familiar sight at weekends and holidays in Pécsely. Households and plots are filled with extra people who, after a
weekend of work and relaxation, pack up and leave, taking
fruit, vegetables, wine, sides of bacon, and cash from the
small farms. The advantages of obtaining residence in some

nearby town compared with the more expensive and problematic solution of settling in Pécsely have already been discussed (p. 160). Quite apart from the other attractions of living in town, this factor predisposes young people to move away.

Pécsely is perhaps less hard hit in this way than other more remote villages, as it is within easy reach of Füred and the town of Veszprém, as well as the circuit round Lake Balaton, since transport was much improved in the 1970s. Pécsely has no nearby train connection and, up until 1968, a single bus service ran to Füred daily. Since then, the bus service has increased to eight per day, and villagers have become increasingly able to afford to buy cars and motor-cycles, so that reaching the nearby centres represents no major problem. This ease of access does not, however, appear to have had much impact among young villagers, the majority of whom prefer to move to be nearer their jobs, to avail themselves of better housing opportunities, and to participate in the more lively urban setting. Many young people also feel the close face-to-face relationships of the village constricting, and the demands of small farming on a daily basis a burden.

The regional development planning of Hungary favours the infrastructural development of chosen regional centres, to the detriment of smaller villages reckoned to be set irreversibly on a decline due to a fall in population. The result of such a policy is not only an acceleration of the decline of small villages, but also the widening of differ-ences between rural and urban areas. As villages lose ins-titutions and functions, and are left behind in development, the educated - for example, teachers, doctors, and so on - move out to the urban centres where people of similar stand-ing and background are to be found. Those less willing or capable of leaving the village are the old, the poor, and those with large families, for whom rehousing elsewhere poses a major problem.

This pattern of decline is at work in Pécsely too, al-though somewhat mitigated, since Pécsely has been selected as a minor regional administrative centre. The council of Pécsely now represents and manages three neighbouring small villages (Dörgicse, Vászoly and Szöllős) as well as Pécsely itself. The village is therefore somewhat favoured as reg-ards development and children from the three partner vil-lages come to the main school in Pécsely as well as to the nursery school which is a recently completed modern estab-lishment, taking seventy children under five. The medical centre of Pécsely also serves the partner villages. As regards road building, schools, public buildings and other amenities Pécsely is being favoured at the expense of the other three villages, which have little prospects in terms of development in the future.

How far this development will encourage the settlement of young villagers in Pécsely rather than Füred or Veszprém remains to be seen. It is perhaps encouraging that during the past five years a wave of housebuilding was started and a new street added to Pécsely, and there is continuing competition to secure houseplots there. All these new houses (14) are modern and well built, reflecting the young owners' material prosperity.

However, those who move away are still in the majority. They leave their parents in charge of the family plot and limit their participation to suit their need and inclinations. They retain significant links with the village through their parents and, on the occasion of their regular visits, they briefly resume former contacts and help out on the small plots - which could probably not maintain the present production level without such a regular influx of additional manpower. These young people who retain an interest in small farming are also more inclined to come home for family celebrations, pig-sticking and even lesser occasions.

This situation is clearly only transitory and adjustments are bound to take place when elderly parents, or other close kin resident in the village who have hitherto been the 'anchor,' die or likewise move away. Two main alternatives are then open: to continue to farm the plot or to sell - and, as a result, cease most ties with the village. Selling often means seeking a buyer from outside the village as there is little market within the village itself. Although there is a demand for cellars - sold on their own or together with vineyards - vineyards or land alone are little in demand.

The tenet that 'the vine dies with its owners' appears to hold true in some cases, but perhaps less so than older gazdas would like to believe. Since 1961 about 22% of the vineyards that came up for sale in Pécsely have been sold to townspeople. However, quite a significant number of non-village residents of village origin remain active plot farmers, even though they have no close relatives left in Pécsely: I identified thirty plots cultivated by owners originally from Pécsely who gave up residence in the village as long as fifteen to twenty years ago, but who nevertheless still retain and work their plot.

The attraction of the vineyard is that vine has been established which has a sizeable value and which may hold significance as family patrimony. Also, there are wine cellars on most good vineyards; these can be converted into weekend houses at relatively little cost. This also means that vineyards with a cellar automatically have better chances of surviving. The best cellars are generally owned by descendants of middle or wealthy peasants; hence these would appear to have better chances of continuity of owner-ship over the generations. Of the thirty-odd non-resident plot farmers of Pécsely descent, twenty-five are descendants of former landowning families.

Apparent continuity in the formal sense masks important discontinuity of meanings, for young people who engage in farming and viticulture do so on very different terms to the previous generation. The plot farm is for them a hobby, 'active relaxation' as Hungarians like to call it, and a profit-making sideline, but not the basis of the family's subsistence. Preference for smaller vineyards is marked, since these make fewer labour demands on their cultivators, and, as a result, vineyards are trimmed to fit their role as weekend 'unwinders.' This relationship is not equivalent to the type of attachment of previous generations to farms, attachment which expressed compulsive commitment and which was constrained by traditional life-style and no alternative means of subsistence.

The second group, that is, plot farmers who no longer have close relatives resident in the village, are removed from the village's social life. Helpers on their plots are not as a rule recruited from the village, for relationships of reciprocal help come about in the course of day-to-day interaction from which non-residents are, of course, exclu-ded and to which they have no access without the mediation of a resident kinsman. The contacts of non-resident plot farmers are usually restricted to a close circle of cellar neighbours and they may recruit occasional help from among their town colleagues and friends who are prepared to do the work for the pleasure of relaxing 'actively' in the country-side.

Town dwellers from Füred, Veszprém and Budapest, who have purchased plots and cellars in the pictureque Pécsely valley, constitute the third category of small plot owners. For such owners, the relaxation element is more of a priority than profit making. To be really profitable, vine cultivation usually requires more labour, attention and expertise than such owners can put into it. To protect agricultural land from precisely such changes of function, buyers of vineyards remain under the legal obligation to keep the plot under cultivation - but this does not necess-arily have to be viticulture. Those unwilling to assume the burden of growing vines, cut out the vine stocks and sow the land with some crop or other, to comply with the rules, and do not really care if their crops do not prosper.

There are also villagers from surrounding villages who are keen buyers of vineyards in Pécsely and who, as has been seen (p. 181) have always occupied the top half of the hills surrounding the valley. They are, in effect, slowly gaining ground lower down the hillsides. However, apart from friendly contacts with cellar neighbours, these plot owners do not participate in, nor are they part of, the village's social life.

Until the late 1970s, the decline of plot farming nationwide has not been significant, and the decline that there has been was compensated for by the intensification of production through improved techniques and specialization. The total territory under plot farming has been reduced by 25% since 1967, and by 13% in the number of farms (Fazekas, 1976:79), and the ratio of plot farm production to large-scale production has decreased from 63.3% in 1970 to 55.3% by 1978 (Varga, 1980:79). However, the gross value of plot farm production has increased by nearly a third since 1967. It is forecast that plot farming will remain at approximately the present level throughout the 1980s (Varga, 1980; Juhász, 1980). The unchanged volume of plot farm production does not, however, necessarily mean that the relationship between the population of the village and plot farming remains unaltered; as it was seen in this chapter, small farming is no longer limited to village residents - but it ties the former residents to the village, and attracts an increasing number of outsiders.

20

Popular and Official Evaluation
of Plot Farming

Plot farming occupies a very ambiguous status in both popular and official evaluation. On the one hand, the fact that it is indispensable within the national economy is generally acknowledged. The population is also aware that the present abundance, variety and superior quality of agricultural products for consumption is directly attributable to the flourishing plot farms. In exports, plot farming products (rabbits, meat, fruit, wine etc.) retain a prime place. The importance of plot farming is not restricted to production but also extends to a chance to exploit production and labour resources that would otherwise remain untapped, and so as to afford additional incomes, over and above regular wages. Both the national economy and the producer stand to gain from plot farming.

Nevertheless, plot farming is widely classified as part of the second economy, and is therefore the object of vague disapproval, mentioned alongside suspect activities such as moonlighting or cheating the State in a variety of ways. Official policies reflect these suspicions: as it has been seen, the fact that plot farming is permitted at all is often presented as a favour, and plot farmers are faced day after day with uncertainty and difficulties in relation to both the production and the marketing of their produce (see Chapter 12).

The ambiguous position of plot farming appears to be related to two main characteristics: first, it is the stronghold of the private enterprise sector as opposed to the collectivized State controlled ones; and, second, through plot farming, the equalizing distribution of incomes of the socialized sector is modified. Official attitudes are therefore ambiguous, and half measures are brought in on the one hand to encourage and on the other hand to restrain its development and bring it under control.

As regards popular beliefs, anxiety about the wealth differentials which plot farming is reputed to generate encourages distorted conceptions; the 'millionaire' plot farmer who amasses huge wealth just by raising rabbits and geese, merges with the other popular caricature of the millionaire owner of the pancake stall (lángossütő). In fact, plot farming should not be equated with such false pictures, as it requires expertise, relentless physical labour and dedication. Income from the plots fluctuates from year to year, and seasonal extremes may play havoc with the year's crops. In spite of more modern techniques employed, the element of uncertainty remains strong. For the plot farmer, engagement in this activity has a different meaning from either the crude evaluations of non-farming townspeople or the ideologically dogmatic official approach.

For the villagers, relentless physical labour is one of the enduring realities of plot farming, and older age groups retain the traditional high regard for diligence and unsparing labour. For them there is a compulsion to work and pride in doing so. Those who are not able to perform physical labour, yet belong to this age-group and occupational category, are heavily criticized in a way that those singled out find hard to take because they themselves share the values in terms of which they are penalized.

Physical labour is not only considered honourable but also a vital activity to the older people who were brought up with traditional peasant values before World War II. Their attachment to the land is strong and farming provides for them a familiar framework of behaviour and day-to-day activity. Leisure and cultural pursuits, or even television, are of little interest to the majority of these older people. Despite such attachment to farming, however, they accept that the small plots they now have are well tailored to their waning strength and on one in Pécsely wishes back the pre-collectivization era of individual farming, although in other villages that desire has been reported (cf. Sozan, 1983).

The most significant trend at present, in relation to the plot farming sector, is to integrate it with collective farming often on a sub-contractual basis. Nevertheless, as far as official evaluation is concerned, the status of plots is far from clear. They are still considered to be in competition with the socialized sectors as regards commitment of labour, and are seen as a potential locus of the much dreaded 'individualism' (Hegedüs, 1977:150) in a system where centralized control over socio-economic processes is still of paramount importance (Kulcsár, 1982:124-127).

At the family level, the main question in relation to plot farming is how far manpower will remain available for its continuation. So far, technical improvements have offset the losses in manpower and plot farming has maintained high productivity. The relationship of the younger age groups to agriculture and particularly to plot farming, will be crucial in this respect. High material rewards are no guarantee against the abandonment of agriculture in Hungary and elsewhere in Europe (cf. Greenwood, 1975; Barić, 1978). It has however been shown that although most young people do not choose agriculture as their main employment and commonly give up rural residence as well, nevertheless they still maintain ties with the village through kinsmen and many, too, continue plot farming (Chapter 19). It is of crucial importance that plot farming is compatible with non-agricultural employment and, indeed, the majority of plot farmers today are not themselves collective members.[1] Non-agricultural employment is the third economic sector in which the villagers of Pécsely are involved, and this sector will be examined in the following chapter.

NOTES

1. The majority of plot farmers are not otherwise employed in agriculture (collective or State Farms) and do not belong to former peasant families. Only 28% of households engaged in plot farming can be described as agriculturalists; 26% are workers; 13% include both. 22% are pensioners, and 11% are non-agricultural and non-manual workers. (Csizmadia G. Valósag, 1978, no.2, p.79).

21

Non-Agricultural Labour

At present in Pécsely, non-agricultural employment is just as important as agriculture. Formerly, non-agricultural employment was not available to any great extent, and up to 1949 the number of villagers in non-agricultural occupations remained insignificant. Going back to the 1900s, those engaging in non-agricultural labour had to seek employment at some distance away from the village, so that continued residence there was impracticable. In the 1920s industries were created within the county and it became possible for villagers to contract for labour during the seasons when agricultural labour was not in demand and to commute back to the village weekly. Such work was somewhat more secure, as regards income, than daily labour in agriculture and could be carried on between autumn and spring, after which time there was ample labour in Pécsely itself during the peak agricultural season. Such temporary jobs were taken up only by the landless and did not result in any significant change in their lifestyle and culture: they remained 'peasant' and village-bound. The villagers themselves do not consider that such sporadic labour in industry was of any major social significance before 1949, and it is only after that time that industrial employment on a permanent basis emerges as a valid and permanent alternative to landowner and landless villagers alike.

The 'flight from the land' can be seen to have been significant in Pécsely between 1949 and 1960. Undoubtedly, the strong emphasis on industrialization, combined with the increasingly anti-peasant State policies of the 1950s, played a great part in initiating the flow. From that time onwards, abandonment of agriculture has been uninterrupted and has peaked with various alterations in rural conditions, mainly in connection with the collectivization campaign.[1]

However, in both Eastern and Western Europe after the War, there has been 'Landflucht' to some degree in practically all countries, and this relates to various factors. In Poland, for example, collectivization has been minimal but, nevertheless, today: '... the rivalry among siblings is not over who gets the farm but who leaves' (Galeski, 1975:66).

The villagers themselves identify major phases of the collectivization campaign as landmarks in the increase of the abandonment of agriculture. The first major wave came about in the early 1950s when pressure to create collectives began to be exerted, coupled with heavy taxes and delivery quotas, which meant that conditions for agriculturalists were very unfavourable. The next significant wave dates to the early 1960s when agricultural occupation became synonymous with collective membership. Industry then came to represent the security of a fixed wage, as opposed to the uncertain payments in kind from the collective and a general feeling of insecurity about the economic future of the collectives. The third wave was in 1973 on the occasion of the merger with Füred, when the collective in a sense became detached from the village.

There were also many members who returned to the collective, unable to adapt to industrial, non-agricultural employment, and movement from one sector to the other appears to have been common, although it is much less so today.

Two kinds of occupational mobility may be distinguished. First, intra-generational, that is, those who gave up agriculture and went into industry; and second, inter-generational, that is, sons and daughters of peasants who went into industry as their first job. The latter had the greatest cumulative significance, for the young had the opportunity to acquire some skill or qualification and were less inclined to opt for the collective. In 1965, only 25 collective workers were under 40 years of age, 24 were between 40 and 50; 30 were between 50 and 60, and the remainder were over 60 (Bodosi, 1965:676).

There is now a wide variety of non-agricultural employment to be found within a fairly close radius outside Pécsely, in the small town of Füred (15 km) and Veszprém (25 km) and around Lake Balaton. These places can easily be reached by private transport or the regular bus service. This represents a situational advantage for Pécsely. In rural areas and in villages which are more remote, non-agricultural workers have to commute weekly to their place of work, be quartered in workers' hostels and return to the village only at weekends (cf. Bodrogi, 1979). No such pattern exists in Pécsely; all workers employed out of the village leave bet-

ween 5 and 7 in the morning and are back by 3 to 4 in the
afternoon.

One major employer in the area is the ship factory in
Füred. About 25 men from Pécsely are employed there in a
variety of jobs as ironworkers, fitters, mechanics, and so
on. Another very popular field of employment is the building trade - where a variety of skills can be practised which
can also be put to use on after-hours private contracts at
good profit, as demand for all building skills is high.
About 40 men from Pécsely are in the building trade. Transport companies employ a number of villagers. Tourism and
service industries offer plenty of jobs, especially for
women who work in hotels, restaurants and shops as cooks,
cleaners and waitresses or in administration. There is a
large clinic for heart diseases in Füred where nurses, cleaners and night porters are required. Apart from these major
employment areas there are jobs on the railways, in the post
office, in commerce and in smaller industries; as there is
a chronic labour shortage, especially of manual labour, the
villagers have ample choice.

The increasing involvement of women in the non-
agricultural labour market is a recent development. Older
women mainly joined the collective or remained housewives
because they had no skills, and child-minding and transport
were not well-organized until the mid-1970s. As collective
members, they could return home quickly at lunch time or
soon after working hours to attend to chores in the home;
therefore, if they considered working at all, their first
choice was the collective. Since the 1970s younger women
are, almost without exception, employed in non-agricultural
jobs.

The development of Füred into an active little town and
tourist centre opened up a wide labour market which forms an
attractive alternative to the hard physical labour of the
collective. Many women welcome the opportunity to work in
Füred, which represents a certain relief from what many feel
to be a monotonous and restrictive village life. Younger
women are often skilled in administration, accountancy or
commerce, or do unskilled work as waitresses or cleaners.
The facilities offered by the local day nursery allow them
to commute daily to work outside Pécsely. Nevertheless, the
majority take advantage of the three-year paid child-care
leave, so they may remain at home for three, six or nine
years on GYES, as this maternity leave is called, depending
on the number of children they have. Most young women use
this time either to work intensively on the household plot
and/or to study for higher qualifications, which allows them

to return to a higher paid position at the end of the GYES. There are seventeen women on GYES at present in Pécsely, eight of whom are engaged in further studies, or catching up with the Hungarian equivalent of O and A levels. On GYES, they receive about 900 forints after each child; this amounts to about one-third of their average wage, which somewhat compensates for loss of income at work. The GYES is a highly popular institution and incidentally it also encourages young women to take up some employment as a matter of course, so that they become eligible for GYES after their children are born. On the other hand, it is difficult for employers to plan and allocate personnel because at any time they may find that their women employees go off on GYES for an indeterminate number of years. And employers remain obliged to keep the same position available to these women at the end of their GYES time. Women may, however, opt to go back before the end of the three-year period, if they wish to.

Pensioners and older villagers who are too frail to continue to work part-time in the collective after retirement may take up jobs - for example, in hospitals - without losing their pension rights. About eight pensioners avail themselves of this opportunity and are employed as cleaners, night porters, etc. in Füred.

In the village itself there are only a very limited number of non-agricultural jobs available and there is much competition for these: in the council, the two shops, the nursery, the school, and the post office.

The nursery offers coveted jobs for qualified pre-school teachers, as well as for untrained helpers, kitchen staff and cleaners. During my stay heavy competition was in progress for two places as untrained helpers in the nursery, one of which was finally secured by the council president's retired wife, the other by his sister - a choice not totally unrelated to official authority support. The post office is run by two women from the village and the two shops and tavern by two young couples. Three village women who hold suitable qualifications are employed in the council. In the school, only the cleaners employed are from among local people; the teachers are all from elsewhere and commute daily to Pécsley. For men there is practically no non-agricultural employment available locally.

Wages in the non-agricultural jobs outside Pécsely vary according to skills and qualifications, but they are approximately in the same range as those that can be earned in the collective and the jobs there are also graded according to skill and occupational branch. The advantage of non-

agricultural labour lies in the wider variety of jobs which
can accommodate individual abilities and inclinations beyond
the more one-sided agricultural work which does not appeal
to all villagers. Since the 1970s the element of security
of income is no longer relevant, as the collective is well
consolidated economically and organizationally, but conditions are still generally better in non-agricultural jobs as
regards the work itself, with the possibility of subsidized
meals, work indoors, and holidays in special resorts. In
the collective, most work is still done outdoors and in all
weathers, with no facilities whatsoever for the workers.

Agricultural labour in the collective, particularly
that undertaken by unskilled labourers and stock-keepers,
carries a fairly low status and it is implied that the young
men who join in such a capacity 'are not fit for anything
better.' Older members, especially those who had been landowners, are less affected by the low status rating of such
occupations, as in their case a more composite evaluation of
status is applied in terms of their ability as gazdas and
the prestige of the entire family. The young men who join
the collective now, tend to do so mainly in the capacity of
mechanics, drivers, etc. and such jobs are rated similarly
to the equivalent occupation in non-agricultural sectors.

As regards educational qualifications, there are 13
villagers at present who have had some form of higher education, 37 who completed gimnazium and 73 who have had specialized training in some skill. But the labour market in
Hungary is such that many young men engage in jobs below the
qualifications they hold, in which they may be better paid
and may have the opportunity for extra income, for example,
as waiters and petrol station attendants. Higher qualifications in Hungary do not necessarily lead to higher pay -
thus, for example, a teacher may be paid considerably less
than a stock-keeper in the collective, not to mention the
workers in the building trade for whose services there is a
very great demand.

There is some difficulty in considering the non-
agriculturalist employees as a separate category in Pécsely,
because it is commonly found that, within one family or
household, some members are agriculturalists, others are in
some non-agricultural occupation, and all are engaged in
plot farming. Since the merger with Füred, as was seen in
Chapter 9, the collective has come closer to an industrial-
type enterprise, so that differences between those employed
in either sector are minimal and differentiation runs along
the line of skilled-unskilled rather than agricultural and
non-agricultural. A broad, common agricultural base is

furthermore represented by plot farming in which non-agricultural workers are also involved.

Occupational mobility in non-agricultural employment is not fully apparent if one only considers the occupational patterns of village residents. The most common form of occupational mobility - away from agriculture - has been also followed by a change of residence. Villagers who have obtained higher education (in teaching, economics, etc.) have moved away from Pécsely. Those remaining residents in Pécsely only represent the section of the population that has achieved lesser occupational mobility.

Non-agricultural employment is increasingly important for the villagers, not only because more and more of the younger age group engage in such employment, but also because within the collectives themselves, employer-employee type relations are evolving (see pp. 125-127). Many of the earlier differences between agricultural and industrial labour, and thus between 'peasant' and 'worker,' are fading within the folds of the socialized, first economy.

It is otherwise with the plot farms, which have pulled in the opposite direction, towards the second economy, as has been seen in the preceding chapters. This has furthered a polarization between the socialized sector - collectives and all State-controlled enterprises - and the private sector which comprises plot farming.

NOTES

1. In Hungary from 1959 to 1965, 450,000 men abandoned agriculture (Donáth, 1977:179).

PART 4

The Collective
and the Community

22

Under One Roof?

The form and function of the family household has been
the slowest to be affected by the post-War changes examined
in the previous chapters. Until the early 1960s, family
life proceeded according to traditional norms with relatively little change, apart from the decline of trust placed in
the ultimate safety and value of the farm and land. To
increase the farm both to and beyond a size allowing self
sufficiency have been primordial aims; the anti-peasant
policies in the 1950s have rendered these aspirations uncertain at best. But the campaigns of collectivization did not
as yet press for the integration of all farms, and up to the
1960s the peasant mode of life went on relatively unchanged,
even enjoying modest, albeit brief revivals in 1953 and 1956
to 1958, when pressures on private farming were temporarily
eased (Chapter 4). The majority of villagers still worked
in agriculture until 1960, and the fact that one or other
member of a family went to work in industry had little
effect on a village household. Non-agricultural labour at
this time was not yet correlated with new skills and qualifications, still less to a career; its function, rather, was
to enable the family to retain the farm. Wages of family
members in industry were very frequently put into the farm
in times of greatest pressure on the peasantry, and afforded
a minimum secure income when little was left from farm produce. Another function of non-agricultural employment was
precautionary, to prepare for collectivization. Younger
household members preferred not to be found in charge of
farms when collectivization reached them. Older people were
left in charge of the farm, while the young provided the
security of a wage. As expectations in relation to collectives were low, the fewer the family members recruited as
collective members the better - it was thought. In these

years therefore the household family in the village was still traditional; successive generations often lived together and there was continuity between the generations - that is, the young were educated into the values and skills of farming life. The family remained organizer of activities, and the daily and weekly schedule of family members revolved around the land and its farming. Women's role had not as yet changed; their involvement in the labour market outside the farm and home was still a rarity and their functions as traditional gazdaasszony continued.

The major changes in the rural family's form and function date from 1960, when mass collectivization reached most villages and practically all farming families. At that time, members of the family household dispersed into different sectors of production and employment; women joined the labour market in significanct numbers, and the farming functions of the family were reduced to the household plots. Reduced, but not to insignificance, as has been shown earlier. The peasant family's life developed in directions quite unrelated to the collective. The daily schedule of the family, authority patterns and the unity of successive generations within the family followed a development of its own.

Dispersement of family labour throughout the different economic sectors may be illustrated through the example of one major kin group of Pécsely, descended from a pair of brothers, Lajos and Imre K. (Figure 22.1). The K. family of Nemespécsely were nemes in pre-1848 terms and they are already to be found in the village in 1779 when registers were started. The family have always been owners of large farms, which were either divided by succession or added to by marrying into other landowning families. They are Protestants and were, and are, of high status in the community. At the beginning of the century, Lajos had 36 and Imre had 26 holds of land and of those, 14 holds were valuable vineyards. Lajos had three daughters and one son between 1920 and 1935, and he lived until the age of 84 (1891-1975). He was categorized as a kulák in the 1950s, but was able to retain his farm until 1959, when he was compelled to join the Petöfi collective of Nemes. His wife also joined and worked the farm until her retirement in 1970. His son married a woman from Nagypécsely and went to work in a wine marketing agency in Füred in 1950. This work helped the family at the height of the kulák period (1950 to 1953) providing at least some steady income. This son, Lajor Jr, joined the Rákoczi collective in 1965, where he was first assistant store keeper and later, chief of the stores. His wife currently works

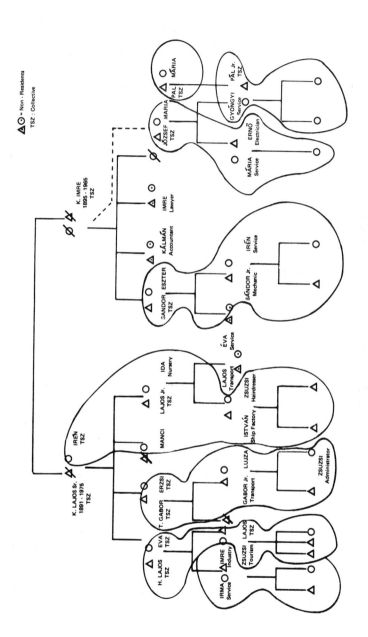

Figure 22.1   The K. family: Household composition

in the local nursery. The family retained some good quality vineyard plots from the household plot allotment of Lajos Sr and his wife, and later from Lajos Jr himself.

Lajos Jr has two children: a son and a daughter. The son works in a transport company in Füred. He married a woman there and now lives in Füred itself. The daughter, a hairdresser, married a man from Füred who works in the ship factory. They have two small children and live in Pécsely, in Lajos Jr's house, which is quite spacious (five bedrooms) and is well modernized. The young couple are waiting for the building of a cooperative flat complex in Füred to be finished so they can move away. A widowed sister of Lajos Jr completes the household, helping with household chores and the family plot. She had been married to a man from a nearby village, who died fifteen years ago. Instead of moving in with her only daughter who lives in town, she joined her brother's household.

This family household is connected to several others in the village, where very similar patterns are found: very active plot farming, retired or semi-retired parents from the collective, and sons and daughters in non-agricultural employment in towns nearby.

An older sister of Lajos Jr is married to a former middle peasant, T. Gábor. He and his wife were members of the collective and have only recently retired. They have one son and his family living in the same household, and they have a very extensive small plot. Gábor Jr has not joined the collective; he works in a transport company in Füred, and his wife is not employed. Their daughter has just taken up a job in the local council as junior administrator, while their son is still in school.

A younger sister of Lajos Jr is married to H. Lajos, former chairman of the Rákoczi collective, and present vice-chairman of the Jókai collective. They have two sons and live in a modern, newly-built villa in Nagy, with their elder son and his family. This elder son works in the collective as a mechanic; his wife works in Füred in the tourist trade. The younger son and his family live in an adjoining house, and are also waiting for a flat in Füred to be completed, where they intend to live. This son did not join the collective, but instead works in industry in Veszprém, a town nearby; his wife works in a department store in Füred.

Imre, who was the brother of Lajos Sr, and his family followed a slightly different pattern. Imre had three sons and one daughter. Even before the War he chose to have two of his sons educated and keep his youngest son on the farm. One son, Kalman, trained as an accountant and moved to

Veszprém. The other son, Imre Jr, is a lawyer in Füred.
Both sons, although not residents in Pécsely, have kept up
plots which they purchased, and work at weekends. The
youngest son, Sándor, remained on the farm and married a
girl from another local landowning family of Nemespécsely.
They were categorized kuláks in the early 1950s and were
recruited into the Petőfi collective in 1959. Sándor developed an excellent small plot, which includes vineyards as
well as livestock. They have an old but well modernized
house where they live with their son and his family. The
son, Sándor Jr, is a mechanic, employed in the ship factory
of Füred, while his wife works in a clerical job in Füred;
they have two young children. Sándor Sr's daughter married
in Füred but got divorced and has no children.

Imre also had an adopted son, Károly, who is a nephew
of his wife. Károly joined the local collective and was a
tractor driver until his retirement. His wife was, and is,
not employed. They have a very good plot farm. Their son,
an electrician in Füred, and his family, both live in the
parental home. Their daughter, married to a young man from
Nemespécsely, who is a mechanic in the collective, used to
live in her husband's parents' house, but moved into a separate house in the village in 1979. They share a plot farm
jointly with her husband's parents.

Family households before collectivization were func-
tionally differentiated in terms of the size and quality of
the farm they owned; since 1960, the occupation of different family members in different sectors of production has
become the major differentiation determinant. There are
several ways in which families can be classified on the
basis of family members' occupation, depending on the labour
opportunities available and favoured in the region and the
patterns most common in the village. In Table 22.1 the family households of Pécsely have been classified according to
whether or not they include wage-earners in different sectors, on the basis of the distinction proposed by A. Hegedüs
(1977:116) between homogeneous and heterogeneous families.
Homogeneous families include members that are all manual
workers in either the collective or industry, or are all
non-manual workers or are all retired. Heterogeneous families are composed of members employed in different sectors
with a combination of manual and non-manual workers. For
example, a husband may be a manual worker in the collective,
while his wife has a clerical job. E. Kovács classifies
families of Varsány into four types:

1. commuting industrial worker husband, collective member

Table 22.1
Occupational composition of households, 1981

		Nagy	Nemes	Both
A:	All members collective pensioners	12	16	28
B:	All wage-earners collective members	22	25	47
C:	Members both in collective & in non-agricultural jobs	30	39	69
D:	All earning members in non-agricultural employment	21	25	46
	ALL	85	105	190

Table 22.2
Occupation of household head, 1981

		Nagy	Nemes	Both
A:	Collective pensioner	12	16	28
B:	Agricultural manual worker	33	43	76
C:	Non-agricultural blue collar worker	32	34	66
D:	White collar worker	8	12	20

wife;

2. commuting industrial worker husband, unemployed wife;
3. collective member husband, seasonal-worker wife;
4. husband and wife both active members within the collective.

I have not found it useful to classify families of Pécsely in this way, because in this village the availability of jobs in all sectors is a great deal less restricted than is the case in Varsány. Occupational combinations within families do not fall into easily classifiable types but are, on the contrary, very varied; the simpler classification given in Table 22.1 proved more appropriate for this purpose. Moreover, it is important to note that significant features of the present day rural family in Hungary cannot be conveyed through classifications such as these.

Definition of the 'family household' is the first problem, as to consider the family units living under one roof as constituting a distinct family household is open to doubt in many instances.

In E. Kovács' definition: 'family household ... is a 'family' one because it contains blood relatives, lineal and collateral alike, whether they live on one plot or several plots; it is a 'household' in that members share the work required for its subsistence and growth, and the income from that growth, both monetary and in kind' (1983:57); and further: 'the extended family is now gradually breaking up but has so far only reached the point of building independent homes' (1983:57). In Pécsely, as in Varsány too, classifying families on the basis of whether people do or do not live under the same roof is inadequate; parents may share accommodation with their married son or daughter but be quite independent from the latter (although this is rare), or they may live in separate houses but have common finances and so many joint day-to-day activities that it is not useful to define them as separate households. In Pécsely, one third of all families that live under one roof are three to four generational, and there are many two-generational households where the young are grown up and employed, or where two older couples live together - the 'third generation' (grandchildren) having left for town. In such cases definition in terms of occupations of husband and wife only is incomplete. In practice therefore, in the construction of even the simple schematic Tables 22.1 and 22.2, arbitrary decisions have necessarily to be made as to what constitutes a family household and which individuals should or should not be considered separately. I chose to count those that

210

Table 22.3
Family households according to the number of
generations

1	2	3	4
79 (41%)	59 (31%)	51 (26%)	3 (1.5%)

live under the same roof as comprising one family unit, as in Table 22.3.

According to Laslett's typology (1972:31) the most common family unit in Pécsely is the 'single family household' consisting of a married couple living either by themselves or with their unmarried children; 97 (50%) are of this type in Pécsely. There are 37 (19%) 'extended family households' with upward extension - that is, with one or more elderly relatives, and 22 (11%) multiple family households, together with 35 (18.2%) solitaries. Finally, there is one household that includes unmarried siblings only.

However, many of the family households listed separately in the classifications above could be taken together, and be considered one single unit rather than two. One example might illustrate this point: JS Sr of Nagy lives with his wife and is retired from the collective. Their son, a truck driver in the collective, and his wife, who works in a clerical job, live with their two children in a villa nearby. They have a small farm intensively exploited with help received from JS Sr and his wife, who are contributing towards the construction of their son's new house. The wife's mother, widowed, lives in the same street and both helps with the household chores and looks after the children while her daughter is at work. In Table 22.3 they figure as one two-generational and two one-generational households, but in fact, their daily schedule, joint finances and common interests and projects would classify them more accurately as one family household rather than three (see Figure 22.2). In the same way, a household classified as homogeneous, including only collective members, may in fact consist of elderly parents, who though they live separately, share common finances and daily activity with their son's family, who may be in white collar jobs.

In Pécsely, as elsewhere in Hungary, the setting up of young people and providing them with independent housing is

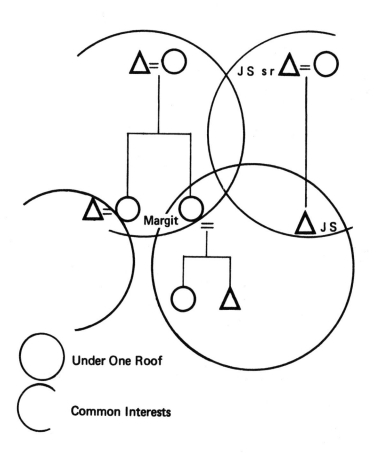

Figure 22.2   The J.S. family: Cooperation between
family households

Table 22.4
Number of children born to women living in Pécsely

Number of children	0	1	2	3	4	5	6+	Total
All women over 15	12	29	69	27	11	7	7	162
Women of child-bearing age (15-45)	6	22	44	19	2	1	-	94

1980 Népszámlálás, p. 576

a process of major importance. The 'softness' of the constitution of the family household referred to in preceding
pages arises from the fact that the ideal model towards
which rural families aspire is very strong, while the difficulties that have to be overcome in order to achieve it are
such that financial and practical cooperation within the
larger family over several years, is a necessity.

In rural Hungary the average family size decreased in
the 1950s and 1960s as a result of both low birth rate and
migration from rural areas. The rate of natural increase
has remained low ever since, in spite of government measures
in the 1970s to improve birth rates, with inducements such
as the three-year paid maternity leave GYES, advantageous
housing for larger families, improved nursery facilities,
etc. The 'ideal' family size in Pécsely today is two children, which is in fact the size of the majority of young families (Table 22.4).

Nationally, the ideal family type in rural areas is
derived from the urban model: a small family, high value on
independent accommodation and its material improvement, independence from the authority of older generations and discontinuity between the life-style and status of successive
generations (Zsigmond, 1978). This ideal draws its strength
from the social and cultural experience of the villagers beyond the village, as well as the mass media. It is adapted
to local, regional circumstances, but bears basic similarities countrywide (cf. Hann, 1980; Bell, 1979; Simó, 1983;
Zsigmond, 1978).

Well before the young contemplate marriage in Pécsely,
funds are set aside for their future home. A new house may
be built or a flat bought, although this is a luxury few can
afford. The finances of housebuilding or purchase of a flat
have already been described (pp. 159-160) as well as how
plot farming profits are used towards the cash needed and
how the houses are built using mainly the labour of family
and friends. Setting up just one son or daughter independently involves the family in a lot of work to raise the
money; if more than one child needs that support the process can continue for decades. Since the parents bear the
substantial costs of setting up the young couple, the value
and form of the potential contribution of the respective
families is a major issue in relation to a prospective
match.

Marriages no longer follow the pre-War pattern, whereby
parents had strong influence over their children's choice of
partners. These partners would have been either local or
sought within a fairly small radius of neighbouring

villages. Since 1960, many marriages have taken place with
non-local partners from a wider radius. Young people today
have a larger circle of acquaintances through school, work
and leisure, and it is often among these that partners are
chosen. Of the 69 marriages between 1960 and 1980, 41 were
with non-local parties, mainly from Veszprém and Füred, the
two towns nearest to Pécsely. Social status, religion and
material circumstances of the families to be bound by marriage were all factors of great significance in the pre-War
period; most have now, however, lessened in importance and
affect the choice of marriage partners only indirectly. Land
ownership is of course of no significance since collectivization, and past social status has only limited relevance.
Nevertheless, the overall economic circumstances of the former landowner families are better today, in general, than
those of former landless families, and this factor at least
facilitates marriages between families who are able to come
up with equivalent contributions. The children of former
middle and rich peasants also tend to have higher educational qualifications, in Pécsely as elsewhere (cf. Sárkány,
1978), and this again tends to bring the youth of similar
backgrounds together. Of the 28 marriages between 1960 and
1980 in which both parties were from Pécsely, 18 involved
families of similar economic and social status in terms of
pre-collectivization evaluation; that is, either they were
from formerly landless families or formerly landowner ones
of the same stratum. In the other ten cases, one party was
from a formerly prominent landowner family and the other
from a formerly landless one, from either Nemes or Nagy
Pécsely. The Nemes or Nagy origin and residence no longer
plays any role - in contrast to the pre-War period when
marriages between parties from the two sides of the village
were rare; between 1779 and 1960, out of 947 marriages,
only 63 (6.6%) were of this type. There have been no marriages between families of either side of the village with
the families of the manor of Kispécsely; to that extent,
pre-War divisions seem to apply unchanged.

In relation to a proposed match, the families have to
assess the size and nature of contributions each side can be
expected to make, the wages of family members, the income
from plot farming, the manpower and skills that can be mobilized in the event of building and, finally, the informal
contacts families may have in order to facilitate, for
example, obtaining a council flat. In any event, a strategy
has to be worked out concerning the future residence of the
young couple. Long drawn-out discussions precede weddings,
in Pécsely as in other villages too (cf. Zsigmond, 1978),

but it is hard to say how far these discussions actually influence a marriage, particularly as all marriages are claimed to be love matches. In Pécsely, while I was there, one contemplated marriage was cancelled, allegedly on the basis of irreconcilable differences between the families on money matters, but disagreement between the youth and his bride was also brought up.

Weddings are major affairs, prepared with great care and at considerable cost. At the time of my fieldwork, a girl from a family of former small peasants was married to a young man from a neighbouring village and the wedding was held in Pécsely. No expense was spared for the event; two hundred guests were invited, a large procession to the church with musicians playing was staged, followed by a lunch in the Culture House. The costs were reported to be around 20,000 forints, equivalent to 4-5 months' wage in the collective. However, some of this expense was recovered through the wedding gifts, which included some major items such as a washing machine from one uncle. Additionally, a very large sum of money was collected through the 'bride dance,' reported to have been in the range of 50,000 forints. It is a matter of prestige to throw in 500 to 1,000 forints to dance with the bride, and it is in that way that such a large sum would have been reached. Grandparents are also major financial contributors to their grandchildren's wedding. They may save up for years towards the event. A wedding staged in grand style is thus not only a matter of prestige for the families involved, but also serves to start off the young couple. In this particular case, villagers were of the opinion that the event was more elaborate than the status of the families involved would have warranted. To a greater or lesser extent, however, weddings usually involve a large number of guests, and young people are given valuable gifts and cash.

Young couples may have to move in with one or other set of parents for a while before their new house is ready; many of the current two or three-generational households fit into this category. An order of priorities has to be worked out if several sons and daughters are contemplating marriage in close succession. One couple may move in with one set of in-laws, while the other may move in with the other; but by this time, in most cases some planning has been made for the new constructions or advance payments laid down for a flat in town. Young people, most of whom have been working for a few years preceding marriage (in Pécsely girls marry usually between 20 and 21 years of age, and men between 21 and 24) set aside money of their own and, when they become engaged, they start buying the houseplot, kitchen fittings, doors and windows. The parents and grandparents contribute larger sums throughout this period and bank loans would be applied for. Very frequently the young couple move into the new house while it is still half ready, living in one room for example while working to complete the house over the years. If a cooperative flat is bought in town, the couple would have to live a longer time with their in-laws, as this takes a long time – and a council flat application might stretch that waiting time even longer. In any event, plot farming is a major cash source towards the solution of these problems. If the young settle in Pécsely itself, cooperation across the generations is more intensive; the plots of the parents and the young may be joined, and, tupically, one of the parents may be the 'chef d'entreprise' (p. 171). If the young couple are no longer locally resident, parents have a greater work-load farming the plots, but occasional help is nevertheless provided by the young. In either case, income from the plots mainly benefits the younger generation. Thus, while traditionally the aim was to integrate the younger generation into the existing economic and social framework, at present the ideal is to provide financial support of such magnitude that the young people are substantially better placed than their parents as regards material assets.

In spite of the financial help provided, the parents do not command authority over their grown up sons and daughters. There is little evidence in Pécsely of parents influencing the young, for example, in their occupational selection. Although parents encourage their children towards better qualified jobs, support them in acquiring training, and may be disappointed if they show little ability and remain content with unskilled labour, there is little apparent pressure in any direction. Education in Hungary is free, and higher education does not require major financial outlays – except in the case of university education when board and lodging may have to be paid for in some large town for the duration of the course.

It is more common, however, for the young people of Pécsely to acquire some vocational training in administrative or technical skills, and their occupation is generally different from that of their fathers. In such families – the majority in the village today – the old landowner gazda's type of authority is inappropriate. The peasant has always been looked down upon by the educated and urban dwellers in Hungary, but he could still derive satisfaction and pride from the independence allowed by owning his own farm. With that ownership having been removed, agricultural work became unambiguously associated with long hours of physical labour under orders. This, in part, accounts for the parents' aspirations for their children and their wish to see their children provided with material trappings which raise them to a higher position in society and out of the paraszti sor (peasant lot), a term which has acquired an almost derogatory meaning. And, in this new type of family set-up, authority is not held by any generation in particular.

From childhood the young are spared the physical work, and are destined for 'an easier life,' encouraged to study and acquire skills. It is the view of some teachers in Pécsely, as in other villages (Sárkány, 1978:308), that children are rather spoiled as regards material well being. As Jávor points out (1978), before 1945 the children's worth was judged on the basis of the worth of their parents; today, the parents' worth is assessed in terms of the material sacrifices they make for their children. Typically, parents expect nothing of their children but that they accept their help and, at the same time, they use them to advertise the family's financial success in the social competition for prestige (Jávor, 1978).

A major development since the 1960s in Hungary has been the employment of women. Countrywide, wages are set so low that most families need to have either more than one member in employment or, in rural areas an intensively worked plot. In Pécsely, of 195 families, 52 women are housewives only. The others are either actively employed, retired or are on maternity leave (see pp. 197-198). Since Pécsely is situated so that villagers can commute daily to work within a small radius, family life is much less disrupted than, for example, in villages such as Varsány. Here, the men in non-agricultural employment are absent during the week and the women have little opportunity of finding work apart from that in the collective (Zsigmond, 1978). Women in Pécsely, however, have ample opportunities to seek work in administration, services, commerce or tourism, and these opportunities are amply exploited. Nevertheless, the burden of 'three shifts' - of paid work, household chores and farming the plots - is considerable. Relief is provided only if advantage is taken of the three-year paid maternity leave, but the GYES payment is only about half to one third of usual wages, and the loss of revenue has to be recovered through even more intensive plotfarming. Grandmother's help is much needed after children are born and often taken advantage of, to the extent that daily schedules of the young family and parental households are inseparable, even if they live in separate houses.

Division of labour by sex is still traditionally defined in relation to both work in the home and the plot. In young families, however, some changes are taking place, with men assuming a more active role around the house and in relation to the children - but not to the extent women would like. Family life in general appears rather hectic and disorganized in many families; the burdens on each member of the family may be felt in the relations between them. The close cooperation and common interests, as much as they bring the family together, also generate innumerable grounds of disagreement: siblings resent apparent favouring of one particular brother or sister; relatives keep note of how much they contribute and bear resentment if the other set of parents do not match their own contribution; temporary accommodation in the home of in-laws creates tensions, and young married couples disagree on whether the wife should stay to take care of the children or take on a job. In many cases husbands do not support their wives' wish to get further qualifications. The exhausting daily routine of all family members leaves little time for relaxing in the family circle, and weekends are dedicated to work just as weekdays are. The young couple are under very great pressure in the early years of their marriage, when they begin their life together. Although divorce in rural Hungary is still rare, tense family situations are very common. This is particularly so if alcoholism is also a problem, and in some cases alcoholism may result from family tensions. The fact that close family cooperation is essential if family members are to advance in social status and that the desired conditions in life cannot be achieved independently of the family, places inordinate strain on family relationships.

Family members who, for some reason, are not thought to be doing their share of work on the plots invite recriminations - as was the case with one young wife who was pregnant at some crucial stage of seasonal work and was blamed by her husband for not helping out. The memory of this incident divides the couple and is evoked years after the event. Siblings keep note of how much parental support each received and resent apparent imbalance, or what is perceived as such. Older sons and daughters who married, say, ten years before their younger brothers or sisters would have done so when their parents could afford less. In the meantime, the ideal standard for setting up young people has been raised, and so has the families' ability to reach those standards. Older siblings bear resentment when the younger children's turn to marry comes and they are fitted out more generously. Or, even if an agreement is reached by the two sets of parents

on the amount they will contribute to the setting up of the
young couple, suspicions and bad feeling may well remain.
For example, in one case, hard bargaining went on when the
parents of a young man gave 100,000 forints towards the
building of his house, while the parents of the young woman
offered only 40,000 forints; eventually, they too contributed 100,000, but relations between the two parental households were irreparably damaged as a result.

Many villagers complain of stress, tension and exhaus-
tion and this is the case even with young women who have
little apparent cause to complain, as for example one who is
on child-care leave; she takes little part in household or
plot chores but, because everyone else in the home works
overtime, tensions run high and morale is low.

In contrast, once the young are settled - and often
they settle away from the village - the opposite problem,
loneliness, arises. A very large number of old people, wid-
ows or old couples, make up the population of the village.
While some are regularly visited by their children and fill
their daily life with plot farming, those who are ill, have
no children, or have children who live far away, live a very
lonely, empty life, only partly compensated by support and
assistance of fellow villagers and neighbours. Relationships with neighbours, although they hinge upon the proximity of houses and courtyards, are nevertheless selective,
and proximity of residence is not enough in itself for the
development of social relations of trust and mutual help.
As one peasant woman put it: 'Neighbours? The C's to the
left are new to the village; we do not know them. The N's
to the right are always drunk unconscious; with the H's at
the back all our chickens were lost; and we have quarrelled
with the O's who live opposite. So we have no neighbours -
if we need something we go to cousin T up the road.' Nevertheless, mutual help among villagers is still common, and
some of the older, poorer people are involved, for example,
in food exchanges to such an extent that they hardly need to
buy anything from the shops. They get eggs from one neigh-
bour, cabbages from another, and milk from yet another, and
they reciprocate with whatever they happen to have. In a
very large number of cases old, lonely people are regularly
looked after and are helped by unrelated fellow villagers in
lieu of family.

Kinship ties which densely criss-cross the village are
of no small significance, even today, and take precedence
over friendship and neighbourhood ties. Kin are the first
to be activated if help or advice is needed, and are called
to participate in family and festive occasions. Clusters of

kin are acknowledged to form groups of common interest and solidarity. Relations with more remote kin have acquired a new significance when informal assistance is sought in certain matters as will be shown later (pp.282-283). An uncle or cousin in some position of influence or even a modest job - but one that allows control over some scarce resource or service - may be appealed to, and help is usually received through such channels. However, relations within the wider group of kin have also, of course, been affected by developments of the last decades. In contrast to the close bonds of common interest and economic cooperation between parents and their married sons and daughters, there has been a marked change in the interactions within the wider kin group. A much reduced circle of kin is usually kept socially activated, as regards participation in family crises, regular visiting, and so on. In other words, there is greater emphasis on more limited family ties than in the past. The greater interest in the children's advancement, often outside the village, and the cessation of the peasant lifestyle which formed a common basis of interest with kinsmen, has caused a weakening of wider kin relations. Relations with cousins, aunts and uncles, apart from the more momentous occasions of births, marriages and deaths, have become more restricted. The weakening of ties within the wider kin group follows mainly from the disruption of the peasant life-style overall, the lapsing of many traditional occasions which brought kinsmen together, and also as a result of the new work schedule. Sundays as days of rest were formerly respected and the winter months eased the pace of work; these were times devoted to social and family meetings, which is the case no longer. Families had very similar concerns and daily occupations so relations with kinsmen were of greater substance. Many kinsmen are no longer resident locally and members of a family are very likely to have gone through very different experiences: some have remained in the collective; others have acquired skills and qualifications and have gone into industry or services. Social mobility of the peasantry away from agriculture has been widespread in post-War Hungary (Ferge, 1969) disrupting the occupational, cultural, locally-bound homogeneity that characterized pre-War peasant families. It is of no less significance that attitudes towards, and participation in, events such as collectivization, the anti-kulák drive and the uprising of 1956 varied considerably, often putting a distance between different branches of the family.

The lives of the families in the village are inextricably linked with the community in which they live, in spite of the many new ties which they have within a larger social environment. In the next chapter, the secular and religious institutions of Pécsely are examined.

23

Community, Society: Institutions

From the late 19th century onwards the local landowner stratum came to dominate both the Church and local government in the village; close overlap between the social elite, village officials and Church representatives developed. Until 1945, the means for the peasantry - in practice the landowner stratum - to participate in public affairs was through the local government. Although villages enjoyed a degree of autonomy, the scope of village administration was increasingly limited from the 1900s onwards. In form and function, however, local administration was an important and integral part of village life.

The nationally uniform system of local administration was laid down by law XVIII of 1871 and amended by law V of 1876. Both were replaced by law XXII of 1886, after which there were few changes until 1950. The local elective body included all tax-paying adult males, domiciled in the village for at least two years. The political community was headed by two councils: the local board and the body of representatives. The village justice presided over both councils, with the assistance of a notary. The village justice and other officials were elected for three years, the notary for life.

The body of representatives was the organ of village self-government, while the village board was the executive organ. In both Nagy and Nemes Pécsely there was a body of eight representatives elected for six years, so that half their number would come up for re-election every three years. Half the representatives were 'virilists,' that is, landowners who paid the highest taxes. One representative from each village was sent to attend the county assembly of representatives.

The office of representative was a part-time activity

performed for a token honorarium. The wealthier gazdas were
therefore more capable of carrying office than the landless
and poorer villagers who were more hard pressed to ensure
their families' livelihood. Older informants strongly
emphasize the 'spirit of public duty' which was implied in
this office, similar to that reported in the village of
Átány by Fél and Hofer (1969:334).

The duties of the village justice included keeping public order and administering justice; villagers could turn
to him with quarrels over boundary lines, thefts or succession disputes, to supervise the division of inheritance and
to summon litigants to court. He could fine or arrest
people for disorderly behaviour. He was chiefly responsible
for the budgeting of village expenditure and the collection
of taxes.

The office of village justice was sought by wealthy
gazdas. This was not only on account of the electioneering
costs but also because they had more leisure time to devote
to public affairs. They were also favoured by the villagers, who held the view that a wealthy justice would be less
likely to divert public funds to his advantage and could
adequately meet fringe expenses connected with the office.
The richer gazdas had greater prestige, could command greater authority, had more experience in dealing with higher authorities and were altogether in a much better position to
represent the village. The advantageous position of the
wealthy in controlling public offices appears to have enjoyed, in Pécsely at least, the support of the majority of
villagers, and was not solely the result of their more
advantaged position. This evaluation, of course, cannot be
more than tentative, since old people's reminiscences may
contain more than a tinge of nostalgia.

The notary's office was the most important by a wide
margin. He was elected for life by the villagers, but their
choice had to be endorsed by the county authorities, who
provided half the notary's salary. In the Pécsely valley
there was only one notary for both villages; he usually
resided in Nemespécsely. The notary was a qualified civil
servant and his job was full time. He had wide-ranging
duties, keeping the land registers, rate books and livestock
records, and authenticating documents and labour contracts.
In conjunction with the village justice he managed the community finances. In practice, he had greater influence than
the village justice, since his tenure was indefinite, while
the functions of the latter were more ceremonial with tenure
of office being limited to a period of three years only. In
Pécsely in the 1930s the notary was a local man who can-

vassed vigorously to get the post and who played a major part in merging the villages of Nagy and Nemes into one administrative unit.

The wealthy gazdas' position of prestige on the basis of their land allowed them to realize fully the ideals of self-sufficiency and independence, which were key values of pre-war peasantry in Hungary (cf. Fél and Hófer, 1969). Their privileged position was acknowledged in a variety of deferential displays in forms of address, church seating order, and so on. For the establishment of prestige, wealth was the decisive criterion, although honesty, good character and civility were also valued.

In Pécsely positions of rank and prestige were not only held by a small number of rich families; a fairly broad section of the upper and middle strata was involved. Until 1912, no Catholic could be elected as village justice and, overall, Protestants of both Nemes and Nagy predominated in official posts, with only a handful of Catholic landowners to be found among them.

The higher administrative authorities presiding over the villages were the district judge and the county council. In the late 19th century the increasingly specialized branches of national administration reached the villages through the district and county offices, and gradually the range of affairs that could be dealt with by local government was narrowed. The county (megye) was the intermediate authority between the ministries and the villages. The County Assembly was composed of elected representatives from the villages, in addition to members who qualified by wealth for virilist membership, just as at local level. The county was divided into járás (districts), headed by the district szolgabiró (judge), who exercised supervision over the village government and relayed orders from the ministries and county authorities. The district judge supervised the election of village officials by opposing the list of those nominated to run for the office. He had wide, direct authority over villages - for example, in relation to permission to assemble and questions of public order (Magyary, 1945:266-296). Lawsuits above a certain value were settled in the district courts, and the superior courts were in the county seat.

The extent to which local administration before 1945 enjoyed self-government is a complex question which has received little attention in post-War Hungarian sociological literature. It is generally assumed that the scope of local administration narrowed between 1867 and 1945, although the extent of diminishing competence is hard to assess. From the Fél and Hófer monograph (1969), the loss of responsibility appears to be negligible, but other authors, such as Horváth (1965), imply that village self-government hardly existed before 1945. Both interpretations agree, however, that the scope of local administration was related to the general subservience of the peasant class as a whole; their burdens in the form of high taxes, the control of local offices by the landed strata and the control exercised by the district judge. The limits of self-government arose from the overall disadvantaged situation of the peasantry as a class and the unfavourable position of rural areas as compared to towns.

In the light of post-War developments certain aspects of pre-1950 local administration gain significance, and changes affecting these aspects deserve attention. In particular, it was characteristic of pre-War village administration that:

1. elected representatives and officials were drawn from the local landowner elite;
2. these local officials were concerned with the interests of their fellow villagers as well as their own, for example, by resisting tax increases or schemes which were a burden to all;
3. the village leaders were farmer-producers themselves, committed to the traditional order of peasant farming;
4. leadership was provided by high ranking families of long-standing residence in the village, who generally aimed to live up to the expectations of village opinion.

In the 1950s, these characteristics of the earlier local administration were replaced by others, and were in sharp contrast to the former:

1. officials were no longer chosen on the basis of traditionally significant criteria, but on the basis of political reliability;
2. the power of the elected village representatives became formal rather than substantive;
3. officials did not represent local interests but were delegated to carry out tasks within a regional economic and political plan;
4. control through local administration extended to areas of farming which hitherto had been free of such control;
5. local administration came under the direct supervision of a large number of non-local authorities who had no direct interest in the villagers' welfare.

The new system of local administration, based on local councils and executive committees, came into force in May 1950. Three levels of territorial administration were set out. The first, at the local level, was to be constituted by councils and executive committees of villages and towns. The intermediate level, the regional administration, was formed by the council and executive committee at district level. Above this stood the county council and its executive committee, members of which were elected from among councillors of the villages and towns of the county. The new system was integrated in a formal structure of 'dual subordination' meaning that each council and committee, at all levels, would be accountable downwards in relation to its constituency and upwards to all higher tiers of the organizational hierarchy (see Hann, 1980).

For all practical purposes, however, the manner in which local administration started to function in the 1950s was determined by factors other than the formal structure. In practice, the paramount factor was subordination to State bureaucracy, the Party, and State Security organizations. The system of vertically integrated levels of administration served as one-way chains of control downwards, with little scope left for local administration to represent or protect the interest of local people or to relay suggestions upwards (see p. 263).

From 1950 onwards, all those who had hitherto been in office, and who belonged to the landowning strata, were excluded from office. The new council was elected from carefully compiled lists, prepared by Party organs at district level, including only people from the 'right' social background, that is, from the lowest landowner strata and the landless - and mainly those who were either Party members or openly supportive of the new regime. The president of the council was also elected from among nominees of the Party election committee, and since in Pécsely only one name was proposed it was an election only in name.

The council appointed in 1950 was large. In Pécsely it included 36 members, mainly landless and poor landowners. Political adherence was the next essential criterion of selection, secondary only in the sense that, in terms of the dogma of the 'sharpening of the class struggle,' no middle or wealthy landowner could be considered, even if he were to declare support for the Party. The council of Pécsely included a very high proportion of recent newcomers to the valley - 25 out of 36 council members - which meant that the old-established Protestant landowner families were excluded from public office.

In the first two years the council president, who was
in practice the central figure in the new administrative
system, was a former landless man known for his communist
convictions. However he only expressed these convictions by
scrupulously enforcing the anti-kulák directives, and by
scraping off the nemes insignia from housefronts. He proved
unable to cope with the administrative side of his office
and was replaced in 1952 by a smallholder from Nagypécsely.
This man was a Catholic, a recent newcomer to Pécsely who
married the daughter of a Protestant landowner in Nagy. He
proved a better choice than his predecessor: a man of ability and moderation. He remained in office for thirty years
and was still in office at the time of my fieldwork. During
his tenure he completed his education and became a very
skilled administrator. In this sense Pécsely may be considered fortunate, in that this office remained in the hands
of a local man and no outsider was brought in as often happened elsewhere (cf. Hann, 1980). This council president
keeps a very strong grip on his office, a fact occasionally
criticized by the local people, but his administrative ability and leadership are admired, as is the stability and continuity maintained by his remaining in office. The main
ability of this president was, in fact, to function in a way
to please outside authorities, for his hold on his office
depended - and still depends - more on these people's approval than on the wishes of the villagers.

More important than the new personnel recruited was the
change of functions, competence and degree of autonomy of
the local administration. Essentially, it became instrumen-
tal in executing the heavy-handed directives issued by the
bureaucratic State apparatus, which could exercise all-
pervasive control through the descending levels of the administrative hierarchy. The main function of the local
administration from 1950 onwards was to see that the part
assigned to the village in the regional politico-economic
plan was fulfilled - from delivery quotas to anti-kulák measures and collectivization. The council president's position was entirely dependent on his ability to apply efficiently the directives handed down to him (see p. 260-261).

These directives were numerous, and functions of local
administration extended into many areas hitherto free of
such control: prescriptions of crops that had to be grown,
the collection of delivery quotas, control over consumption
(for example, pigs could not be slaughtered with permission
from the council), marketing of goods, the implementation of
kulák policies, and pressure in favour of collectives and
their surveillance.

The council and its president were in no position to dispute the contents of the directives handed down for execution, even if these were injurious to the majority of the locals, an example being the excessively high delivery quotas of 1952 which left the majority, not only the kuláks, without enough wheat for the year.

Local administrators were responsible for the adequate fulfilment of delivery quotas assigned to the village as a whole, but how these were actually collected was left to their discretion. For example, they could assess a family's holding for father and son separately, or consider it as a single unit, thus using a higher measure of assessment. The council could also justify defaulters as destitute, incapable or ill. This allowed council members to alleviate burdens selectively or increase pressure to gratify personal grudges. To encourage quotas to be met, 'shaming boards' were set up in front of the village with the names of those who could not meet their quotas in full; this was offensive to the proud gazdas. Inclusion or exclusion was not the only point of honour involved, for defaulters were denounced in the compulsory public political meetings as 'saboteurs,' a charge which all knew from personal experience to be unfounded. To meet quotas in full was not altogether good either, for it invited arbitrary increases on quotas the next time round. And kuláks who did meet their quotas to the full were not praised on the appropriate board. Such events - some serious, others trivial - caused villagers to look upon the council with weary distrust.

In addition to the set delivery quotas and taxes, various other arbitrary exactions were made, such as the 'peace loans' or 'voluntary offerings.' Scores of collectors regularly descended upon the village and were told by the council to visit the houses where some surplus was suspected.

In 1956, both the local Party cell and the council were shaken by the impact of the national upheaval, and many Party members, including senior Party officials, tore up their membership cards. In the village itself, political action was restricted to a march, and a gathering of all villagers around the village monument chanting nationalistic slogans and songs. The son of a former landowner was asked to make a speech which subsequently led to his being roughly handled by the police, and his surveillance for five years afterwards.

After 1956 the village council and the Party re-emerged in a slightly altered form, with more narrowly defined functions which were more administrative in nature. With the cessation of the anti-kulák system and the delivery quota system their more intrusive functions were over, although, as was seen in Chapters 6 and 8, they maintained control over the collectives until the mid-1960s.

In the council the individuals whose only claim to membership was the right social background and political reliability were replaced by a more representative body, where ability and character were taken into account to a greater extent. Pécsely appears to have been fortunate in that the first group, thrown into power in the troubled 1950s, was replaced relatively quickly by a second, more moderate group with generally recognized abilities. Once in office, the second council president and his close associates were able, by upgrading their education, to fill their offices to the reasonable satisfaction of most villagers; this was not generally the case in other villages (cf. Márkus, 1968).

In 1960, the original large council was replaced by a smaller body of twelve people, and the members were more representative of all sections of the village. The village was divided into small constituencies of streets or parts of streets, and those living there elected members from their own numbers to send to the council. The list of council members for 1969, for example, includes several members from former larger landowner families and, generally, a much broader cross-section of Pécsely's residents is represented than formerly: six had been formerly landless, four had been middle peasants and two had been <u>kuláks</u>. Today, while there is moderate public interest in the election of council members, there appears to be complete lack of interest in what the elected council members do subsequently, even though it is their function to inform constituency members of topics of communal interest. The council meetings are poorly attended, except for those that are compulsory, and mainly petty affairs are brought up for discussion, which appears to indicate that the council has not recovered from the feeling of impotence engendered during the 1950s. The yearly community assembly is even less well attended - in 1979, only thirty non-council members turned up. Discrepancy between public interest in council elections themselves and subsequent council performance indicates that, although there is some satisfaction in seeing respected individuals elected, little faith is placed in their ability to influence community affairs, with the exception of the most trivial - such as maintenance of roads and wells, availability of fuel for the elderly pensioners, etc.

The council of Pécsely was merged with those of the neighbouring villages of Vászoly, Dörgicse and Szöllős, so they have a joint council and administration headed by the president from Pécsely. There is a standing staff of seven salaried administrators, two dealing with finances and taxes, four secretaries and a vice-president of the council (a woman) from Pécsely. The office of council president is at present a salaried, full-time job not, as previously, an honorary public office.

The council controls community finances and development, the maintenance of roads and communal buildings, and allocates building permits in the village. On all major issues decisions are made in conjunction with the district and county authorities, who have large regional development plans with which the development villages has to accord. At the moment the possibility of bringing Pécsely into the administrative circuit of Füred is under consideration, in which event the village would be reduced to no more than a suburb of this small but lively town.

Local administration runs a modest welfare programme for the elderly and destitute, and people in need of institutional care apply for it through the council. Registers and property deeds are kept by the local administration and minor complaints (small thefts, disorderly behaviour or infringement of property) may be lodged there. In practice, the council president and salaried staff retain all control of community affairs which the system allows, partly because it is they who liaise with the district and county officials and have acquired skills in routine administrative procedures, and partly because council members and the villagers whom they represent are not interested in communal affairs or, rather, are not interested enough to try to exert some influence. Of course, it remains questionable how much participation and influence the system would allow if the interest were there to exert it.

The scope of deliberative participation of village administration itself is significantly determined by its financial dependence on higher regional authorities. Since 1968, local councils have revenues from taxes which are non-alienable; that is, local administration may dispose of them without interference. Other sources of revenue originate from the county and the State. The county centralizes all local revenues that are alienable and redistributes them. In Veszprém county, to which Pécsely belongs, this redistribution has been found to operate on the basis of ad hoc decisions of the county council, and in effect only a very small portion of the total revenue is directed back to the villages; as much as two thirds is used for development projects in the county seat itself (Szegő and Wiener, 1978: 72-94). The county council decides on the allocation of

funds, and these are supplied only to village development
projects which fall in line with county plans. Non-
alienable funds referred to above are usually small sums,
which have to be supplemented by State grants, and acceptance of plans is essential for grants to be forthcoming.
Since 1971 district councils have been reduced to intermediate administrative organs of the county council in order to
increase the independence of local administration in villages. However, it has been found that, because the functions of district officials are not only limited to administration but also involve carrying out organizing functions
and supervising the execution of development policies, local
administration remains almost entirely subservient to their
control (Szegö and Wiener, 1978). No doubt in Pécsely in
particular, very generous development projects have been
carried out which have been to the benefit of the villagers,
because Pécsely has been earmarked from among its neighbours
for development. But it was certainly not an initiative with
which the local council can be credited.

A committee active in community affairs is the local
Party cell. In the 1950s it totalled about thirty-five members, including some communist Party members of 1919, with
the majority comprising landless members, many of whom had
been members of the Land Reform Executive Committee (KFB).
They had priority of place in the council and chairmanship
of the collectives and were generally active agents of political agitation and control. The importance of the Party
cell of Pécsely itself, however, does not appear to have
been overwhelming. Its true power lay more in its being a
representative and mouthpiece of the country-wide Party organization, and in relaying information and directives from
higher non-local authorities to the village.

Since 1956 the Party has receded to a more discreet
position, claiming priority mainly over political matters,
which in Pécsely are few and far between. Nevertheless, the
importance of the Party cell should not be underestimated
since it is very capable of mobilizing powerful influences
in conjunction with higher Party cells, if the need arises.
Party influence is mainly exercised through the fact that
most of its members are office holders in the council, collective or school – out of fifteen members only five do not
hold any particular office in Pécsely. A certain secrecy
appears to surround Party affairs and members do not usually
volunteer their membership status. Whether or not Party
members have grown into an 'elite' group and how the villagers relate to them will be discussed in Chapter 24. In
this chapter it remains to examine the village's religious

institutions, and the changes that have affected them since 1945.

The residents of the Pécsely valley were divided between membership of two Churches. The elegant silhouette of the Protestant Church dominates the landscape, standing between Nagy and Nemes, at once uniting and separating the two parts of the village. Catholics of Pécsely congregated in the church of the neighbouring village of Vászoly, journeying there over a wooded hill-path. In Pécsely, Catholics have only a belltower and a cemetery; formerly they also had a school.

The Protestant Church was the village institution of greater social significance. By 1665, already the village was Protestant and the Protestants had taken over the ancient, originally Catholic church building, dating back to the 15th century (Prokopp, 1963). The old church was smaller than the present one, graced by a stylish wooden tower and frescoes; its demolition in 1860 was opposed by archeologists who had hoped to preserve it for its stylistic value and beauty (Floris, 1860).

The Protestant Church owned about 40 holds of land and 5 holds of vineyards. These were partly worked by the villagers on a voluntary basis, and partly contracted out to share-croppers. A reasonable revenue was provided and out of this fund the clergyman's and cantor-teacher's pay was met; it also contributed to the upkeep of the local school. Church and school matters, as well as the administration of Church funds, were entrusted to a body of councillors, the 'presbyterium,' under the chairmanship of a curator. The presbyters were a leading group of the parish in both 'material and spiritual matters,' as defined by the present clergyman. Beyond that, to be chosen as presbyter was an honour, a public recognition of status, rank, and moral uprightness and, at the same time, a source of prestige in itself.

The presbyterium met regularly to discuss church affairs, check accounts, allocate funds, etc. In the presbyterial log-books, issues brought up for discussion were entered. They often seem to be of a rather trivial nature such as, for example, the number of times the bells should toll for high-ranking (i.e. nemes) deceased, and how many times for ordinary villagers. There are many notes on school matters and frequent discussion about school children's lack of attendance because they were kept at home by their parents to work in the fields. In 1849, the visiting doctor wrote about the measures which villagers should take against cholera, which was spreading in the region. Major events and calamities, such as a destructive flood in 1855,

are described in detail. The church council thus had a
fairly broad involvement in many aspects of community life.

The most ambitious undertaking by the Protestants was
the building of a new, and larger, church. This project was
carried through in haste before the authorities could prevent the demolition of the old one on account of its archaeo-
logical value. The new building was started in 1861 and was
accomplished entirely through the villagers' contributions
of materials and labour, and money. In 1864, the new seating order of the congregation was carefully compiled, with
the prestigious front seats being allocated to the wealthy,
who were then expected to secure them by way of generous
contributions. It is clear that the building was very much
of a burden, for the matter of debts, contributions, and the
building's progress became regular issues and sources of
strife for decades afterwards. Presbyters were accused of
embezzlement, some resigned, and one family even converted
to Catholicism rather than pay a heavy contribution. The
building was eventually completed after 12 years, but heavy
debts remained unpaid until 1920, when an energetic clergyman put an end to the matter by forcing each family to pay a
certain sum of money in proportion to its wealth. The church
building venture is an indication of the importance of the
church for the villagers and their confident optimism that
their small, old church would not be able to hold their
growing congregation in the future.

The Protestant church in the pre-War period faithfully
expressed and harmonized with the socio-economic hierarchy.
The landholding elite and village officials were the same
men who occupied the honorific offices in the church organization, and formal participation in church affairs was
clearly an expression of the rank and status system outside
it. Up to 1848, the presbyterium included only nemes members; hence all the men from Nagypécsely were excluded. Up
until 1828, all the presbyters were nemes. Following the
emancipation of the serfs, half the body of presbyters was
chosen from Nagypécsely, from the wealthier men of the
village, in accordance with directives issued by the central
Church authorities. Although this meant that henceforth
both villages had equal formal participation in local church
affairs, the congregation itself remained separated and did
not mingle socially. For example, the order of seating in
the Church was carefully ordered, the residents of Nemes
occupying the left side and using the entrance on that side,
while the residents of Nagy occupied the right side and used
the entrance opposite. This arrangement also meant that before and after the services the congregation of each village

would gather on opposite sides of the building, and not mingle to exchange greetings and friendly gossip.

The Catholic Church of Vászoly did not offer such a strong institution to its members from Pécsely. The relationship of the Catholics to their church was looser, with fewer communal and social interests, being more restricted to purely religious practice. The Catholics' only institution in Pécsely was their school, which was controlled and financed by the Bishop of Veszprém, until the Church sold its land in 1912 (see p. 27). The buyer of one of the larger portions of that estate, the Marton family, accepted financial responsibility for the upkeep of this school, which they did somewhat half-heartedly, this being the cause of innumerable disputes.

Religion in the village since the war is best approached by distinguishing two separate domains that have developed differently. The first may be defined as that of individual religious practice, which has withered into insignificance as far as the overwhelming majority of villagers is concerned. The second is the domain of the Church as a community institution, aspects of which have shown greater resilience throughout the post-War years.

From 1949, the State dissociated itself from all Churches. Both Catholic and Protestant parishes were affected by the loss of the lands they had hitherto controlled. Village schools were taken over by the State and religious education became optional.

The vision that inspired the Protestants of Pécsely to destroy their small ancient church building in 1860, and to replace it with a much larger building was sadly misguided. The ten elderly ladies who at present form the core of the Sunday congregation have requested that services be held in the shabby little room attached to the parish which at least can be heated in winter. The doors of the church itself are opened for services only at Christmas, Easter and other major holidays, and even then the building is too large for the modest congregation of seventy to eighty people.

Before the War, service attendance was the norm for both adults and children. In the 1950s those who associated themselves with public affairs or the Party were expected to discontinue Church attendance, and many did. Others, not so motivated who grew away from the church for other reasons, were also able to discontinue church attendance without creating a stir. In the 1950s, however, the decline of church attendance was not yet significant, and members of the prominent Protestant families attended services regularly. Baptisms, weddings and funerals were also invariably religious,

and even Party members resorted to religious funerals -
instead of asking the Party secretary to conduct the funeral, as official propaganda suggested.

Villagers maintain that the Catholics were more assid-
uous in religious practice than the Protestants after the
War, which is also reported to be the case elsewhere in Hungary (Jávor, 1978).

Informants unanimously mark 1960 as the turning point
in religious practice and relationship to the Church, both
for Protestants and Catholics, without however agreeing on
the cause of this specific timing. Church attendance fell
sharply at this point, coinciding with mass collectivization. One reason often invoked for this coincidence was
that the dual arrangement of main employment/plot farming
turned Sunday into a major working day for those in individual vineyards thus making attendance at services difficult.

The early 1960s were also the years when many sought
non-agricultural employment outside the village, the locals'
social environment thus extended beyond the village so that
'What will everyone say?' came to matter less.

In 1960 there was a crisis concerning the appointment
of the new pastor when the previous one retired after forty
years of service. The villagers showed keen interest in the
appointment and two candidates emerged as possible success-
ors. One was a young man who had already conducted services,
helping out the old pastor; the other candidate was unknown
to the majority of villagers. A very strong group of parishioners teamed up to support the latter, including the local doctor and most of the former landowner nemes families.
They went as far as organizing outings to a nearby village
where their preferred candidate was preaching, in order to
make him popular. The other parishioners, outside the
circle of these higher ranking families, stood by the young
assistant pastor, whom they described as 'a man of the
people' - although there was in fact little in either candidate to make this description relevant. Competition was
fierce, with signatures being collected and so on. This was
a somewhat futile occupation as the Church authorities could
appoint the pastor without reference to the villagers' preference. There was never any question of an 'election.'

Eventually the young assistant pastor was appointed
with the nemes faction losing the day. The village was so
divided on this particular issue that whatever the outcome,
it was bound to cause offence. As a result of this affair
all those who supported the loser stopped church attendance
and most of these have been unremitting ever since.

This appointment 'crisis' was to all appearances a last

attempt of the formerly influential families to exert control over a matter of community interest; it appears to have had symbolic rather than substantive significance.

The coincidence of collectivization and the appointment crisis enhanced the negative influences of each, which jointly strengthened the tide of secularization taking place nationally at that time through education, the mass media and so on.

From this time onwards the decline in Church attendance has been rapid. At present service attendance is practically nil, with religious education minimal, and baptisms, confirmations and religious weddings are rare. Only funerals, where the ceremony is invariably religious, draw the usual crowds; in fact, this is the only religious area which if anything has shown a revival of interest. Unprecedented concern and money is lavished on tombs which are made out of fine stone and marble. Often they are completed during the lifetime of the people for whom they are meant so that these people can bask in their fellow villagers' admiration. Traditionally, tombs were marked only by carved wooden crosses or simple headstones, and these contrast strikingly with the row upon row of recent lavish large headstones.

Decrease in religious practice does not mean that all villagers have become unbelievers, but belief or otherwise has become a private affair and is not translated into socially visible action. Older villagers feel compelled to offer unsolicited justification for their absence from services: 'I am too old/ill/tired ...Eight o'clock is too early (!) ...I have to work ...but I listen to the service on the radio.' Younger people, not having had much religious education, are mostly complete unbelievers and do not feel bound to justify their absence at all.

On important religious occasions, when a more numerous congregation than normal is assembled, the pre-War traditional seating order is retained; Nemes and Nagy residents occupy different sides, and the formerly higher-ranking families occupy the first pews. Disregard of this pre-War seating order is talked about.

On the Catholic side, similar developments have taken place: the Mass held in the school building every fortnight draws just as low attendance as the Protestant service. Coincidentally, the Catholics also had a crisis in 1960, when an old and much esteemed priest was replaced by a younger man. Many Catholics also discontinued attendance at Mass at this time, although in this case there were no rival contenders.

So far we have looked mainly at one religious domain:

that of individual religious practice. There is, however, another domain which has to be considered separately: that of the Church as a community institution.

Even after 1949, the Protestant parish in Pécsely owned 10 holds of land and a 1-hold vineyard, in addition to various buildings: the Church, the parish hall and the wine cellar. These properties continued to be managed by a presbyterium of twelve and a curator. The revenue obtained from the land and vineyard, as well as church dues collected from those willing to pay, is today managed by this church council. In practice, all Protestants continue to pay the small annual dues to the Church, regardless of whether or not they attend church services. The larger revenues from the vineyard and the land (which are rented out) are set aside to cover repairs and the upkeep of the church building, while the pastor's pay is met by the Protestant Bishopric of Veszprém County.

The cultivation of the vineyard is no small matter and, since 1945, it has been cultivated by the voluntary labour of the villagers. The pastor himself is not a keen plot farmer and does not take part in its cultivation. It is left to the villagers, who have so far worked it impeccably under the coordination of the curator, who calls on people in turn to accomplish a particular work-phase. At vintage time a very large number of villagers turn up, people who are never seen in church. In 1978 the roof of the church cellar burned down and was promptly repaired by the parishioners.

The Church building is looked after by a group of women who in 1978 initiated a collection in order to have a new altar cover made in fine velvet embroidered in gold. They collected a very large sum (about the equivalent of £400 - which in Hungary has considerable purchasing power). All Protestant villagers contributed to this venture and the festive inauguration of the new altar cover drew the largest crowd seen in the church for decades; even the local Catholics came to view it.

The constitution of the presbyterium remains reminiscent of its pre-War order and principles of recruitment; its members are the most respected former gazdas. The present collective's vice-chairman, who was chairman of the Rákoczi before the merger of 1973, has also been a member of the presbyterium since 1961. Among the members is the only smallholder from Nagy who had been a communist all his life, even before 1945. He never went to church as an adult but has nevertheless been a member of the presbyterium for thirty years. His membership has of course invited queries from both the Party and the Church, but he has taken a stand, explaining that he considered the church to be a village institution and the community patrimony to be separate from individual belief and practice - a division which appears to be a valid distinction.

Although the church councillors continue to be recruited from among the more respected parishioners, there are significant differences. More important than status, continued attachment to, and involvement in, village life are essential prerequisites; all presbyterium members were or are members of the collective and their families remain closely associated with the village not only in terms of residence, but also plot farming, kinship ties and daily interaction with fellow villagers. It is these factors rather than former or present status which predispose them to be active in relation to the church. Most members are now over fifty, and their replacement appears problematic. Recently a highly respected young villager was approached to become a presbyter, like his father and grandfather but he declined. He holds high office in the collective and he felt that presbytership was incompatible with his career. He was probably right, since he is reckoned to be the successor to the present council president.

In terms of our description therefore it would appear that the Church as a community institution, symbolic of the village as an ancient, proud community, has shown more resilience and has remained of more importance to the villagers than individual religious practice.

Among the Catholics somewhat similar trends are apparent, although they have neither local Catholic Church property to look after nor presbyterium. All their efforts and care are therefore lavished on the local Catholic cemetery, which compares favourably with the rather neglected Protestant one. The Protestants have other church property to look after which exhausts their interests.

The enforced withdrawal of the Church from secular community life and the narrowing of the scope of its activities compared to the pre-War period has certainly accelerated secularization, though it would be futile to argue about which process has determined the other. The Church as a symbol of communal patrimony, however, has withstood the tide of secularization better than individual religious belief and practice.

24

Community, Society:
Competing Paradigms

In Hungarian villages, patterns of social differentiation can no longer be defined using a single point of reference - that of the distribution of land - as this was possible in relation to the pre-War period (cf. Fél and Hofer,
1969; Sárkány, 1978; Bell, 1979). By the 1980s the dismantling of the stratification system based on the ownership
of land appears to be complete. It has been, if not a
gentle, certainly a gradual process, stretched over several
decades. Reforms were introduced through successive stages
as has been shown in the previous chapters which traced
their path in Pécsely from the 1945 Land Reform to the <u>Jókai</u>
collective today. Post facto knowledge of what these reforms have actually amounted to is the privilege of the latter day observer; outcomes that are certainty today were a
mere probability while in the making. As the government
programmes unfolded, the villagers upon whom they were inf-
licted made adjustments that, at each particular juncture,
appeared to be the most appropriate to exploit some newly
available advantage or to defend themselves against disadvantages. More than once throughout the post-War period,
rural families were forced to rethink their own and others'
positions and the prospects open to them. The 'maze effect'
applied (Barić, 1978) that is, it was impossible to foresee
where any chosen path might lead, since the rules and circumstances were prone to change without warning. The villagers' responses to successive government policy changes
helped to form the present-day patterns of social differentiation, endowing the temporal dimension of post-War developments with special significance. Here I am thinking of the
sequence of government programmes and reforms and their com-
pression within a relatively short period of time. However,
the various material and non-material dimensions of life

change at an unequal pace – a peasant can become a collective member overnight, but it may take years, even decades, for him to shed the life-style, habits and values of the independent farmer. As was seen in the earlier chapters, development of the different production sectors reflect these inconsistencies in their differing principles of operation, the groups they mobilize and the attitudes to labour and income they foster. Plot farming mobilizes small informal kinship and friendship groups, has precarious status within the formal table of socialist institutions, is a sector where optimal effort and labour pay direct dividends and, finally, remains a repository of traditional values, techniques and networks of mutual help. The collective sector, the socialist answer to the problem that the peasantry as a class represents in the ideology, has failed to realize the promise of grass-roots democratic control by members and of collective ownership; on the other hand it has successfully made the transition towards large-scale modern agricultural enterprise forms. Lastly, sectors of non-agricultural employment have opened up the village to the larger social environment and have introduced aspirations of urban models of living.

Technically, these sectors are integrated at the family level through engagement of family manpower in the various sectors. However at the level of community life, the heterogeneity of these different sectors, the often opposing values they represent and attitudes they encourage, come into view. In the village today, different systems of values and frames of reference coexist simultaneously which, for want of a better word and to avoid long-worded terminology will henceforth be referred to as 'paradigms.' This will be with reference to:

1. socially accepted values and aspirations formulated in terms of these values;
2. the ways in which others and self are categorized, and ways of relating to kinsmen, family, fellow workers and villagers;
3. attitudes to labour, ownership, possessions and towards the formal political and economic institutions.

In brief, the traditional paradigm includes all attitudes and forms of interaction carried over from the pre-War period. The socialist paradigm consists of the political concepts, ideology and ideals with reference to which the formal politico-economic organizations have been reformed since 1948. Lastly, the urban paradigm is reflected in the striving towards urban models of living, with emphasis on material accumulation and urban consumption patterns which owe something to influences from Western Europe. Some families lean with greater emphasis towards one or other of these paradigms, depending on their age group, levels of education, engagement in plot farming or perhaps because one or other family member holds office in one of the formal political or economic organizations.

But no family or individual conducts his or her life in terms of only one paradigm to the exclusion of the others. Competing paradigms are not exclusive to present-day Hungarian rural society, or even to socialist societies in general, but the specific features of life in the community and social differentiation in the village today follow from the nature of the competing paradigms to a very large extent, the examination of which is the theme of the chapters that follow.

25

The Traditional Paradigm

The land reform of 1945 has, as it was shown in Chapter 2, decapitated the landowning hierarchy by dispersing the large estates, but did little to change the social fabric of the rural communities. From the beneficiaries' point of view, the significance of the land reform was that it settled the 'thousand year long dispute' of the Hungarian peasant for the land and gave an impetus to post-War recovery. Nevertheless, the majority of land recipients remained deprived; with very few exceptions, neither their material conditions nor their position within the community was greatly affected by the changes. In these immediate post-War years the peasantry as a whole was strengthened and the categories of the peasant system were unchanged in meaning, content and prospects.

More significant were the changes gathering momentum from 1948 onwards when political power in the government was definitively secured by the Communist Party. From then onwards there was intense pressure on the peasantry which impinged on the traditional old order and community life. Land ownership became a liability and the peasant was often in a position where it became advantageous to extricate himself from the penalties and burdens attached to the ownership of peasant farms. Conflicts within the peasantry were artificially augmented and 'sharpened' - to use the much used political jargon of the time. This assumed a two-pronged approach: on the one hand the foremost landowning strata were put in an impossible position both materially and psychologically; on the other hand the former landless were given public offices and were recruited as executive agent of the multiple directives and control to which villages were subjected. Neither policy in practice had quite the effects intended on the life of the community.

Those who had been kuláks tried to comply with the demands made upon them as best they could. Most experienced psychological strain as a result of the shame officially attached to that status. Yet, they were not as badly damaged, materially or psychologically, as one might have expected on the basis of the severity of the measures directed against them (see Orbán, 1972). The kuláks did not, as had been intended, fall to the lowest position in the social hierarchy, which suggests that a man's place in the traditional farming community is determined by more complex factors than merely those of prestige and advantages accruing from the ownership of large farms. Many kuláks enjoyed a great deal of support among fellow villagers in Pécsely, and this was the case in other villages as well (Pápai, 1984; Orbán, 1972). The richer gazdas appear to have had a pool of assets - both material and non-material - which was not caught up in the net of laws set against them. On the material side, the quality of their houses, land, equipment and livestock remained advantageous even though they had been reduced considerably. On the non-material side, their experience, skills, wide social and kinship networks and patron-client relationships came to their stead.

The kulák persecutions were, however, of paramount significance for the farming community generally. The model of the independent gazda was central to the value system and normative order of the Hungarian peasantry; it was the ideal model towards which all aspired - not the worker or the intelligentsia. The kulák laws struck hard at this model, unlike the land reform of 1945, which affected mainly the landlords who had not been part of the villages' social life and who blocked the villagers aspirations to acquire more land. The majority of the villagers do not appear to have adopted the official condemnation of kuláks, particularly because of the 70,000 people put on kulák lists, more than half are estimated to have been middle peasants rather than rich peasants (Orbán, 1972:78). Many of these gazdas were respected members of the rural community, who embodied ideals of success, diligence, self-sufficiency and a lifestyle that most villagers, including the landless, hoped to attain. The kulák laws not only put the rich/middle peasant gazdas under sentence but also the ideal model towards which the villagers aspired. Although the policies at the beginning of the 1950s were claimed to differentiate between the 'democratic middle peasant' and the 'reactionary rich peasant' (Rákosi, 1947 speech/1950:211), in fact 'hard measures' affecting all peasants were in the pipeline even then.

In these early years of reform, the internal divisions

of the peasantry were assumed to be far more important than in fact they were. For example, landowner gazdas and the recipients of the land reform of 1945 were officially viewed as irreconcilably antagonistic to one another. In fact, the landowning gazdas did not oppose the land reform in any organized way; thereafter it was found that more than two-thirds of the land recipients were satisfied with the help given to them with equipment and draught animals by the gazdas and that only one third reported lack of, or not enough help (Orbán, 1972:58). This would indicate that the traditional patron/client relationship and solidarity were far stronger than officially admitted. As one Party report notes in 1949, the possibilities afforded by the kulák laws were not taken advantage of in the majority of villages 'to sharpen the class struggle' (Orbán, 1972:80). Rather, in reaction to the extreme measures and often unlawful excesses against landowning peasants, in Orbán's words: 'peasant solidarity of a negative kind was generated' (1972:97) - negative, that is, inasmuch as it went against the aims of official policies of the time. In actual fact throughout the 1950s pressures on the peasantry were not differentiating but generalized: taxes, requisitions, confiscations, fines and pressure to join collectives affected the entire rural population, which had the effect of uniting all rural strata to some degree. Paradoxically, government measures themselves worked unintentionally towards fostering better relations between, for example, the richer peasants and the labourers they employed. The richer gazdas were bound to pay higher rates to their labourers, to observe set hours of work, ensure rest days, etc, while State Farms were not so bound. So, in comparison, the individual gazdas appeared to be the less exploitative employers. Hence, when the Agricultural Labourers' Interest Protection Association was formed (DEFOSZ), membership was sought only by State Farm labourers (Orbán, 1972:110).

Agrarian policies of the 1950s also generated new divisions within the peasantry. For example, both collective members and private farmers suspected that the other was receiving benefits from the State at their expense. The exceedingly weak collectives of the 1950s relied heavily on State subsidies and loans, not only for the purposes of production but for a minimum pay for members, so peasants farming individually thought that collective members lived on State money. Individually farming peasants also resented the collectives' land consolidations which often affected their best fields. On the other hand when, between June 1953 and 1954, high level government changed briefly and concessions were given to individually farming peasants, these were perceived to be a betrayal of collective members. And this type of policy change was repeated again in 1957 to 1958, generating much the same response. Dissent was also generated between collective members themselves, some of whom, at various stages (mainly between 1953-54 and 1956-57) opted out of the collectives, while others remained behind. It was in the interest of those who remained to keep the collectives' property undiminished, and they were therefore reluctant to let the leaving members take with them the animals, land and implements that they had brought in. Members leaving sought, on the contrary, to recover from the collective they were leaving at least enough to re-start individual farming. Disagreement too was common, over how much of the collectives' debts should be shouldered by leaving members. Throughout the 1950s and well into the 1960s, collectives were in permanent debt to the State and this debt reached vast proportions; for example, countrywide in 1953 the fines for non-completion of delivery quotas alone amounted to over 10 million forints. Members leaving the collectives were charged with a proportion of such debts, which was a considerable burden to assume. Tensions between old and new members were common; members forced into the collectives were reluctant workers and they were not made welcome by long-standing members. Members recruited in 1952-53 were forced to bring all livestock and implements they owned into the collective and, if they refused, an equivalent value was deducted from their share of income, creating yet more tension. The vast movements of peasant property changing hands in these years, into and out of collectives, back and forth from the State, created a situation whereby each individual felt himself to have lost out in favour of someone else.

Following mass collectivization in 1959 these divisions between collective members acquired an even greater significance. The former gazdas had the know-how and higher standing that qualified them for the better positions, but this invited adverse reactions from former landless members: 'Are we to be ordered about by the gazdas again?' On the other hand, the gazdas were reluctant to take orders from those who 'had not even been able to obtain a proper farm.' In Pécsely, as has been seen (Chapter 6) traditional community social divisions were carried over and operated within collectives for a very long time.

The former landless, who constituted the majority of collective members until 1959, throughout the 1950s were not successful in improving their situation; even though the

State supported the collectives to some degree, members'
incomes averaged only 67.5% of that of private farmers (A
Magyar Népi Demokrácia Története, 1978:195). Only from the
1960s onwards has this stratum of the rural population been
able to improve its position considerably, through the combination of plot farming, collective membership and industrial work divided up within the family. Nevertheless,
throughout these years a certain confidence germinated in
members of this stratum: through their involvement in the
collectives' management, from the fact that they were primarily eligible for offices, and that their social background
was no longer a liability. How each family could and did
take advantage of the new possibilities is much more difficult to determine; within one village, for instance, there
is a wide range of individual destinies, each of which
proves either too much or too little. The rise of social
status through political office applied to only a small minority and this will be examined in the next chapter. The
majority of landless did eventually improve their lot
through their children attaining better positions but many
were unable to seize upon the new opportunities available.
It needs to be said again, however, that deprivation in
rural Hungary today is not what it was in the pre-1945 period and, indeed, throughout the 1950s. It is a deprivation
measured against much higher standard of living expectations
compared with the former near-starvation levels. Deprivation of that severity is virtually unknown in Hungary today;
in the relatively few cases where it is actually encountered, such deprivation is associated with personality,
health or other disorders. In Pécsely there are many examples covering the entire spectrum of success or failure in
the improvement of former landless families' standards of
living. However, the anti-peasant policies of the 1950s coincided with the former landless being brought to the fore-
front of community life, with fairly negative consequences.
Suspicions, bitterness, and a defensive turning away from
community matters and towards the closer family circle were
typical reactions according to villagers' reminiscences of
this decade. Over the years such attitudes hardened into a
tendency to look outward beyond the local community to a
less personal urban environment, and a recoiling from
community life, careful movements, and small circles of
friends.

Completion of collectivization in 1959 was a major
landmark in the life of the community. The peasantry as a
distinct social category came to an end at that time and the
villagers had to start thinking in entirely new categories.

Middle peasant, landless and so on, lost all material basis.
So too did the concept of gazda, which had hitherto defined
a man's place not only in relation to the community, but
also to his family, with implications of authority, responsibility and independence. Since collectivization has been
completed, ownership or control of farms has only indirect
bearings on social differentiation. C. Hann shows (1980)
that in the szakszövetkezet collective, based on vertical
type cooperative integration (that is, continued individual
farming, cooperation limited to marketing, services and
supplies and a small collective sector), full time farming
households continued to be the most prosperous, in a way reminiscent of pre-collectivization patterns. In Pécsely too,
similar trends are found, that is, marked and continued
advantages for former landowners. This is in spite of the
fact that, in Pécsely, the collective is of the horizontally
integrated artyel type (see p. 54) and that in practice most
land is farmed collectively. This would suggest that private control over the means of production needs to be understood in a very narrow sense in Hungary today; on the other
hand, the lack of such control, associated with the artyel-
type collectives, is also less complete than one might sup-
pose. Even in the szakszövetkezet community of the Tázlár
type (Hann, 1980) the farms operate within very narrow limits: their expansion is controlled, hired labour is scarce,
and the threat of enforced incorporation of individual farms
into an artyel type collective is ever present. In contrast,
in villages with full collectives, as in Pécsely for instance, plot farming possibilities have increased to the extent that a 'maximizer'-type farmer (Hann, 1980:97-98) can,
by judicious choice of production and accumulation of plot
allotments, build up a plot of considerable size and output.
And, just as in the szakszövetkezet communities, in the
artyel-type collective villages too, those most likely to
undertake and succeed with such intensive farming, are the
former gazdas rather than the former landless. Thus the
patterns of social differentiation in both szakszövetkezet
communities and fully collectivized ones are very similar.
In both cases however, the formal ownership structure existing since 1959 has removed the material, structural basis of
peasant social categorizations and relegated them to a shadowy existence within the minds of villagers. Much of the
malcontent and difficulties of adjustment to collective
membership stemmed from the persistence of these traditional
categorizations in the villagers' thinking and nostalgia for
the now idealized memory of peasant life. Only since the
1970s has modernization of agro-techniques and internal

organization of labour in the collectives reached a point where comparisons with peasant farming became irrelevant. Nevertheless, relegated out of the new, formal economic structure, these traditional attitudes still live on, exerting influence in indirect ways.

In the micro-events of day-to-day existence, informal contacts between families and patterns of interaction tend to proceed along the well-worn traditional grooves. The former landowner families, densely connected through kinship ties, prefer to retain contacts among themselves. Greetings containing subtle meanings of familiarity and respect are exchanged and this is regardless of the fact that the former gazdas are now mostly workers in the collective. Some kinship and neighbourhood ties are kept in socially working order, while others are ignored or only intermittently activated. The former leading gazdas and their families habitually exclude people within the former landless category, with the smooth consistency of the 'habitus' (Bourdieu, 1977) and even among the younger generations friendly groups prefer to include members with established long-standing ties.

Coexistence of parallel systems of reference are well illustrated by the nature of affinal ties. Considerations of former status of families linked by marriage are of diminishing, limited relevance (pp. 213-214). But as regards marriages that took place twenty or thirty years ago which involved parties of unequal status, paradoxically, social disapproval continues to function. Note is kept in Pécsely of matches that went counter to the accepted pattern of marrying within a given stratum. Affines of a considerably lower former social status are less often invited, for example, to help out with plot farming or vintage. On family occasions the parties from disadvantaged backgrounds, if they happen to be present, assume roles congruent with their former social status. One example might illustrate both this point and some aspects of traditional patterns of interaction among kinsmen.

The occasion concerned was a pig sticking in the house of one of the former prestigious gazdas on the Nemes side of the village. On such occasions participants necessarily include close kin and affines, who are allocated tasks in the day-long proceedings of slaughtering the pig(s) and processing the meat. Finely shaded considerations of each participant's place within the household, or in relation to it, determine the part each person is given to play throughout the day, and the occasion assumes a highly complex ritual precision. There are two central male roles. One is the

specialist (bőller) who slaughters the pig(s) and is the
chief decision maker regarding all procedural matters, such
as seasoning, carving the meat, and so on. This role in the
present example was assumed by an old uncle, a former prestigious gazda. The other important male role is that of the
head of the household who remains in charge of the 'social
management,' acting as host, seeing that no one is given
offence and that all are liberally and continuously supplied
with drinks. His wife is the central figure among the women.
Tasks are allocated according to age, sex and status of the
participants. Central tasks which place inside the house,
involving procedural decisions, tasting, seasoning, etc. are
the privilege of only a few people - the bőller, the household head and his wife, and their parents. Other people
present for the occasion are allocated the more routine,
unskilled, peripheral and outdoor jobs in order of their
decreasing importance. Teamwork is coordinated with precision, requiring little explicit verbal interference; all
know what, how and when to do - and which tasks are appropriate to assume and which not. Considering the cramped
conditions, the variety of jobs done simultaneously and the
speed required - it all has to be done within one day - the
high level of coordination bears witness to the well-worn
technical and social traditional grooves. The mistress of
the house on the occasion in question had married into this
respectable, rich family from a small peasant family on the
Nagy side. Her mother, according to observations made on
other such occasions, should have assumed a privileged position within the inner ring of activities on that day. However, she conspicuously assumed the lesser, menial tasks
outdoors, hardly ever going into the house. Other participants made a point of noting that she did not 'belong.' This
marriage has been one of the more unequal in the village in
terms of status of the parties; although it dates back 25
years, in a family event such as this, old and possibly
erstwhile judgements were replayed once more.

Similar considerations coloured many relationships
within the village: small day-to-day affairs, in participation in family or friendly gatherings, and terms of address
used. There are many occasions for groups of kinsmen and
neighbours in the village to come together (see Chapter 17)
and to a very large extent these are conducted with reference to pre-War usages and social networks. In comparison
with the past however, essential differences of the present
tend to reduce the meaning of these traditional social
interactions. They are not in harmony with, or grounded in,
the formal economic and social structure of the present,

hence they apply only to specific contexts. The traditional values and organizing principles of social relations are today only one among competing alternative frames of reference. In the past, for the majority, the traditional paradigm was the only one available. Throughout all villages in Hungary this order was replicated; if a man moved from one village to another he would find the same order as in his village - and fit precisely into his place. Movement out of the traditional peasant paradigm was only possible by emigration or leaving permanently for town and working in industry. However, even in villages such as Varsány (Jávor, 1978), where land scarcity forced men to look for jobs in industry even before 1945, they did so as commuters, remaining socially attached to their native village and unintegrated in the urban, industrial working environment.

This is no longer the case. People can move with much greater ease into a different social environment and are much more exposed and receptive to alternative frames of reference and values. Taking up employment outside the village inevitably weakens the hold and relevance of the traditional values of the rural community of origin - and this community itself is no longer a strong viable peasant community. Others increase the distance between themselves and the village's little world by education. Sons and daughters settled away from Pécsely, in white-collar occupations or even in managerial status, also serve to weaken the relevance of the traditional paradigm for the parents left behind. Yet others may stay in the village but seek advancement through the council or the Party, having acquired some administrative skills; as has been shown, these offices are today quite different from their pre-War equivalents and the traditional paradigm is of no relevance in relation to them. Which of these avenues a family exploits depends on where their assets or weaknesses lie, but all families in the village today have other frames of reference beside those of the traditional paradigm.

Villages in Hungary today have an ageing population, as a very large proportion of the young have continued to leave the village for the towns over the last two decades. Older parents remaining behind still have access to a significant resource denied to town dwellers: plot farming. This subsidiary economic base has contributed to the preservation of the traditional paradigm, albeit in a shadowy, free-floating form. The existence of the traditional paradigm is, therefore, both elusive and very real; it has tenuous legitimacy vis-à-vis the formal socialist economic and social institutions, yet it both impinges on and flows into them through

countless channels. The economic base of the traditional
paradigm is the plot farming sector, which brings together
people who are, during formal work hours, related to and
living in quite different social environments; the agronomist, the Party secretary, the worker in the ship factory
and the hotel cook may be found pruning their vines side by
side in the after work hours stint on the plots. And in
relation to the plots and principles of social interaction,
daily routines and rhythm of work are ordered in terms of
the traditional paradigm. The good plot farmer is admired
for his efforts, dawn-to-dusk physical labour is respected
and networks of mutual help are of a traditional type.

Residing in the village in itself constitutes a ground
of uniformity and there appears to be relatively little
variation in the life-style and everyday existence of families, even though various members of a family may have very
different occupations in the collective, in industry or even
as higher cadres of village and collective administration.
Although income varies within a fairly wide spectrum, residence in the village endows daily routines and material conditions of life with a certain homogeneity. Shared advantages and disadvantages of rural living mean that families
have very similar concerns: problems of lonely old people,
bad housing, problems of young people planning moving away,
transport problems and insufficiency of services and leisure
and cultural activities. The majority of villagers live in
a shared life situation, and differentiation of families in
terms of material and non-material assets is lessened by the
homogenizing effects of rural living. Nevertheless, some
thirty families in Pécsely may be considered disadvantaged
more than average on several counts (income, housing, education), while a number of families may be said to have
achieved more than the majority. Different material and
non-material circumstances however are not correlated with a
more leisurely, easier life-style; at all levels overbur-
dened work schedules are the rule, and the limitations of
rural living apply.

Regarding the differentiation of families, the disadvantages and advantages in the different spheres of material
and non-material assets do not tend to balance out. For
example, in the families considered deprived, disadvantages
are reinforced: provenance from the landless stratum, low
position in the occupational hierarchy, as well as low standards of education tend to be present conjointly. And elements that define a family's overall current situation do not
originate wholly in the objective socio-economic circumstances of today: the past reaches into the present through

innumerable channels. Features of the traditional paradigm are built into the society of today in a fragmented and disjointed manner, yet are no mere 'survivals' but active components of the villagers' lives. It was presumed, however, that the socialist paradigm would replace the traditional peasant system of reference, and in the pages that follow the extent to which that expectation was fulfilled is examined.

26

The Socialist Paradigm

In the following pages I will not be considering socialist theory, ideology and its praxis in high level politics,
but only those elements of socialism that have reached the
village and the form in which they have done so. What
interests us here is what the villagers have experienced of
socialism and how they have incorporated that experience
into their daily lives and that of the community as a whole.
'Socialist paradigm' therefore, is used here only in the
limited sense of the villagers' perception and understanding
of socialism.

The socialist paradigm was introduced into the life of
the villagers of Pécsely in the post-War years, mainly
through the reformed local institutions and the new personnel recruited as official and executive members (Chapter
23). The new council, the Party and the collectives were
the most important institutions among them. These establishments executed policies, plans and directives issued by
higher authorities outside the village, and it was through
them that ideological messages and political exhortations
were relayed to the villagers. Indeed, these institutions
and their personnel were the main channels through which
ordinary villagers first became acquainted with the workings
of the new order. Their experiences of these in the 1950s
helped to form the villagers' attitudes towards the State in
general, local officialdom in particular and the new 'elite'
- the local staff recruited to official positions.

The socialist paradigm lacked the well-worn finish of
the traditional paradigm that was seen in the previous chapter. It comprised many elements imported from the Soviet
Union, which had no tradition in Hungary and hence were unfamiliar and not well adapted to local conditions.

When it made its first appearance in the 1950s the

socialist paradigm consisted largely of concepts unfamiliar to the majority in the rural community, and of rough-and-ready stereotypes of an exceedingly abstract kind. The values propagated, such as 'socialist man' and 'community spirit,' as well as the goals set - 'building socialism,' achieving the norm,' 'towards a country of iron and steel' - were of limited relevance to the villagers' everyday existence. Social categorizations also based on ideology - kulák, 'class enemy,' 'good cadre' - were alien to the majority, and it was seen in the previous chapter how these failed to be adopted by the majority (p. 246). Although respect for private property was often evoked by government propaganda, the policies followed in the 1950s in fact caused a vast proportion of peasant property to pass to State and collective control (see Chapter 3). The villagers did not successfully assimilate the socialist morale and the failure was reflected in their disregard for collective and State property and a belief that they had licence to plunder these without compunction. Even today villagers say that to help oneself to State property is no great shame; it is referred to as 'getting' rather than stealing and it is a sign of resourcefulness rather than dishonesty. 'Stealing' means taking someone's private property. Collective property has become synonymous with that which nobody owns, not that which is owned by all. Currently, these attitudes are changing somewhat. Since the 1970s, the development of collectives into independent enterprises has impressed upon the villagers that they do now have 'owners,' in the shape of a strong managerial leadership, which look after the resources of the collective with greater zeal than hitherto.

The more extreme terminology of political propaganda faded away with the passing of the 1950s, without much of it being assimilated by the villagers.

Socialism did, however, introduce concepts and values that were internalized and integrated into community life. For example the rejection of class prerogatives, the 'caste'-like hierarchical divisions and the subservience of the landless. The majority of villagers today assert: 'We are all equal now' with some conviction, even though further into the conversation more subtle distinctions are admitted to prevail, and as one observes daily life in the village, one in fact comes across many manifestations that run counter to that optimistic assertion. Equal access to, for example, education, medical treatment and pensions are today felt to be inalienable rights and socialism is credited with them. Common interests in relation to the collectives have, in the last few years acquired greater substance but the way towards realizing this was not through the realization of the 'collective ownership principle' but development of the employee attitude of members (see Chapter 11). The aims of the socialist government are a great deal better understood today than was the case before the 1960s, and there is some pride in relation to the country's economic and social achievements. Nevertheless, the way towards the integration of elements of the socialist paradigm was far from being a smooth process and even today it is not complete, mainly as a result of the negative burdens carried over from the 1950s.

In the 1950s the villagers were divided according to the manner in which each family was placed in relation to the new order and official institutions. In practice, radical distinction between members and non-members of the Party was less important than a whole spectrum of political reliability. Rather paradoxically, the first criterion for gaining that reliability was to have been born into one class rather than another; declared political allegiance was only second to that. This type of classification was applied to every individual and family throughout the 1950s, based on files (that is cadre records) compiled about each and every person. These cadre records were crucial to a man's life and to all members of his family. Several criteria went to make up a man's cadre record, the most important being his class background, occupation, political background and religious behaviour. A good cadre record opened the way towards offices, higher education and exemption from disadvantages such as kulák laws. A good record and declared ideological convictions were, however, no unconditional guarantee for advancement in the new order; enthusiasm as such was not welcomed as much as enthusiasm for appropriately sanctioned goals (cf. Humphrey, 1983:169). For example, in Pécsely a communist of long standing was expelled from the Party in 1952, seemingly for excessive idealistic initiative and refusal to go along with the political programme of the day. Those with unfavourable files went into great lengths to have them changed, some with success. A man in Pécsely who had been a gendarme, for example, went to work in the mines so that his cadre-record entry would show 'miner' as his occupation. This move paid off years later when his son applied for and gained admittance to higher education, which would have been very unlikely if the 'gendarme' still figured on the cadre record card. Since the 1960s, these considerations have receded in importance and political reliability is no longer of crucial relevance in everyday life. No one is in principle disqualified from any office in

function of his or her family background. Children of former kuláks or clergymen have as much chance of university
entrance as those of miners. The question of Party membership comes up normally in relation to only those seeking
posts in political, educational or managerial spheres, and
stringent political evaluations have been greatly relaxed.

Today, people of ability and promise are often invited
to join the Party, but there is no compulsion to do so. How
far refusal of or compliance with this invitation influences
a man's subsequent career is hard to say and would require
deeper study than is possible from the vantage point of one
village. Joining the Party is certainly not a rigid precon-
dition for attaining higher posts; some vague indication of
progressive views is all that is needed.

For the majority in the 1950s the problem of everyday
existence had greater urgency than ideological concerns and
most people limited themselves to defensive strategies:
keeping out of the view of officialdom, non-participation in
public affairs and turning inwards towards the close family
circle. The horizontal networks of relationships between
families were to some extent preserved in the recesses of
everyday life due to the majority's inability to participate
in a positive way in local common affairs and institutions.
Those who were formerly leading members of the community had
no longer any place in the new community institutions but
this was not an unqualified disadvantage, since the new
official personnel came to be associated with the most un-
popular measures directed against the peasantry. Although
'the 1950s' - a term that carries weighty meaning in Hungary
even today - are over, attitudes and strategies evolved in
these years have left lasting marks. The non-participation
and lack of interest in community affairs is one such consequence, so is the continued attachment to traditional informal interest networks.

The Party, the council and, somewhat later, office holders in the collective became the holders of formal authority, but their power is a lot less than one might imagine.
The function of these local institutions was not, broadly
speaking, to deal with the problems of the community, as was
the function of the pre-War council (Chapter 23), but to
ensure that delivery quotas, taxes and requisitions were
collected, that kulák laws were enforced, collectivization
campaigns were under way and that appropriate political
messages were disseminated. Their activities were closely
monitored by higher authorities and their powers limited to
the scrupulous execution of orders. To take initiative in
solving local problems and represent the villagers' inter-

ests was beyond their competence (A Magyar Népidemokracia Története, 1978:166-167). As C. Humphrey shows, holding public office in a socialist system often lacks some of the 'sweeter' aspects of power, since '... the competence ascribed to any given position is always less than the responsibility ascribed to it ...' (1983:8). Officials were accountable for deficiencies which were not wholly in their power to control: for example, collective chairmen in the early years were responsible for meeting certain production quotas, despite possible lack of manpower, equipment or the possibility of harvest being ruined by the weather. Council presidents had to account for full delivery of compulsory quotas even if there was little to collect, and they earned the epithet 'loft sweeper' in their zealous efforts to collect reserves to the last grain. Local officials had the entire vertical chain of power hierarchy bearing down on them and it was a pressure they could only partially pass on to ordinary villagers. Unlike the higher echelons of authority issuing the orders, however, they lived in face-to-face contact with those they pressurized by virtue of their position. The former chairmen of the collectives in Pécsely in the early years remember these years with bitterness, and even in 1961 the man elected chairman of the Rákoczi collective was a reluctant candidate. Equally, the first council president in 1950 had much to live down in subsequent years and his two year tenure of office did not bring him much in terms of either moral or material advantage. In the 1950s, to be appointed to office was not to be envied, and these episodes in a villager's life tend to be remembered against them to this day. For example, on the occasion of the death of one prominent executive agent of these years, which occurred during my stay, his activities were remembered by all; in spite of the usually large attendances at funerals, this man's funeral was ignored by everyone except his closest kin.

For many years public offices remained undefined in terms of formal competence, actual power and criteria of appointment, and these uncertainties conspired to render the exact meaning of office holding highly ambiguous. The personal attributes of those who filled the posts assumed great significance, shortening or lengthening the period of unsettled conditions in each village. In some villages disastrous appointments followed successively; in others, the first batch that came to office stayed too long. These settled into a routine which was desirable in the 1950s but no longer justified or required later, and thus perpetuated 'the 1950s' atmosphere beyond the calendar. In yet other

villages, officials were brought in from outside and these
were even less likely to be sympathetic to community problems, or at least were not given credit for sympathy by the
locals. Pécsely in this respect was quite privileged, in
that the first batch of officials gave way to a second very
soon; these held their positions well into the 1970s, thus
ensuring a certain stability yet at the same time adapting
their methods with some flexibility in the improved political and social conditions of the 1960s.

In the 1950s, the personal prestige of a man was passed
to the office he held, not the other way round, since the
status of the new offices was as yet blank. The office itself was enhanced or demeaned by virtue of the qualities of
the man who occupied it, in some reverse order to the common
model of office conferring status on its holder (Parkin,
1972:34). From accounts in different villages, together
with the example of Pécsely, types of officials emerge at
this time: the puritan man with ideological convictions;
those using office to settle past wrongs; opportunists ris-
ing with the tide of events; former gazdas, usually reluctant recruits. Not until the 1970s are these types replaced
largely by the qualified administrators, technical specialists and managerial professionals that exist today.

The functioning of local institutions and the features
of office holding just described left their mark on present
day local authorities. The inclination to abrogate decision-
making to somewhere higher up the chain of official hierarchy is still marked, and this is not wholly unjustified in
the light of some examples of how decisions in public
matters are arrived at. Oláh and Vágvölgyi (1984:42-52)
examine the procedure followed in relation to the introduction of gas mains in a village in 1982-83. The costs of the
installation were to be shouldered by the villagers at the
rate of 20,000 forints per household, the total of which
would represent 60% of the costs. In addition, the households faced the expense of converting internal fittings to
gas combustion, a further large outlay. In principle, such
an operation can be initiated if 90% of the households
indicate their consent. The local collective needed this
installation, the county council wanted to promote this village of 15,000 inhabitants to 'town' category and the existence of a gas network would help to achieve this. Preparations were started, such as securing permits, bank loans and
making engineering plans at the cost of 18 million forints,
long before the population had been consulted. To obtain
the consent of the majority was not felt to be urgent and
the outcome was not in doubt. As the authors show, the

local council was first presented with the project when it was well under way and the council's role was merely to legitimize decisions made elsewhere and obtain some semblance of popular consent - although popular consent should have been the first requirement, not the last. When interviewed by the authors on this issue, the villagers showed remarkable ignorance of most aspects of the case and, although the majority declared against it, it was not at all clear to the villagers that they had the right to refuse consent. Despite this, the authorities claimed to have obtained the necessary majority for the project.

Decisions made by higher authorities apply equally to matters related to consumption cooperatives and collectives. Plans are made by county-level Party and council authorities, all preparations are set under way and it is when these are at the point where rejection is no longer a practical option that the project is presented to the local council and the members involved. Mergers of local consumption cooperatives, where in principle members are shareholders and decision-makers, are shown to have been engineered through the national consumer cooperatives' authority (MÉSZÖV and SZÖVOSZ), in conjunction with county level Party authorities (Seres, 1985:78-86). In Pécsely, mergers of the three collectives in 1961 (Chapter 7) and the merger of the Rákoczi collective with the Jókai of Füred in 1973 (Chapter 9) are examples of decisions forced upon the locals. Neither merger was the initiative or wish of either the local members or the local leadership. In fact, they were against them, but the local leaders' resistance was probably weakened by the fact that they were given valuable plots in the Füred area at the time - a coincidence that cannot be unconnected with the successful mergers. In none of the cases relating to Pécsely did local officials take the initiative to find out local members' views so they could arrive at some definition of what members felt to be in their interest and obtain validation of those interests. Local officials do not appear to consider the representation of local interests as their principal function. This was confirmed by a research in 1974 among local council members delegated to a county council. About half of them declared that they did not believe their function in the county council was to represent local interests; another quarter admitted seeking validation of local interests, but believed this was probably wrong; only one quarter acknowledged that their function was indeed the representation of local interests as against competing interests at the same level (Bogár, 1983: 130-131). The majority of officials therefore appear to have adopted an attitude regarding their function amounting to the admission of the limitations of their competence, despite the recent efforts of central government to widen the scope of local self-government (Dányi, 1975).

The villagers are well aware of the limitations imposed on local officials and hence their status within the community is relatively modest. They have certainly not taken the place of the pre-War elöljárok (leading men) and köztiszteletben állok (those held in public honour). The components that make up the status of public office holders today constitute different elements than was the case in the past. The de facto limitations of their functions, and the negative connotations associated with the authorities in the 1950s, have made dealings with official organizations something to be avoided. In fact, this avoidance is no longer justified. Ordinary villagers have a near total lack of concern for communal affairs, when in fact it would be in their interests for them to know more about the rights to which they are legally entitled.

Nevertheless, those in official positions do enjoy certain advantages by virtue of their position (Chapter 18) and are an elite group in terms of material assets. This is particularly true of the managerial group of the collective, who are in control of far greater resources than the village council. Components of the traditional paradigm too, go to make up the status of office holders; many are plot farmer gazdas of repute, linked throughout the village by kinship and friendship networks. In Pécsely, office holders are a fairly cohesive group, more or less marked out from the ordinary villagers, and often linked by kinship. The son-in-law of the Party secretary is a branch manager of the collective, for example, and the vice president of the collective today is brother-in-law of another administrative official. Office holders have their plots on the same stretch of vineyards (Chapter 18), which brings them into regular informal cooperation and potential ties of friendship.

Many elements of the socialist paradigm have been incorporated into the life of the villagers, which coexist with the surviving elements of the traditional system. The latest addition to this amalgam has been what might be called the western-urban paradigm, which we are examining in the chapter that follows.

27

The Western Urban Paradigm

The urban paradigm is relatively new and owes much to the consumption-oriented Western European model of living. The aspirations it fosters are more materialistic; evaluation of others' status tends to be made in terms of their apparent material achievements and the self is also presented in that light. Relations with others in terms of this paradigm places the focus on the mutual advantage of transactions, which is different from the traditional approach where transactions are expressions of ongoing social relationships. The attitudes to labour are focussed on the income derived from it; labour merely regarded as a means towards a material goal, not, as in the traditional paradigm a source of prestige in itself, or, as in the socialist interpretation a means towards some collectively defined goal.

In rural Hungary the major post-War social and economic reforms were launched in conjunction with a sudden increase of external intervention and control through a number of non-local agencies and personnel, on an unprecedented scale. The consequences were twofold: first the villagers received a great deal from a larger social and political environment, and second, the pressures generated by that intrusion were the root cause of many villagers leaving for employment or residence elsewhere. The two-way flow between village and town increased sharply, though the inflow was mainly intrusive and the outflow was defensive, with the villagers attempting to move away from the path of the worst anti-peasant measures. This no longer obtains today, but as a result the village is no longer isolated, but bound to a much wider social, cultural and economic environment by innumerable individual, familial and institutional ties.

Since the 1960s mass media have augmented the flow of influences into the village, carrying in components of the western-urban system of values and references.

In the 1950s, the urban models of living did not have much impact on the villages, since these models were themselves changing in the towns, with the majority of urban residents uncertain of the present, let alone the future. Individual farming was still significant and those who left for industrial jobs joined the lowest rungs of unskilled labour with not much change in their attitudes or lifestyle. As was shown in the previous chapter, the socialist paradigm was the only alternative in those years and it had not yet significantly displaced the traditional paradigm. Socialist policies had an overall levelling effect and material possessions that had formerly been a source of pride and prestige were best kept out of view. Even though few had much after the devastation of World War II, the few animals remaining, for example, were likely to be a liability to their owners when compulsory delivery quotas were set. Hence, attitudes to material possessions tended towards concealment and avoidance of display. With the passing of the 1950s, these cautious attitudes did not change overnight. When the villagers first had opportunities to acquire luxury goods, such as televisions or cars in the 1960s, such goods were not flaunted but hidden. The first television bought in the early 1960s was kept, it is recalled, under the bed, and viewed behind closed shutters, much to the other villagers' amusement. The first car bought in Pécsely was purchased by two families jointly and, as informants relate with relish, this was done not for lack of means, but to diffuse the 'burden of ownership.'

Today, the majority are no longer so inhibited, and achievement of material progress has been elevated to a major aim in life, even if the intention defeats itself by self-imposed dawn-to-dusk labour undertaken to fulfil those aspirations. The prestige value of material possessions is high, and good housing, cars and small children dressed to kill, are unambiguous statements of a family's worth. Achievement of material success and the ideals of urban style living are much more general among the villagers today than aspirations either towards traditional or socialist values. The three paradigms are, however, inextricably linked. The plots and starting point advantage of former landowning families (see pp. 166-167) play a significant part in a family's success in achieving material progress, and leading positions in socialist institutions may be converted into material advantages. Wealth in Hungary needs to be understood, of course, in a narrower sense than in Western Europe. It means proper housing, a holiday cottage, modern household equipment, a car, and the means to travel abroad. Those who achieve all these are those who have outstanding positions in management, public life, art or the sciences. In the rural context, however, even leading families have only achieved one or two of these goals, never all of them.

Large incomes derived from plots are achieved only at the price of unstinting physical labour - which stands in sharp contrast to the comforts of the villa-style house built from the proceeds. New houses have no place for the pigsty in the backyard, hence these are often in the parents' backyard, alongside the plot farming equipment. The young people who live in the new houses do not have the leisure to enjoy their hi-fi set, television etc. in the living area, which remains under-used and unlived-in. Today, as before, the kitchen remains the most lived in place in the house.

Cars bought at great expense are hardly ever used, because people tend to move within a relatively small radius, even if they work away from Pécsely, and there is little time for leisure trips. Often cars are no more than a temporary investment and are re-converted into cash when cash is needed for a house; during my stay, three cars that had hitherto been sitting in their owners' garages were sold for downpayments on houses. This is therefore not to say that people strive for things that they do not need, merely that the means available to reach those goals stands in the way of their full use and enjoyment.

Magazines, newspapers, films and television stimulate interest in new fashions, patterns of behaviour, and tastes in music. There is great interest in anything from Western Europe: gadgets, clothes, etc. are sought after and become prized possessions. Travel to the West is increasingly becoming a prestige achievement but is still the privilege of the few. For years, jeans were coveted symbols of modernity, urbanity, and material success among young people, alongside Western drinks and cigarettes. A wider distribution of such goods has been achieved in the last few years, since they have started to be produced in Hungary itself under license, and they have been incorporated into the life-style of young people, together with pop-music and soft drinks. The visitor to Hungary over the years was able to measure the pace at which the home market reoriented production and imports to meet those demands, according to the list of desirable gifts. Earlier, jeans, cigarettes or spirits were asked for; more recently pocket calculators have headed the list. These trends are more than mere fashions. They appear to express an orientation towards a new style of living, which fills the void created by the weakening of the traditional paradigm, and the inability of the socialist paradigm fully to take its place.

The urban model reaches deeper than the outer trappings of everyday existence. It is reflected in the manner of relating to work, for example. In the traditional paradigm work was not a nine-to-five affair, in an environment separate from the home, family and local community. The socialist paradigm emphasized the communality of work, in which individual interests were subordinated to, or achieved through, collective goals. Sacrifices were demanded in the name of higher interests of the community or of society - the higher the level of generality the better. Individual and micro-group interests were not sufficiently legitimized to allow them to be sought openly; in the spirit of the 1950s, the entire Hungarian nation was conceived to be labouring towards some united goal and the vertical chain of hierarchical institutions from community to district, county and central government level were re-structured accordingly (see Bogar, 1983). Opposing interests do exist nonetheless, at all levels of society, and, to further these, covert, quasi-legitimate networks have been developed, both within and outside the formal table of institutions. The strategy of posing individual or micro-group interests as common interests of a higher level of generality has been developed to a fine art. In the last instance, however, the majority look neither right nor left but pursue individual aims, towards which work is no more than a means. The prime consideration in relation to work is the income it generates, which may even override the next important consideration - the avoidance of unskilled or physical labour. In fact, young people with high qualifications are found employed as garage attendants, working in the building trade or in the collectives' high income stock farming sector. They do not obtain work which requires their diplomas as this work would bring them far lower remuneration. Here, the motivation is not only the wish to fulfil objective needs of better housing, for instance - but to fulfil it to the high standards set by modern urban living.

The urban model is gaining ground fast and many aspects of it are in fact being incorporated into the socialist paradigm too. Official policies today aim to break with the association of socialism with low standards of living and the individual striving towards material success is being legitimized. The string of reforms since 1968 aiming for greater autonomy of collectives and enterprises, encourage-

ment of competitive policies and support of small scale enterprises, all reflect this new trend. So material success
no longer stands in contradiction with the socialist paradigm. Full integration of these three paradigms with one
another is, nevertheless, still to be achieved, and is the
task of the next generation.

28

Social Differentiation

The most recent research programme on social stratification in Hungary concludes that social and material advantages and disadvantages are not evenly distributed throughout Hungarian society (Kolosi et al. reviewed by Andorka, 1984). It has been found, for example, that although families' situations were determined by a multiplicity of material and non-material components, advantages in one respect tended to be reinforced by advantages in other; conversely, disadvantages reinforce rather than cancel each other out.

The current assumption that Hungarian society consists of a wide middle stratum flanked by smaller strata of the more prosperous on the one hand and the deprived on the other is unfounded. It was concluded, on the contrary, that a relatively small middle stratum (17%) is sandwiched between a markedly prosperous stratum (7.2%), a large stratum that is more than averagely prosperous (28.8%) and the large stratum of the averagely disadvantaged (32.2%), followed by those most deprived (14.4%) (Andorka, 1984:100).[1]

This analysis of patterns of stratification in Hungary - the most comprehensive study on the subject up to date - prompts reflection on the difference between the results of statistical methods and participant observation. The results of statistical macro-studies are very different from social differentiation observable in everyday community life. One of the features that catches one's attention during fieldwork is the scarcity of categorizations ordinarily used in the community which would signal people's situation and status in society. In the pre-War period such categorizations were precise to the point of caste-like rigidity; for example, a man might describe himself as small peasant (kisgazda) and, in that description, the extent of his material assets, social status and rank, his exact position in relation to all other strata and his life-style, would all be contained. Categories used by the villagers themselves would also be found in the sociological literature virtually unchanged or possibly with some added refinements, but they would still be easily recognized by those to whom they applied.

That this is not the case in Hungarian rural society today confirms that the former rigid hierarchical social system has indeed been successfully dismantled. It also confirms that clear articulation of social groups in new ways is still in the making. Present analyses of social stratification do not generally make use of popularly used categorizations as the point of departure for their studies but are forced to make them up artificially as they go along and these categorizations would not be recognizable by the majority of those in question. Doubtless this is also a consequence of the more refined socio-analytical techniques developed during the last few decades and it is not the aim of sociologists to reflect popular notions. Nonetheless, the lack of popular agreement as to what social categories exist in contemporary Hungarian society, and how they are placed in relation to one another, is a noteworthy feature that deserves mention.

Through the example of Pécsely it has been shown that families are engaged in different sectors of production, and their situation overall as regards material and non-material assets is made up of very diverse elements, some related to the traditional, others to the socialist, and yet others to the urban paradigm. The multiplicity of coexisting frame-works of reference, which often pull in opposing directions, endow social life in the community with a singular flexibil-ity and softness. It is no longer perceived to be nearly impossible to break out from the social situation into which a man is born, or that this can be done only at the price of inordinate effort and chance, as was the case before 1945. All informants now believe that 'he who wants to forge ahead can do so; he only needs to work,' and 'everyone has a chance to improve their lot.' This optimistic perception of their life chances fuels the often gruelling, self-exploita-tive labour schedule that villagers impose upon themselves, not without some justification, witnessed by the excellent results many have achieved.

However, the fact that people have little perception of the overall situation of others and self within society also fosters the belief that society is a great deal more 'open' than in fact it is. In other words, the objective limit-ations that hinder certain categories of people, or allow situational advantages to others, are lost from sight. For example, although peasant social mobility (not necessarily upward) has been prodigious since the war, today a rural peasant background is regarded as being 'unequivocally a disadvantage' (Kulcsár, quoted in Andorka, 1980:178). Indeed, disadvantages for the rural populations have been reproduced over many generations, in terms of lower education, lower chances of acquiring skills, greater likelihood of remaining caught in the the dead-end situation of unskilled commuter workers. Not that villagers are unaware of these limitations or that they believe all is possible for them; on the contrary, their daily experience is one of unending struggle against such limitations. But they tend to perceive these limitations on a one-to-one basis, and do not perceive them as part of a larger pattern. For example, they measure their own position in the community as set against some other family or individual only, and not in terms of a specific category of individuals. They know that the 'X' family is more prosperous and more advantaged than they are, and that, on the contrary, the 'Y's are less advantaged than they are, but they do not perceive the X family to belong to some named category that is above them or the Ys as members of a category below them.

Town dwellers are not categorized in a generalized way either, as many families from Pécsely have children living in a town and they know that in terms of income for example, town dwellers are not necessarily that much advantaged, since most lack the possibility of plot farming. As will be shown in greater detail (p. 281), ad hoc descriptions and categorizations of an impressionistic kind are most frequently used in everyday life.

In Pécsely only two clearly defined categories of people are fairly consistently acknowledged: the professional intelligentsia (doctor, clergymen, teachers) and the managerial and administrative elite (agronomist, council president, collective chairman). Socially the intelligentsia are not part of the village, and in fact are far less so than before 1945. At that time the teachers, for example, lived locally and were even bound by kinship to some local families; although members of a higher stratum, beyond office hours they participated in village life and were intimately involved in the life of the community. Today however teachers no longer live locally; they come in the morning and leave in the evening and their relationship to the village is strictly professional. The clergyman no longer lives in the village either, and his appearance in the village is limited to the Sunday service and funerals.

The doctor does live locally, but mingles little with the locals.

The managerial/administrative elite is linked to the village in more complex ways, as has been shown throughout previous chapters. These people are, as a group, placed in a more prestigious position in relation to ordinary villagers in function of their position. Apart from these groups, no other categories are used consistently to differentiate families. Ordinary members of the collective, skilled and unskilled workers and white-collar workers are generally not perceived to form distinct groups. Incomes earned in the various sectors, with various levels of competence, vary within a narrow spectrum, and occupational qualifications are not shown to result in significantly higher pay; in fact the income of the collective member in the stock breeding branch may be higher than that of a teacher. Plot farming equalizes as well as differentiates; low wages in a job may be compensated for by working a plot, or on the contrary the latter may be added to higher wages, thereby increasing income differentiation.

Intensive plot farming however, as has been seen, also stands in the way of realizing de facto the urban life-style in pursuit of which it is undertaken in the first place (Chapter 26).

The former patterns of stratification have ceased, or at least have been relegated to a shadowy existence, and new ones are still in the making. As most recent research shows (see p. 271), objectively identifiable strata have already been generated; what is still lacking is popular perception of these objectively existing patterns. In the community, the lack of such perception has the effect of inhibiting the development of informal, voluntary interest groups, as will be examined presently.

NOTES

1. The stratification study referred to here has been made by a team of the Social Sciences Institute in Hungary, headed by T. Kolosi. Extensive questionnaire-based data was collected from half a per cent of the population, in 1981-1982, the conclusions of which are to be published in three volumes, as well as one volume in English, prepared for the Conference on Stratification in Budapest in September 1984. The data referred to in the present work is based on a review and summary by R. Andorka, in Valosag, 1984/9, pp. 97-104. The mathematical and statistical data has been collected on the basis of eight dimensions which enter into the definition of the social position of individuals and families: (1) character of place of residence (from village to the capital); (2) housing conditions (space, comfort, amenities); (3) wealth and income; (4) consumption (meat, toilet goods, entertaining); (5) culture and education (qualifications, cultural pursuits, hobbies); (6) place in the occupational hierarchy (occupation and conditions of work); (7) ability and competence in interest-validation (in political institutions, place of work, etc.); (8) participation in the second economy. On the basis of these criteria, several kinds of analysis are made. Most importantly, Kolosi has established an index ranging from one to seven, and divides status groups on the basis of their advantages; for example, those consistently advantaged in all dimensions would constitute the uppermost group (1.5%) and those consistently disadvantaged would form the lowest group (8%). On the basis of cluster analysis, twelve status groups have been arrived at: (1) elite; (2) upper urban; (3) provincial upper; (4) provincial affluent worker; (5) urban affluent worker; (6) interest validating middle; (7) urban middle; (8) interest validating rural; (9) affluent rural lower; (10) urban lower; (11) moderately deprived; (12) very deprived. These status groups are defined not only in terms of occupational place but are a composite of variables such as place of residence, consumption patterns, interest validating competence. The hierarchy model referred to on p. 271 of the present work is based on the scales constituted from these groups, and it is on that basis that stratification patterns are arrived at by the authors. The full complexity of that study need not be conveyed here; the above sketch is only given to indicate the nature of this study to which we are referring.

29

Community, Society:
Voluntary Associations

Pre-War rural Hungary was overloaded with, rather than deficient in, categorizations in terms of class, stratum, wealth, religion and locality of origin. Rigid categorizations, however, not only divided the community, but also ordered relations within groups and, perhaps more importantly, allowed clear self-classification. Identifying one's own position in relation to others, and identifying those with whom one's interest and goals coincided, were essential for the integration of local communities. Informal associations based on self-selected membership were numerous in pre-War rural communities in Hungary, integrating horizontally all members of the community.

The local Circle of Farmers, Firefighting Association, the local cells of Consumer Cooperatives, Grazing Associations and informal cooperative groups (Chapter 4) were local interest groups with concrete sets of organizational rules and an economic, cultural and cooperative agenda. There were also reading circles, a choir, and meetings organized by the local teacher with agronomists invited to discuss innovations in agro-techniques. On the more informal level, in the Transdanubian area, there were regular 'pinceszer,' that is, gatherings of gazdas in the hillside wine cellars, equivalent in some ways to the 'tanyaszer' which were usual in the Plains region where such gatherings took place in the stables (Fél and Hófer, 1973:787-801). These gatherings were not, as Fél and Hófer also show, merely occasional drinking parties. They were regular gatherings of a select number of habitual guests in the stables or cellars of respected gazdas, in the course of which community affairs, farming problems, as well as political questions were debated, with information exchanged and disseminated.

The farming community had a variety of common affairs

which were managed jointly, for example, in relation to the vineyards. One gazda of repute was appointed 'hegybíró' (justice of the hills) and settled small disputes connected with the vines, supervised the quality of wine produced, announced the day on which vintage could start and dispensed the blue vitriol (rezgalic) used as pesticide. Grazing associations were self-managed, the gazdas buying shares in the pasture lands according to the number of animals they pastured. Grazing land was kept in good order, watering places kept clean, and shepherds were contracted to look after all animals.

Religious affiliation was another criterion that brought people together and served as a basis for the formation of common-interest groups. Catholics and Protestants, as has been shown, had separate congregations that cooperated with each other in pursuit of common goals, for example in the building of a new church (p. 234). Villagers were also activated in lesser ways in their parish, in cultural, charitable and educational activities.

Interest groups based on locality were also significant. Residents of Nagy, Nemes and Kis Pécsely had a strong sense of pride and solidarity with their locality (Chapter 1). Even as late as the 1960s, residents fought for advantages for their localities when for example it was a question of where the new surgery, nursery and the new centre of the collective should be built (p. 104).

In the post-War period, horizontally integrated informal interest groups and associations equivalent to those operating formerly have not been generated. From 1945 onwards the majority of associations such as these were dissolved as a result of either direct measures or indirect influence. The Farmer's Circle, for instance, was prohibited and dispersed in 1949. The local consumer cooperative cell – Hangya before the War – was replaced by the ÁFESZ and was gradually merged with other local units into larger cells, which had little local autonomy left. The informal cooperative groups were not revived after the war and there was no continuity with the socialist collectives formed from 1949 (see pp. 54–56). The less formal voluntary meetings withered of their own accord in the 1950s, when all such gatherings were regarded with suspicion to the highest degree by the authorities. Gatherings of friends in cellars has revived recently to a small extent, but many former gazdas merely sit in their courtyard day after day, if they are not working on their plots and say: 'Why should we get together when there is nothing left to be discussed? Now mainly those get together who are either young or drunkards.' Such attitudes only confirm that pre-War gazda gatherings had other functions than mere entertainment. Today, the bar (kocsma) remains the focal gathering point, where drinking is the chief attraction, and if someone with personal networks exhausted wants to find a labourer for an occasional job, the bar/café is the place to go to and ask around. The former gazdas however are rarely seen in the bar; they drink in their own cellars.

Other informal or semi-informal gatherings lapsed as a result of indirect influences, for example, the non-existence of different political parties and the change of the schools' organization. Teachers no longer activate after school hours social and cultural events or, if they do so, they are merely fulfilling part of an educational programme imposed on them. This factor is undoubtedly something that depends on the personality of the teachers in the villages. In Pécsely for instance, there were two teachers, one Catholic and one Protestant, in the 1930s to the 1950s, who were, on the basis of accounts, exceptional personalities who contributed greatly to the community over several decades. No characters of such stature are to be found among the teachers today.

It has been seen how the roles of religion and parish have changed (Chapter 23), and how the Protestant parish has remained possibly the most resilient and active community interest group.

The vacuum that has been created with the demise of the informal community groups has not been filled. The associations promoted officially were artificial cells of nationwide organizations, with specific political agenda. Such were, for example, the short-lived FÉKOSZ (National Association of Agricultural Workers and Smallholders) and the UFOSZ (National Association of Land Recipients) in the early 1950s. These included members mainly from the agricultural labourers' stratum or poorer landowners, were controlled by the Party and were merely cells of national level political organizations. Such is also the local cell of the Patriotic People's Front, which is closely monitored by the Party and adheres to pre-set programmes with only limited authority.

Youth organizations in Pécsely well illustrate the difficulties of spontaneous group formation. The youth organizations officially promoted, (DISZ, MADISZ and finally KISZ) in the 1950s and 1960s, had their dynamism flattened by the political purpose to which they were put; since then however, in some communities at least, KISZ organizations may have grown into organizations of greater substance. This, though, is not the case in Pécsely. There has been no youth

organization since the 1960s. Since the mid-1970s, young
people in the village have pressed for a youth club, but
permission and assistance have been refused by the local
council. Finally, in 1977, the initiative was taken by a
most unlikely character - the man who runs a horse-riding
school in the village. He has about thirty horses and cat-
ers for foreign tourists who come from the hotels surrounding lake Balaton. He is a newcomer to Pécsely, has rather
rough manners and is a great crusader against alcoholism.
His idea was to gather the youth of Pécsely together to form
a riding club, on the agreement that he would teach them to
ride, while they would groom and exercise his horses - so it
was not an entirely selfless plan. It would however have
brought the village's youth together in some common pursuit
and sport; typically, the youth of the village has hitherto
never learned to ride or groom a horse. As soon as the
first moves were made towards this plan, the council stepped
in, stopped the initiative, and ordered the foundation of a
KISZ (Communist Youth Association) club instead and assigned
a room for the purpose. The group of young villagers split:
some remained in the horse riding school as individual helpers, while others joined the KISZ. The most positive programme of the KISZ group has been the redecoration of their
centre. Since the first year, however, club activities have
been half-hearted, lacking in leadership, programme and
enthusiasm. Since the riding club idea was thwarted, the
council lost further interest in the KISZ club. For example, the Centre has been asking for a television in vain
for years. The older villagers look upon both the riding
school and the KISZ club with suspicion and do not support
either.

In contrast to the poverty of voluntary local associations generally, those in relation to cultural pursuits have
been successful. Between 1950 and 1956 in Pécsely for example, the villagers had most successful and active dramatic
societies which mounted several productions each year, and
even toured neighbouring villages. There was wide participation in these productions; stage props were made locally;
and these events today are remembered with affection. In
other villages, such as Tázlár, such groups exist today
(Hann, 1980:124-125). In many others there are choirs,
folklore dance groups and folk-craft groups. All these are
specialized groups, however, which are not socially exclusive and do not serve political or community functions. None
of the informal groups and associations found in rural Hungary today are of a kind that bring together a self-selected
voluntary membership with the aim of validating or articula-

ting micro-group interests or of furthering common goals.

In part, this is related to the formal structure of Hungarian society, which is based on vertical, hierarchical subordination. That is, power, directives and communications flow downwards along vertical channels. If two units placed parallel at any point of the hierarchy want to cooperate or communicate formally, they can do so legitimately only through the mediation of an authority higher up the hierarchy; for example, two work brigades wishing to cooperate can do so only through the mediation of the collective leadership, two villages through the mediation of the county, and two counties through the government (Hankiss, 1983). Horizontal linkages have tenuous legitimacy and are not encouraged, or alternatively they are incorporated into the vertical hierarchy, which generally deflects their dynamism - as has been shown through the small example of the KISZ club, which has been made into merely one cell of the nationwide KISZ organization.

Life in the community is such that it discourages the generation of informal voluntary groups. The three coexisting paradigms described in the previous chapters endow community life with a characteristic amorphousness, a lack of a unified system of reference. Each family had widely spread attachment in different sectors of production and the traditional, socialist and urban paradigms operate simultaneously, inhibiting delineation of interest groups and common goals. Makeshift, quasi-classifications of an impromptu kind abound: 'those-who-have-power and those-who-have-not; those-above-us; those-enriching-on-the-plots, us struggling-on-a-fixed-wage' (Hankiss, 1970:40). Through the plots, workers are tied to agriculture; agriculturalists on the other hand increasingly do mechanical, industrial type jobs in the collective. Office holders themselves are involved on the plots, a 'second economy' domain (Chapter 12). Hence a sense of lack of belonging to a definite category renders the structure of the local community amorphous, with a lack of clear articulation of common interest groups.

The majority of informants in Pécsely emphasize that 'we live for ourselves' (magunknak élünk), meaning that they do not identify themselves with any group, that they concentrate on the advancement of the family in both material and non-material terms, and are self-contained. The rural family appears to emphasize its function as a 'defensive' unit. Members rely on one another unconditionally, advancement of one member has repercussions on all the other members. This interdependence is not without its own problems, as it was shown in Chapter 22.

Networks of reciprocal help flowing along traditional grooves do not tend to crystallize into distinct groups that include specific categories of people and not others. Groups forming currently have an ephemeral, personal character and are not represenative of the objective social categories of the present society. For example, old _gazdas_ who get together are _gazdas_ no longer but retired members of the collective or industry.

An added dimension of community life is that people have de facto interests which they seek to validate against competing claims. Legitimate channels for the validation of such claims are not well developed enough, therefore quasi-legitimate hidden networks have come into being. Positively manifested, these networks relate to kinship, friendship and neighbourhood cooperation; negatively manifested, they shade into corruption, nepotism and illegality. A very large number of everyday problems and routine affairs are solved by these hidden networks of reciprocal help, and affairs that do go through formal channels are reinforced - given a little extra push - through the hidden networks. To get some coveted job or piece of work, obtain scarce goods, arrange for services, transport, to get a necessary permit or priority in the health services, 'contacts' are deemed to be essential. Perhaps they are not, but people have become used to resorting to the hidden networks 'just in case.' As a problem arises, the family asks: 'Who do we know in that office/department/hospital/school who can help?' Many affairs of everyday life are a matter of manoeuvring (_kijárni valamit_), with all the implications of ingeniously activated informal networks. Public as well as private affairs are dealt with in this manner. For example, if a community or county council is committed to some project, informal networks are bound to be activated to secure distribution of resources to their advantage rather than to some other competing unit (Bogár, 1983:120-123). Material possessions are not an individual's only assets: connections, access to information, even the most modest competence in decision-making may be negotiable. The shopkeeper who sells his stock of scarce goods to some people rather than others, the brigade leader who assigns lucrative jobs selectively, the council president who gives priority to building one stretch of road rather than another, are all in control of some non-material asset that they can trade with. Access to information may be ingeniously exploited. At its most trivial: '... to be a Party member is a good thing, because one knows about price increases and other essential matters. The Party members run to the stores. Everybody runs after.'

(Sozán, 184:30.) To know where plots for housebuilding are about to be allocated is of greater significance.

The launching of a community development project that affects everyone would benefit from more free-flowing information yet, as has been shown (p. 262), preparations are often set in motion and carried to a point where reversal is no longer a practical option, before the public is informed. That these things happen is not exclusively the result of official attitudes; they are partly determined by the lack of interest and apathy of the majority in relation to community affairs, in contrast to the keen interest in matters perceived as private. That, in the last instance, public affairs have consequences for private affairs does not seem to induce involvement with public affairs. In sum, the present situation generates the impression that the community is 'atomized,' that family and individual interests are fought for on a day-to-day basis, for quick results, without any long-term view of the kind of life people hope to achieve.

Inconsistencies of the simultaneous, contradictory frames of reference also have disorganizing effects on people's everyday interactions. Notorious among these has been the failure to develop some uniform code of the use of terms of address. The Hungarian language has a rich store of forms of address, from the familiar '<u>te</u>' to the more formal, third person '<u>maga</u>,' through to the more ceremonious variety of the third person '<u>ön</u>' and lastly to the '<u>tessék</u>' signifying the most assymetrical relationships of all in terms of age and status. These forms determine grammatical construction of sentences and cannot be circumvented in the course of ordinary speech with the aid of some ingenious neutral grammatical form. Terms of greeting are a first hurdle. The highly differentiated forms of the pre-War era, with its '<u>Tekintetes</u>,' '<u>Méltoságos</u>,' '<u>Nagyságos</u>' (Honourable and its variants) express subtleties of an untranslatable kind. The majority of these terms have lapsed alongside the entire hierarchical social system that gave rise to them, although some old people in the village, sometimes surprisingly, use anachronistic terms. In the 1950s, when the old terms had been only recently discarded, the new term 'comrade' was introduced. Originating in the pre-War illegal worker-movements, and within the Communist and Social Democratic Party, 'comrade' signalled ideological commitment. After 1949, the term was spread throughout all levels of society; not to use it was considered reactionary and those not so addressed were politically stigmatized. Since then its use has receded considerably, but it has not become easier to decide when it is appropriate and just how it should be used - is is 'comrade Kovacs' or 'comrade John' or just 'comrade'? The problem is tempered by the fact that the term is used mainly in official dealings, but even here it may be considered as inappropriate or too formal. The major problem however is: if comrade is not widely used, what term of address is? A timid revival of some of the old terms fill some of the gaps, the 'úr' (Gentleman, Sir) for example, but it is never clear when to use it would be considered an offence and when not. This term can be used with some assurance only with reference to some professional people, such as teachers, doctors or Catholic priests, in conjunction with the addressee's profession (e.g. Doctor úr: respected doctor). It would be offensive to use this term when addressing a council official. In practice, the majority of villagers in Pécsely use familiar terms among themselves, first names with some added qualification such as 'bátyám' (elder brother) or 'néni' and 'bácsi' for old people. Traditional grooves ordering daily interaction are not so problematic; the difficulties arise mainly in connection with people outside the village, which occurs with increasing frequency. The inadequacy of terms of address and greetings is a result, paradoxically, not of the scarcity of terms available but because of their abundance - anachronisms, old terms revived, and new terms compete with one another. What is lacking is a consensus regarding appropriate usages in a whole array of new situations. Even after careful consideration one cannot rest assured that one has chosen a form of address that corresponds with precision to the nature of the relationship and status of those involved. Which brings us back to the softness of the social structure arising out of competing value systems, aspirations and models of living.

These last chapters have aimed to present some of the features that make up the everyday existence of the villagers in their community. What may be possible using macro-scale statistical methods is not possible at the level of a village study. The two methods, that is, micro and macro-level studies, however complement one another. Events and processes originating at individual family and community level, may, if replicated in large enough numbers, give rise to the trends that the statistician is there to record, without perhaps the means to define the grass-roots level processes that have given rise to those trends. These chapters have aimed to make a contribution towards understanding this problem.

Conclusion

The village of Pécsely today bears little resemblance to the three small communes which existed in the valley before World War II. Chapter 1 aimed to dispel the appearance of unchanging stability even in the pre-war period, but also aimed to show that 'change' took on a new meaning after 1945, a difference that lies in centralized planning and the way it was carried out, compared to the far more gradual and unguided changes which occurred before that time.

Pécsely has remained a relatively vital community both in its people and its physical growth but, as Franklin (1969: 22) writes, 'a vital rural community is not synonymous with a vital peasant society.' The distinction is apt, for the relative vitality of Pécsely springs from its successful collective, the commercial value of its plot-farming products and the availability of non-agricultural employment near the village. This specific combination of features preserved Pécsely from the massive depopulation and slow death that have been the fate of many Hungarian villages of similar size.

The resilience of traditional values undoubtedly hindered the introduction of new forms of production and social organization in the post-war period. In Pécsely, social divisions based on landownership lapsed very gradually and affected the course of collectivization (Chapters 4 and 7). Post-war changes, however, did not merely amount to the gradual dissolution of old structures and values; the new socialist policies themselves went through successive stages of development, as has been shown. The ability of individuals and groups to absorb, reject or alter the outcome of social and economic policies has been a pressing problem in socialist states (cf. Tepicht, 1957; Barić, 1978) and this present work also suggests that the roles played by the

285

peasant family and the pre-War community structure throughout these changes have been crucial.

The way that families have integrated work in the three economic sectors - collective, non-agricultural and plot farming - into their everyday life is a major feature of the social structure of the village today. Engagement in the three sectors determines people's ties - both individually and as a community - to the world beyond the village. On the one hand plot farming enables families and individuals to continue to relate to each other in traditional ways; on the other hand work in the collective and in non-agricultural labour opens up a wider social and economic environment.

Yet, this wider economic environment is split in two, not unified. The 'first' and the 'second' economy (pp. 6-7 and 135-146) are not only different but in conflict. The socialized and private economies in Hungary rest on different principles, and the operation and control of one economy calls for methods that are inapplicable to the other. The collectives for example are vulnerable to direct control and regulation by the State and, although they strive for profits, they do not respond sensitively to the needs of the market (pp. 115-116). Their resources and opportunities for expansion are, ultimately, controlled by the State although, conversely, they do not have to bear the full penalties of inefficiency. Because the State does not regulate its cost-effectiveness, the socialized section is hungry for resources and manpower. It can use - or squander - a large number of workers, without being forced to insist on peak efficiency or being able to reward it adequately (see Gábor, 1985). Wages, levelled and controlled throughout the socialized section of the economy are not as crucial in setting a family's overall prosperity as the ratio of workers versus dependents in the family and the extent of the family's engagement in plot farming. As rewards for effort invested in the private sector are more sensitive to market and price conditions, attitudes in the two economies towards labour are very different (see pp. 126 and 169-70). As regards State control and regulation too, the logic of each economy's operation differs; the second economy cannot be so strictly regulated as the first. Controls through taxation have led to widespread slow-downs in production and consequent shifts of pressure onto the socialized sectors which it could not carry. The private sector remains hedged in and, on reaching the barriers, the operators have the choice of either shifting towards illegality or reducing their activity of production. As R. Gábor shows (1985) the problem is that the ideological charter of the State does not allow the private sector to grow into the socialized sector. The private sector may contract or expand according to the political and economic circumstances of the moment, but cannot achieve true integration with the socialized sector. Vacillating government attitudes (pp. 139-143) have not been reassuring to the private sector - even though these have usually been supportive since the mid 1970s. Emphasis is on keeping the plots flexible, able to adjust to changes from moment to moment and aiming towards quick profits rather than long-term investments and expansion.

As far as individual operators are concerned there is only a single economic field, with a variety of advantages and limitations. But while the work force engaged in both the first and the second economy is essentially the same, the attitudes to labour encouraged in each and the rewards and opportunities they offer are very different. The duality of the economy - a crucial feature of Hungarian economy - is closely related to the ways in which individual families exploited chances available in both socialized and private sectors of production. Judicious allocation of family manpower and its dispersal through the various sectors has, arguably, powerfully shaped the structure of the economy in general and of its constituent sectors in particular.

First, peasant families did not commit their full labour force to the collectives as they had done hitherto to their peasant farm. The term 'multi-family peasant farm' used by Galeski (1975:19) to define collectives needs some qualification here: it does not fully convey the change caused by collectivization and implies that the peasant family's entire labour force was transferred to the collective. Similarly, Tepicht (1972:69) has emphasized that peasant farms are merely agglomerated and not transformed on being incorporated into the collective. It needs to be taken into account that from the outset collectivization of peasant farms brought fundamental changes for the rural family. The way in which the family began to allocate its time and energies to different sectors of production was a major departure from the peasant farming system, a change that can be attributed only partially to the subsequent modernizing of agriculture. It is also interesting to speculate how far the withholding of a major part of the family manpower from the collectives stimulated the development towards an enterprise-type structure - for example, through the need to employ non-members in order to compensate for manpower shortage and demands for mechanization which in turn have speeded up occupational differentiation and growth of specialist management.

The second change of significance in shaping the
economy was that family power withheld from the collectives
should be redirected towards plot farming; this enabled
plot farming to acquire strength within both the national
and the household economy. The rapidity with which plot
farming has been redirected towards commodity production has
been a major factor in its growth (Hegedüs, 1977:142). This
is less apparent in Pécsely than elsewhere in the country
because plots are mainly vineyards, which were market
oriented from the beginning. It has not therefore been possible in this book to show how significant has been the
redirection of plots from subsistence towards commodity pro-
uction. Yet even in Pécsely it is apparent that plot farming rapidly outgrew the limited role it had officially been
assigned. Through the development of plot farming, the
rural population also acquired a strong bargaining position
vis-à-vis the government (Hann, 1980:170-172).

Lastly, the manner in which former peasants and their
children sought employment in non-agricultural sectors deserves attention. Since most families are active in more
than one sector, it has become very difficult for the government to isolate non-agricultural workers from the effects
of policies designed for agricultural workers, and vice
versa. Government programmes from the late 1940s were aimed
very specifically at the various social strata and were
almost punitive towards the peasantry as it has been seen
(Chapter 3). In Hungary the term 'worker' is even today
heavily charged with ideological implications and is often
used in political jargon to exclude the former peasant, the
plot farmer or member of a collective, although in everyday
usage it might be used in a less restricted sense. But selective policies, designed to affect one stratum alone, are
no longer possible. The limitations of such selective control have been apparent, for example, in the outcome of the
restrictive measures against plot farming in the early
1970s. Incomes from plots were substantial and, in view of
the lack of possibilities and incentive for re-investment in
production, plot farmers turned profits mainly into consumer
goods. It was considered ideologically ambiguous that the
'peasant' rather than the 'worker' should be so highly
rewarded and substantial taxes were imposed on plot farm
profits. Plot outputs were promptly reduced, causing shortages, price increases and loss of revenue all of which hit
the worker - the very stratum of society that the taxes
aimed to protect (Kulcsár, 1982:148-149). As Kulcsár pointed out, this example showed the extent to which the distinctions of 'worker' and peasant were now irrelevant; the

majority of workers are plot farmers too, or belong to families which include plot farmers.

Although the majority of rural families are engaged in all three sectors of production, they differ in their degree of participation in each. Advantages in the different sectors are exploited while disadvantages are balanced through dispersal of family labour among the different sectors. Each sector of production offers certain material and non-material advantages but not others - and in this respect the sectors vary considerably.

Plot farming is the sector in which most family members are involved, yet, while it brings within reach material advantages that other sectors do not, it has inherent limitations. Many of the assets of plot farming cannot be converted into other kinds of material and social advantages. Plot farming is, indeed, bound to specific disadvantages. First, those of living in a village. The capital assets of plot farming consist of land, implements, livestock, etc. Non-material assets include farming expertise and the habit of physical work, as well as local networks of reciprocal help. These assets are exploitable only insofar as family labour is available and they are largely tied to the village; they cannot be increased much and what can be sold has limited cash value. All these assets are of concrete value only while they are worked; without human labour and beyond the village boundaries, they are not.

In spite of numerous improvements since the 1950s, the rural population in Hungary remains disadvantaged compared to townspeople. Take housing, for example. In the villages 83% of houses are owned by the residents, while in Budapest the proportion is 32% and in towns 58%. This means that the overwhelming majority of houses in villages have been built and financed through private means and, as has been seen, building work is done to a very large extent by kinsmen and friends (pp. 160-161). Village dwellers are entitled to considerably fewer bank loans for housebuilding than town dwellers. Thus, while in the towns the State assumes a good proportion of the burden of providing housing, in the villages this burden is shouldered entirely by the families living there. Once completed, houses in the villages compare favourably with the small cramped flats of subsidized residential estates in towns but they also tie down the energy of the entire family for years, even decades. During that time, the workload of the family engaged in building is staggering, many starting work at 3 or 4 o'clock in the morning and working until late at night, including weekends and holidays (cf. Simó, 1983).

Villagers are at a disadvantage in other respects too. Until 1979, electricity rates were almost double those of towns and even today they are still higher. Mains water supply is lacking in 83% of villages, even in a village such as Tard, for example, where all wells are contaminated by high nitrate content and the water is unsuitable for drinking or even bathing babies (Simó, 1983). Although incomparably better than anything available to villagers before 1945, medical services, schools, nurseries and leisure facilities are inferior to those in towns (Társadalmi Struktúránk Fejlődése, III, 1981). The majority of small villages still have only one or two local stores, and the production of vegetables, fruit, eggs and meat on the plots is therefore a necessity. Thus, although plot farming may be the source of income, the profits serve to a large extent to compensate for the disadvantages of living in a village. The rigorous pace of daily labour itself stands in the way of converting the gains from the plots into advantages such as a more relaxed life-style, in which cultural, educational, and leisure activities are included. Plots consume both energy and time but are not, for example, of any help towards a career. This is not so in all socialist countries. As C. Humphrey shows (1983) in Buryatiya, USSR, what she calls 'manipulable resources,' many of which are generated through the plots, are assets which can be converted into other kinds of advantages, such as a higher rung on the occupational ladder, help and protection in times of need, fostering good relations with influential people, access to scarce goods and services. In Hungary, although personal contacts are significant (pp. 282-283), job alternatives are not scarce, and allocation and use of cash and products are not regulated by the State to the same extent as in the Soviet Union; hence, social relations do not need to be fostered so actively, and the profits from plots are not generally employed for that purpose.

Non-agricultural employment holds the greatest advantages for the younger age groups, for whom it offers the prospect of a career and a wide choice of jobs to fulfil personal talents and inclinations. Acquiring qualifications and training in some chosen skill is the general rule among young people and many have made excellent progress in their fields.

The limitations of non-agricultural employment vary regionally; in villages like Pécsely, where industrial and service jobs are plentiful in nearby towns, limitations are few. In more remote villages, however, non-agricultural employment requires either residence in workers' hostels

throughout the week, as for the villagers of Varsány (Bodrogi, 1978) for instance, or exhausting daily commuting
which has to be added to regular work hours, as in Tard
(Simó, 1983). Non-agricultural employment leads often to
moving out of the village, limiting the possibilities of
plot farming; in Pécsely as in other villages too, this is
compensated for by participation in plot farming as described in Chapter 19.

The problems facing the members of collectives have
been set out in previous chapters; these have been greatest
for the older generation of former gazdas for whom, if anything, membership has meant downward social mobility: from
self sufficiency, independence and authority on the family
farm, to the subaltern position of unskilled labourer.
Engagement such as this in the collectives, however, is on
the wane and the younger age groups, mainly semi-skilled or
skilled workers, relate to the collective quite differently
and are without most of the frustrations that the older members have experienced. They regard work in the collectives
as any other kind of contractual job.

The collectives in Hungary are irrevocably integrated
into the rural social structure and in Pécsely no evidence
was found of a desire to revert to individual farming. The
question - so pressing in the 1950s - of collective versus
individual farming does not arise in the village today. On
the other hand, the future of plot farming remains problematic for the villagers. In contrast to the unsupportive
government policies until the 1970s, plots today have an
acknowledged place within the framework of national economic
planning, and it is generally forecast that they will continue to produce at their present levels into the foreseeable
future (Juhász, 1980; Varga, 1980). The villagers themselves think otherwise however. In Pécsely it is believed
that decline in plot farming will accelerate as the older
generations reduce their participation. This loss is not
expected to be compensated for by the young, many of whom
are unwilling, unable or uninterested in maintaining plot
farming at its previous level. It has been seen that plot
farming is nevertheless of considerable significance, for
example, in solving the chronic housing problems. The housing shortage has been crucial in motivating plot farming and
shows little sign of abatement, despite massive government
and private effort devoted to its relief. As long as the
housing problem persists, plot farming offers a major means
of solving it, although a solution to the problem increasingly through other channels cannot be ruled out.

Since 1980, and particularly since January 1982, a

series of new regulations has come into force which allow
unprecedented scope for small, individual enterprises and
small trades, both within agriculture and outside. These
recent reforms encourage individual and family enterprise
through several types of concessions and incentives. Firstly they extend the enterprises in which private small businesses and tradesmen may engage and lift some of the restrictions that operated hitherto.[1] A number of new forms of
small businesses and trade associations have been legalized,
such as, for example, small service cooperatives, industrial
and service groups, and business work associations.[2] New
forms of cooperation and contractual relationships between
State enterprises, collectives and individuals or groups
have been devised.[3] These alternatives are often innovative
and original, and widen the scope of small family and group
enterprise well beyond the domain of plot farming. Although
the full effects of these reforms still lie in the future,
they are generally believed to hold potentially significant
profits. They may also be expected to have important consequences for the future of plot farming and thus to affect
the economic structure and the functions of the family. The
recent reforms may also contribute towards the full integration of the 'second economy' and resolve some of the contradictions of the duality of the present system.

NOTES

1. Decree no. 14 of 1977 has been amended by Decree no.
16 of 1981 allowing 'small enterprise-type industrial activities' in the manufacture, maintenance and repair of industrial products and transport of passengers and goods. This
considerably expands the scope of activities for private
enterprise. Six family members and six employees may be engaged. Licences for private artisans (kisiparos) cannot be
refused if required qualifications are met and the proposed
activity is not against the law. Social insurance has been
extended to private artisans, entitling them to pension,
accident insurance, and maternity benefits (Magyar Közlöny
nos. 43 and 53, 1981). The availability of bank loans for
private artisans has been increased (Heti Vilaggazdasag,
October 1982). The aim of the reform has been to increase
this sector, an expectation partly fulfilled; there has
been an increase of private artisans by 1,000 in Budapest
alone during the course of 1982 (Magyar Nemzet, July 17,
1982).

2. Small cooperatives are legal entities that have 15 to 100 members, involved mainly in the manufacture of goods in short supply which are not produced in sufficient quantities by State enterprises. Industrial and service groups are formed within existing State enterprises or collectives but are independent as regards management and accounting. They may contract to use the equipment and workshops of the host enterprise outside working hours. They consist of a minimum of five members. Business work communities are associations of between two and thirty members. They mainly provide services such as, for example, in the tourist trade (letting rooms, renting boats, guide services). They may also contract for services such as garbage disposal or private transport (Mezőggazdasagi Szemle, 1981).

3. New schemes for private initiatives within collectives include, for example, initiatives to improve land use through share-cropping, contracting collectives' land for growing poppies, onions, etc. (Sopron, Magyar Hirlap, 1980 Dec. 18,19); vineyards (Borsod, Kertészet es Szőllészet, July 23, 1981); apple orchards and pastures (Győr, Radio Budapest, 1981, March 23). Entire production units may be leased by private contractors (e.g. chicken farms, fodder mixing units); bids were open for twelve such units in one collective in October 1981 (Népszava October 24, 1981). Machinery not used to full capacity by the collective or state enterprise may be leased (Magyar Nemzet, October 28, 1981).

Glossary

forint	Hungarian currency introduced in 1946
gazda	peasant household head, farmer
gazdaasszony	peasant housewife
határ	the land and territory enclosed by village boundaries
háztályi	collective farm household plot
hold	measure of land: 1 hold = 1.42 acres = 0.57 hectares
jobbágy	serf
kis	small
kisgazda, kisbirtos	smallholder
koma	the godfather of one's child; friend
kőzepparaszt	middle peasant
kulák	wealthy peasant, pejorative, from Russian 'fist'
nagy	large, great
nagygazda	wealthy peasant
nemes	noble
nemesség	nobility
puszta	manorial estate
termelőszővetkezet	collective of production
zseller	landless serf

Bibliography

Andorka, R. 1984 'A társadalmi szerkezet és rétegeződés vizsgálatai a Társadalomtudomanyi Intézetben' (Studies of social stratification and structure in the Social Sciences Institute) in Valóság, no. 9, pp. 97-104.

Barić, L. 1978 Traditional groups and new economic opportunities in rural Yugoslavia in Themes of Economic Anthropology (ed) R. Firth ASA Monographs no. 6, pp. 253-277. London: Tavistock.

Barth, F. 1965 Models of Social Organization. Royal Anthropological Institute Occasional Paper no. 23. London: Royal Anthropological Institute.

Bell, P.D. 1979 Social Change and Social Perception in a Rural Hungarian Village. Ph.D. Thesis, University of California.

Berend, I. 1979 A Szocialista Gazdaság Fejlődese Magyarországon, 1945-1975 (The development of socialist economy in Hungary, 1945-1975). Budapest: Kossuth.

Beli, Z. 1977 Földreform Zala Megyében (Land Reform in Zala County) Zala Gyűjtemény no. 4.

Bogár, L. 1980 Erdekviszonyok, másodlagos gazdaság, korrupció (Interest relations, second economy, corruption) Valóság, no. 8, pp. 37-46.
1983 A Feljlődés Ára (The price of progress). Budapest: Közgazdásagi és Jogi Könyvkiado.

Bodrogi, T. 1978 Varsány: Tanulmányok egy Eszak Magyarországi Falu Tarsadalmonéprajzához (Varsány: Ethnographic studies of the society of a Northern Hungarian village). Budapest: Akademiai.

Bodosi, Gy. 1965 Mit lehet kiolvasni a Matribulábol? (What do the Registers tell us?) Kortárs, no. 12, pp. 1930-1941.

1975 Pécsely, in Jelenkor, pp. 671-684.

Bourdieu, P. 1977 An Outline of a Theory of Practice. Cambridge University Press.

Bourdieu, P. & Boltansky, L. 1978 Changes in social structure and change in demands of education, in Contemporary Europe: Social Structure and Cultural Patterns eds. Giner, S. & Archer, M.S. London: Routledge & Kegan Paul.

Chayanov, A.V. 1966 The Theory of Peasant Economy (1925) eds. Thorner, D., Smith, R. & Kerblay, B. Irwin.

Dankovits, L. 1963 A Háztáji Gazdaságok és a Mezőgazdasági Termeles (The houseplots and agriculture) MSZMP Gazdasági tanfolyam Budapest: Kossuth.

Dányi, P. 1976 A Községi tanácsok működése, szervezete feladataik in V. Kulcsár (ed) (A Váltózo Falu), pp. 287-319. Budapest: Gondolat.

Donáth, F. 1976 Gazdasági növekedés és socialist mező-gazdaság (Economic growth and socialist agriculture) Valóság no. 9, pp. 18-28.
1977 Reform és Forradalom. Budapest: Akademiai.
1980 Reform and Revolution - Transformation of Hungary's Agriculture, 1945-1970. Budapest: Corvina.

Erdei, F. 1952 A termelőszővetkezeti kőzségek és városok kérdése (Problems of the collectivized communities and towns) in Szővetkezeti Irások, 1979. Budapest: Akademiai.
1969 A mezőgazdasági szővetkezetek néhány kérdése (Sociological questions of agricultural collectives) Valóság, no. 2, pp. 74-89.
1974 A Magyar Falu (The Hungarian Village). Budapest: Akademiai.
1977 Mezőgazdaság és Szővetkezet (Agriculture and Collectives). Budapest: Akademiai.

Erdélyi, S. 1979 A másodlagos elosztásrol (On the secondary distribution), Valóság, no. 12, pp. 38-52.

Enyedi, Gy. 1977 The transformation of the Hungarian village, New Hungarian Quarterly, vol. XVIII, no. 67, pp. 69-86.

Fél, E. & Hőfer, T. 1969 Proper Peasants. Chicago: Viking.
1973 Átány: patronage and factions, American Anthropologist, no. 75, pp. 787-801.

Fazekas, B. 1976 A Mezőgazdasági Termelőszővetkezeti Mozgalom Magyarországon (Collectivization in Hungary). Budapest: Kossuth.

Féja, G. 1961 Sárköz Tája (The region of Sarkoz). Budapest: Szepirodalmi.

Ferge, Zs. 1969 Társadalmi mobilitás - a társadalom

nyitottsága (Social mobility - the openness of society) Valóság, no. 6, pp. 9-20.
1978 Keresetek, jővedelem, adózás (Incomes, wages and taxation), Valóság, no. 3, pp. 27-42.

Fur, L. 1965 Jobbágyfőld-parasztfőld (Serf-land, peasant-land) in A Parasztság Magyarországon a Kapitalizmus Koraban, ed. Szabo, I. Budapest: Akademiai.

Frankel, S. 1955 The Economic Impact of Underdeveloped Societies. Cambridge: Harvard University Press.

Franklin, S.H. 1969 The European Peasantry: The Final Phase London: Methuen.

Foster, G.M. 1967 Peasant Societies and the image of limited good, American Anthropologist 1967, p. 293.

Galeski, B. 1975 The Basic Concepts of Rural Sociology. Manchester: Manchester University Press.

Gábor, R.I. 1979 A második gazdaság (Second economy), Valóság, no. 1, pp. 21-36.
1985 Második gazdaság: a magyar tapasztalatok altalanosithatonak tűnő tanulságai (Second economy: some generalizations on the basis of the Hungarian experience), Valóság, no. 2, pp. 20-38.

Gáldonyi, B. 1970 Pécsely 25 eve (Twenty-five years of Pécsely). Unpublished manuscript: Pécsely Council.

Gonda, I. 1979 Kistermelés és Kistermelők (Small farming and small farmers), Valóság, no. 12, pp. 66-73.
1984 Kistermelés-kérdőjelekkel (Smallfarming - with question marks), Valóság, no. 5, pp. 82-91.

Greenwood, D. 1976 Unrewarding Wealth - the Commercialization and Collapse of Agriculture in a Spanish Basque Town, Cambridge: Cambridge University Press.

Hankiss, E. 1979 Felemás világ (Ambiguous world), Valóság, no. 5, pp. 30-44.
1984 Második társadalom (Second society), Valóság, no. 11, pp. 25-44.

Hann, C.M. 1980 Tázlár - a Village in Hungary. Cambridge: Cambridge University Press.
1983 Progress towards collectivized agriculture in Tázlár 1949-1978, in New Hungarian Peasantry eds. Hollós, M. & Maday, B. Social Science Monographs, New York: Brooklyn College Press.

Hársfalvi, P. 1965 Tőrekvesék a parasztbirtok védelmere (Attempts to protect peasant holdings) in A Parasztsag Magyarorszagon a Kapitalizmus Koraban (ed.) Szabo, I. Budapest: Akademiai.

Held, J. 1980 The Modernization of Agriculture: Rural Transformation in Hungary, 1848-1975. Eastern European Monographs, New York: Boulder.

Hegedűs, A 1977   The Structure of Socialist Society. London: Constable.

Hollós, M. & Maday, B. 1983   The New Hungarian Peasants - an Eastern European Experience of Collectivization. Social Science Monographs, New York: Brooklyn College Press.

Hollós, M. 1983   Ideology and economics: cooperative organization and attitudes towards collectivization; in New Hungarian Peasants (eds) Hollós, M. & Maday, B., pp. 93-123. Social Science Monographs, New York: Brooklyn College Press.

Holzman, F.D. 1981   The Second Economy: A Terminological Note, ACES Bulletin , no. 1.

Horváth, Z. 1965   A községi önkormányzat és a parasztság (Community, self-government and the peasantry) in A Parasztsag Magyarorszagon a Kapitalizmus Koraban (ed) Szabo, I., pp. 565-615. Budapest: Akademiai.

Humphrey, C. 1983   Karl Marx Collective: Economy, Society and Religion in a Siberian Collective Farm. London: Cambridge University Press & Editions de la Maison des Sciences.

Jávor, K. 1978   Kontinuitás és változás a társadalmi és tudati viszonyokban (Continuity and change in society and consciousness) in Varsány (ed) Bodrogi, T., pp. 295-373. Budapest: Akademiai.
1983   Continuity and change in the social and value system of a Northern Hungarian village in New Hungarian Peasants (eds) Hollós, M. & Maday, B., pp. 273-301. New York: Brooklyn College Press.

Juhász, J. 1980   A Háztáji Gazdálkodas Mezőgazdasagunkban (Small Farming in our Agriculture) Budapest: Akademiai.

Kolosi, T. 1980   Uj tendenciák a társadalmi szerkezet fejlödésében (New trends in the development of social stratification), Valóság, no. 3, pp. 37-50.

Kovács, E. 1983   Types of households in Varsány in New Hungarian Peasants (eds) Hollós, M. & Maday, B., pp. 57-69. New York: Brooklyn College Press.

Kovács, I. & Kuczi, T. 1982   Gazdálkodoi előnyök átváltási lehetőségei a társadalomban (The possibilities of converting farming profits into social advantages), Valóság, no. 6, pp.46-55.

Kulcsár, V. 1976   Változo Falu (The Changing Village). Budapest: Gondolat.
1982   A Mai Magyar Társadalom (Hungarian Society Today) Budapest: Kossuth.

Kunszabó, F. 1970   Elnoktipusok a Szovetkezetben (Chairmen types in Collectives). Budapest: Akademiai.

Laky, T. 1980 A recentralizació rejtett mechanizmusai
(Hidden mechanisms of recentralization), Valóság,
no. 2.

Laposa, J. 1979 A zártkertek sorsa (The future of protected
farm areas), Valóság, no. 6, pp. 92-99.

Lewin, M. 1980 The kolkhoz and the Russian muzsik in
Peasants in History (ed) Hobsbawn, pp. 55-68. Oxford:
Oxford University Press.

A Magyar Népi Demokrácia Története 1944-1962 1978.
Budapest: Kossuth.

Magyary, S. 1942 A Magyar Közigazgatás (Budapest).

Márkus, I. 1969 Ezt Láttam Falun (What I saw in the
Countryside). Budapest: Gondolat.
1968 A mezőgazdasági fejlesztés és helyi viszonyai
(Agricultural development and its local conditions),
Valóság, no. 2, pp. 42-52.

Marresse M. 1980 The role of the second economy: lessons
from Hungary. Lecture in the IV Hungarian-American
Economics Meeting, Cambridge USA.

Moore, S.F. 1983 Law as Process - an Anthropological
Approach. London: Routledge & Kegan Paul.

Newby, H. 1977 The Deferential Worker. London: Penguin.
1980 Green and Pleasant Land?. London: Penguin.

Oláh, M. & Vágvölgyi, B. 1984 Egy helyi döntes körülményei
(Circumstances of a decision), Valóság, no. 6, pp. 42-
52.

Orbán, S. 1958 Adatok a Balaton Felvidék parasztlakos-
ságának specialis arculatahoz (Contribution to sociological aspects of the Balaton highlands peasants)
Veszprémi Szemle, vol. 2, pp. 40-58.
1972 Két Agrárforradalom Magyarországon (Two agrarian
revolutions in Hungary). Budapest: Akademiai.

Orosz, I. & Schindele, M. 1977 Időmérleg a háztáji
gazdaságokban (Hours of labour on plots), Statisztikai
Szemle, nos. 8-9.

Pápai, L. 1984 Hagyományunk megújulása (Revival of our
traditions), Valóság, no. 2, pp. 58-71.

Parkin, F. 1981 Class Inequality and Political Order.
London: Granada.

Prokopp, Gy. 1963 Adatok az elpusztult Nemes Pécselyi
templomrol (Notes on the destroyed Church of Nemes
Pécsely), Műemlék Védelem, no. 4, pp. 203-212.

Paukert, F. 1973 Income differentials at different levels
of development, International Labour Review, nos. 2-3.

Puky, K.B. 1930 Honi Törvény Szótár (Dictionary of Law).
Pest, 1930.

Rákosi, M. 1950 Válogatott Beszédek és Cikkek (Selected

Speeches and Writings). Budapest: Szikra.

Romer, F. 1860 A Bakony. Veszprém Muzeumok Igazgatosága, 1971.

Sárkány, M. 1978 A gazdaság átalakulása (The transformation of the economy) in Varsány (ed) Bodrogi, T., pp. 63-150. Budapest: Akademiai.

Seres, A. 1985 Egyesülések vagy Egyesitések? (Mergers: Forced or Voluntary?), Valóság, no. 3, pp. 78-86.

Simo, T. 1983 A Tardi Társadalom (The community of Tard) Budapest: Kossuth.

Sozán, M. 1984 Falu (Village) in Irodalmi Ujság Sorozata, pp. 20-26.

Smelser, N.J. 1967 Towards a Theory of Modernization in Tribal and Peasant Economies ed. G. Dalton, pp. 29-48. University of Texas Press.

Swain, N. 1982 The evolution of Hungary's agricultural system since 1967 in Hungary: a Decade of Economic Reform (eds) Hare, P., Radice, H. & Swain, N., pp. 225-251. London: Allen & Unwin.

Szabo, I. 1965 A Parasztság Magyarorszagon a Kapitalizmus Korában (The Peasantry in Hungary in the age of Capitalism). Budapest: Akademiai.

Szego, A. & Wiener, G. 1978 Public administration and interest relations in Hungarian Society and Marxist Sociology in the 1970s (eds) Huszar, T., Kulcsar, K. & Szalai, S., pp. 72-92. Budapest: Corvina.

Szent-Gyorgyi, K. 1983 Ranking categories and models in two villages in Northern Hungary in New Hungarian Peasants (eds) Hollós, M. & Maday, B., pp. 181-211. New York: Brooklyn College Press.

Társadalmi Strukturánk Fejlödése: Gazdaság, Település, Társadalomszerkezet, III. 1981. Budapest: MSZMP KP Társadalomtudomanyi Intezete.

Tagányi, Z. 1975 A faluközösség helyzete és jövöje egy Nograd megyei faluban (The situation and future of the community in a village in Nograd), Ethnographia, LXXIX 1978, no. 3.

Tepicht, J. 1973 Le Marxisme et l'Agriculture: le Paysan Polonais. Paris: Armand Colin.
1975 A project of research on the peasant revolution of our time, Journal of Peasant Studies, Vol. 2, no. 3, pp. 257-269.

Toma, P. & Volgyes, I. 1977 Politics in Hungary. San Francisco: Freeman.

Unger, M. & Szabolcs, O. 1973 Magyarország Története (A History of Hungary). Budapest: Gondolat.

Varga, Gy. 1980   Small-scale farming in Hungary, New
    Hungarian Quarterly, no. 78, vol. XXI, pp. 77-87.
Volgyes, I. 1980   Dynamic Change: rural transformation 1945-
    1975 in Held, J. The Modernization of Agriculture:
    Rural Transformation in Hungary 1848-1975, pp. 351-442.
    Eastern European Monographs New York: Boulder.
Wolf, E.R. 1968   Kinship, friendship and patron-client
    relations in complex societies, in Banton, M. (ed)
    Social Anthropology of complex societies. ASA
    Monograph no. 4, pp. 1-20.
Wylie, L. 1977   A Village in the Vaucluse. Harvard: Harvard
    University Press.
Yanov, A. 1972 qu. by Hookham, M. in Osipov Town, Country
    and People. Soviet Studies London: Tavistock.
Zsigmond, G. 1978   1960-1970s évek fordulojának családtipusa
    (Family types in the 1960s and 1970s) in Bodrogi (ed)
    Varsány, pp. 151-172.   Budapest: Akademiai.

Index

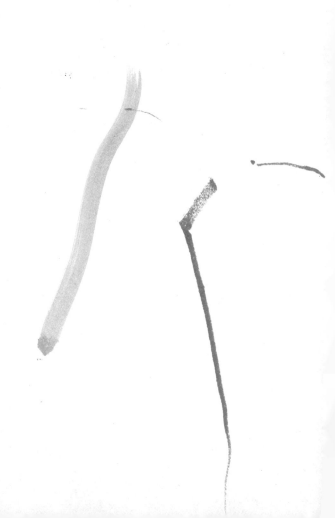